PATERNO
LEGACY

PATERNO
LEGACY

ENDURING LESSONS
FROM THE LIFE AND
DEATH OF MY FATHER

Jay Paterno

TRIUMPH
BOOKS

TRIUMPHBOOKS.COM

Library of Congress Cataloging-in-Publication Data
Paterno, Jay.
    Paterno legacy : enduring lessons from the life and death of my father / Jay Paterno ; foreword by Phil Knight.
       pages cm
     ISBN 978-1-60078-974-8 (hardback)
1. Paterno, Joe, 1926-2012. 2. Football coaches—United States—Biography. 3. Pennsylvania State University—Football—History. I. Title.
    GV939.P37P38 2014
    796.332092—dc23
    [B]   2014006253

This book is available in quantity at special discounts for your group or organization. For further information, contact:

    Triumph Books LLC
    814 North Franklin Street
    Chicago, Illinois 60610
    (312) 337-0747
    www.triumphbooks.com

Printed in U.S.A.

ISBN: 978-1-60078-974-8

Design by Amy Carter

Photos courtesy of The Paterno Family unless otherwise indicated

This book is for my mother and father. We will always love you and remember that you both always strove to do what was right, no matter the price. That is more important than anything. You are giants who will have left the world around you a dramatically better place through the lives you've lived.

This book is for my wife and children. Kelley, I love you more now than I ever loved you. Your loyalty, strength, and willingness to fight for me and for my family will always shine in my memories. Fleeing would have been a lot easier. For my children, know that your smiles and your love are the greatest of gifts. The love of my wife and children has been the sustaining force in my life through the darkest times.

For my brothers and sisters and for their children, I hope this book helps you remember the man that Joseph Vincent Paterno was and the lessons he shared with so many.

This book is for journalism students. In a world where the pressure to be first often outweighs the responsibility to be right, I hope you always look in your heart and pursue the truth. It is the most solemn responsibility of freedom of the press. Realize your mistakes will have consequences for real people.

Finally, I hope that this book helps people talk about the issues of child welfare in this country. Abuse is all around us, but if the last days of my father's life raised awareness to protect even one child's safety, he would have told you it was all worth it.

Life can only be understood backward; but it must be lived forwards.

—*Soren Kierkegaard*

I'll end with the deepest lesson this case taught me. When I think back through the whole complex history of this episode, the scariest thing to me is that actual human lives were at the mercy of so much instant moral certainty before the facts had been established. If there's one lesson the world should take from the Duke lacrosse case, it's the danger of prejudgment and our need to defend against it at every turn.

—*Duke University president Richard H. Brodhead*
at a Duke Law School conference
on September 29, 2007

Contents

Foreword

Six months after the eulogy, it is 6:00 in the morning. I sit in my small hotel room in western Idaho, watching. The man on the TV is finding the worst things to say about an old friend. The TV blinks on and on, and the man goes on almost an hour. The calls to Beaverton have begun at the 15-minute mark.

By the end of that hour, there have been a half-dozen phone calls with me. At the home office, calls pour in from all over the world. What are you going to do about the name of your child-care center?

We are going to get blasted for aiding and abetting pedophilia. For sure. How does it get worse than this?

Every public appearance, every news interview for the next six months, a question will come up on this subject. For 38,000 employees—when they go to summer barbecues—the question will come up. And every single one of those 38,000 will ask him or herself, *What kind of a company do I work for?*

I can make that all go away. I can protect the company that I devoted my life to. I stare at the wall and think: *Why am I pausing?*

• • •

I first met Joe Paterno a third of a century ago. He was already established as one of the greatest football coaches of all time. But it had not always been so.

He had come to his school in 1950 out of Brooklyn by way of Brown to this place as far from Brooklyn as you can get: a land of thick forests and wide streams, an idyllic landscape appropriately named "Happy Valley."

An area with a significant Amish population. Sometimes on a Saturday night, after the furniture sale, a young man would steal into town for a couple of secret pops. Later that evening you could see him pulling irregularly on the reins, his surrey weaving all over the country road.

In 1966 when he, at last, got the head coaching job, he started what he called, "The Grand Experiment," setting out to prove that academics and athletics can co-exist, even enhance each other. It included these goals: recruit without cheating, make your players go to class, graduate them, and compete.

How did that work out?

He went 5–5 his first year.

Then he won. Oh, how he won. Four hundred and nine times. If Nick Saban coaches 20 more years and averages 12 wins a year, he will still be four wins short of 409. Joe belonged to Our Lady of Victory Catholic Church in State College. I used to kid him, "What did they call it before you got there?"

And in those years, the people of Penn State built a world-class university, and Joe was one of its chief architects.

So when I walked in the door, it was for me, as well as many others, about that Grand Experiment, not just winning. Over a couple years I was drawn, not just by the champion of that Grand Experiment, but also to a man with a great sense of humor, including about himself, and a deep sense of doing the right thing in all areas.

I watched him make numerous hard decisions. Keep an All-American running back out of a game because the kid missed study hall, kick his two best defensive players off the team—a team rules thing—when he had just finished back-to-back losing seasons for the first time. Fans, donors called for him to step down. *You are too old.*

And then he takes what is left and goes 11–1.

I remember one Friday before a game. I am back there with buddies Ken O'Neil and David Frei. We have gone over to the house to wish him good luck, and much of the family is there. The driveway is jammed with cars, and as we maneuver out, we stop to let a college student pass on the sidewalk. He pays us no attention. As he crosses the boundary between Sunset Park and the residence, he takes off his baseball cap, places it over his heart. When he moves into the neighbor's space, he places the cap back on his head.

At the 2010 National Football Coaches Convention, when he enters the room, 800 coaches spontaneously rise to give him a standing ovation.

When he passes they invite all the lettermen back for a private dinner the night before the memorial service. Forty-five years at 25 players a year, they are expecting as many as 750; 1,250 showed up.

Simply, he was the gold standard by which all other football programs were measured.

When Jay Paterno read Kenny Moore's wonderful book, *Bowerman and the Men of Oregon*, he called me to say, "Man, there are a lot of similarities."

For me, too.

They both won multiple national championships—plural. They both lived in their first houses long after they could afford much more. "What do I need more space for? Tell me that, huh."

They had mutual goals: to change the world for the better, one athlete at a time.

When Bill Bowerman passed, he bequeathed to me one thing: his green cowboy hat. It was in his later years a trademark, wearing it to track meets, in his lab, out on the farm. Green was for his alma mater and employer, cowboy for childhood and learned values. A physical reminder of his most memorable line: "Do right and fear no man."

Joe Paterno never heard Bowerman say that. He just lived it. For 85 years.

And somewhere in my mind the two men began to morph together: Bowerman and Paterno, the two most moral men I ever knew.

• • •

But that guy on TV. He has a good reputation, too. Former district judge, former head of the FBI. Credentials to impress anyone.

After five hours I make the 12th and last phone call of the day. *Take the name down.*

• • •

I walk now.

I used to run. In my mind I still do. It is just that I keep getting passed by the fast walkers.

With walking it takes a lot of time to get a good workout. So I download audiobooks. One summer I read/listened to over 5,000 pages on U.S. history.

But these days I go miles before I turn on my iPod. My conversations with myself take a long time. It is not happy talk. One thing about walking alone: there is no one to hide from.

When I returned to Oregon, I re-read the 16 pages summarizing the grand jury testimony. First of the oh-ohs. It has not been characterized accurately in the presentation I witnessed two days before.

Then I read the Freeh Report. All the pages. Double and triple oh-oh. Joe Paterno-Gary Schultz-Graham Spanier are treated as if they are one person. Joe's guilt is dictated primarily by emails written by others—what in Judge Freeh's court-room in an earlier day would be tossed out—not just a hearsay, but double hearsay. This is not the document of a judge; it is a plaintiff's brief.

So I walk and talk to myself. I try to avoid the obvious. I did what I had to do. Didn't I?

And it is there at other times as well.

Like when I am in my den at home. That green cowboy hat. It sits on a shelf at eye level. Whenever I pause at my computer, that hat glowers at me.

Until at last I have to recognize myself. I am a child of the west, who grew up to be the sheriff with the lynch mob outside the jail. "Give us the prisoner or we'll kill you both," is the cry of the mob. I forestall for hours, then say, "Take him."

No rewinds. I have to live with this.

After six weeks I call Sue. *I am coming to the East Coast, can I come by?*

I am glad her kids Mary Kay and Jay are there. They make it easier. Sue is more than gracious. Of course. It is expected. But Jay surprises me. *Dad would have told you to take the name down.*

More than surprised, I am stunned. But after thinking about it, I conclude he is right. Joe would have said that.

Jay has said that to make me feel better, which it does at first. But not for long. Because I believe if the situation had been reversed, Joe Paterno would have left my name up, lynch mob be damned.

Forgiven or not, I cannot escape that I was, at least for a time, "one of them."

Today we are in that period between current events and history. I console myself with the belief that like the girls of Salem, Captain Dreyfus, and Hurricane Carter, history will contradict earlier current events.

In the meantime: look around at State College. He is there. Immortality is just timeless ubiquity. So they—and sadly I—through our actions have narrowed the scope and degree of this immortality. But nobody can make him go away.

—Phil Knight
Nike Co-founder

Prologue

Early morning I walked my dog & saw

the glow of the stadium. I will never lose

Joe's light in my life.

—@JayPaterno on January 23, 2012

When you watch someone you love slowly die from cancer, it is the changes that stay with you when they are first gone. I thought of my father without his hair, his raspy voice and silent presence on a ventilator the last two days of his life, communicating with nods.

Now when I visit his grave, I think of him walking, running, laughing, his thick head of dark hair, and his voice, an unmistakable guiding force in my life. I talk to him. I pray, but mostly I want to hear his voice.

It happens sometimes. As I stand by his hillside grave, I hear him in a gust of wind, a rustle of leaves, the sound of geese flying overhead.

Mostly I want to obliterate the wall that went up in his life on November 4, 2011. On one side of that wall, everything good and bad in my life before that day is bathed in light. After that day everything both good and bad is in the dark shadows.

My life will forever be bisected by the wall and the events of that day and the days after it. But in a true display of his character, in the last months of his life my father never allowed himself to feel bitterness or hatred. In a world that wanted him to spew venom, he never allowed it to touch his soul.

For over six decades, Joe Paterno conducted his professional life in a principled way. In seven days those decades would recede into the background as he became the object of an all-out assault in a scandal not in any way of his making. His only goal was to see that justice be carried out without regard to what it would mean to him or his football program.

But Joe Paterno's life stands far taller than the events of the last months of his life. He carried himself as though Rudyard Kipling's poem "If" was encoded in his DNA. He shared that poem with me when I was young, and it has always resonated with me.

No one ever walked with kings but never lost the common touch better than he. No one ever kept his head about him while all others were losing theirs better than he. Joe Paterno could have been anything he wanted yet he chose to settle in State College, coach football, raise a family, and teach the thousands he coached.

More than that, my father had a way of explaining things and talking to you that at times wasn't easy to understand, but he was always blunt in his assessments. Self-esteem wasn't something you were given. You earned it through achievement of worthy goals.

One morning in ninth grade, I complained to my siblings about a teacher in front of my parents. That afternoon he called me into his den. He sat at his desk while I stood. He had a blue pullover sweater and tie on. He wore a tie just about every time he left the house when I was a kid. As I stood in front of him, the late afternoon sunlight was coming in through the window behind him, finishing its daily journey over the horizon of Sunset Park behind our house. At times the rays gave my father's den an other-worldly glow.

As I stood in front of his desk, I knew a friendly conversation was not in the offing. This meeting had begun by the dreaded beckoning, "Jay, come in here and shut the door."

Nothing good was ever discussed behind the closed den door—at least for me. If I had to come in with Mom and shut the door, I feared I may be packing my bags. At least today my mother wasn't summoned. "Jay," my father began looking up from his desk. "Look, you're not in trouble."

Relief. However, I sensed there had to be a "But" coming. There was more to this story.

"But..." he continued.

I knew it.

"But you said something this morning that bothered me."

"What was that?" I asked.

"You were complaining about one of your teachers."

"Yeah."

"Yeah? You mean *Yes*. Don't talk to me like I am one of your friends."

"Yes."

"You were complaining."

"Yes, I was. He kicked me out of class for something that wasn't my fault."

"It wasn't your fault?"

"No. Someone had moved his chair before I came into class, and when he went to sit down he missed the chair and fell on the ground."

"So why did he kick you out of the room?"

"I came in and saw him on the floor and laughed. I couldn't help it."

My father's expression changed from inquisitive to one of slight anger.

"You couldn't help it?" he asked in a voice with just a trace of ire.

"I just couldn't. Then he got up and said, 'Out, Out, listen you little S.O.B. that hurt like hell.'"

"So he kicked you out?"

"Yes, I had to stand in the hall the first half of the class and I didn't do anything bad."

At this point I expected him to side with me and commiserate on the injustice I'd endured. After living in this house all my life, I should have known better.

"Jay, it probably did hurt him, and the last thing he needed was some smart aleck kid laughing at his pain. You're going to go in tomorrow and apologize to him."

"But Dad, it's not fair."

"Jay, life isn't fair, and the sooner you learn that the better. Here's what I want you to know. I am not interested in being your friend now. I don't particularly care if you like me now. When it is important, you'll understand, and when it is important, then you'll like me."

My 14-year-old mind was lost trying to get a grip on the concept. The puzzled look on my face must have conveyed my lack of understanding.

"What I am trying to say to you is this: don't expect me to side with you when you have a conflict with a teacher. They work hard to help you and they don't get paid a lot of money. You have to learn in this world that sometimes things may not be your fault, but you have to deal with them."

"Okay."

"What I also want you to understand is this: there will be times in your life when I make you do things you don't understand or things that don't seem important. Trust me: they will make sense to you and be important when you have a job, a wife, and a family of your own. When you are on time for meetings and disciplined enough to get things done when you're supposed to get them done, then you will understand. Whether or not you like me now, and whether or not you get what I am trying to teach you now, isn't as important as you getting what I want you to know when you're older."

His tone was forceful but not angry. It was a statement; it was a declaration of what it was to be a father. I knew I wasn't in trouble; he just wanted me to understand him.

Twenty-eight years later I was having a discussion with my 11-year old son about his school. I found myself giving him a lecture about not wanting to be his friend now. Halfway through I knew exactly where I had heard that before.

That is the beauty of Joe Paterno—his enduring lessons never leave you. In his days as a father, a coach, or a mentor, there was always a lesson to impart. The lessons work their way into your brain and subconscious. Years later they reappear and you smile as you pass on his lesson, knowing exactly where you learned it.

For nearly 62 years at Penn State, he passed along his lessons to everyone he could reach. There were no single teachable moments in his life. It was a constant stream of teaching that never required a particular moment to trigger it. The trick was always to listen to him—always. Very few of his lessons were the type I just mentioned where he had a moment to grab you and let you know he was imparting some big wisdom.

Most of the time they were drive-by types. If you were alert, you got it. If you weren't, then you missed it. The best learners were the best listeners. It was all part of his mantra about paying attention to details. If you paid attention, you'd reap big rewards.

As the last few months of his life began to unravel, the lessons kept coming. The week after he died, we became aware of just how far his lessons reached. As tens of thousands of people filed past his casket to pay their respects, I listened to stories and hugged those who were crying.

The visitors hailed from down the road to places in faraway lands. All had a story or a connection to this man whom many had never met or had met briefly. But all shared how Joe Paterno's words or life example had reached them. His classroom was the world, and he may not have even known it.

As I got older, I listened more and more carefully to my father's stories and jokes and learned to appreciate them all. At a dinner table or in a meeting, he'd speak softly but deliberately. He challenged you to pay attention, maybe even lean in to hear him better, like he was letting you in on a secret. He usually was.

In early February 2011, he and I were talking about the speech President Obama had given in Tucson after congresswoman Gabby Giffords had been shot by a mad gunman. In my bi-weekly column for StateCollege.com, I'd written about it, and my father liked the theme of what I'd said.

"Jay, I admire how the President handled that speech. Do you know how tough that was? The event was in a basketball arena and was part memorial service and part rally for the people of that community. To give a speech that was upbeat but respectful was tough. He had to give a speech that mourned the death of a young girl but not bring everyone in the arena down. That is so difficult. I admire what he did."

Little did I know that less than one year later, I'd be standing in a basketball arena giving a speech about my father's life that had to be hopeful and respectful while also being mournful.

It was my father's lesson. The President's speech was something I thought about before writing my father's eulogy mainly because my father had recognized its power and strength.

That lesson stayed with me when I needed it most. And even now, many months after his voice is gone, his lessons continue to keep coming to me, and his work lives on.

As I wrote on Twitter the morning after he died, "Joe's Light Will Never leave my life," and neither will the words he gave that guide me.

This book is the story of those words and of a life example that not only survived but thrived in the onslaught against him. It forged his example in a way that made it stronger and more enduring.

As 12,000 people stood and held hands at the Memorial For Joe, I led them in the the Lord's Prayer. I could not have known what I would learn from many people after the event.

But in that moment, Joe Paterno's life came through as I spoke the words that many tell me was a moment they will never forget:

For 45 years he led this program. He always ended his postgame remarks with the same thing. He'd say, "Let's thank the good Lord." And we would kneel down, hold hands, and say that Lord's Prayer. One time, just out of curiosity, I said, "Dad, why? Why that prayer?" He said, "The words, Jay, the words:" "*Our* Father," "give *us* this day our daily bread," "forgive *us*...as we forgive," "we," "us,"—every pronoun is plural, "we" and "us." There is no "I" or "me."

Then it clicked. Here in the last act after every football game we play is a reminder from Joe that it was never about him. It was we and us, unselfish to the core. The current and former players in this room know that, and they know that scene. They've had those moments. But this afternoon I want us all to have that moment. I ask that if you are able to stand up, hold the hands of the person next to you and step into that locker room and feel the bonds of Penn State. Let's say one last "Our Father" as a team for Joe Paterno:

Our Father, who art in Heaven
Hallowed be thy Name.
Thy Kingdom come,
Thy will be done on Earth,
As it is in Heaven.
Give us this day our daily bread.
And forgive us our trespasses,
As we forgive those who trespass against us.
And lead us not into temptation,
But deliver us from evil.

> For thine is the kingdom, the power, and the glory,
> For ever and ever.
> Amen.

Every time I say that prayer, now I can hear him. I stand by his grave on my visits and I say it aloud so he'll know I remember his lessons. I hope he smiles when he sees me.

Chapter 1

The Elephant
in the Room

Many of you landed on this page because you are a Penn Stater, a college football fan, or a sports fan wanting to know more about Joe Paterno's life.

I also know some are here because you're interested in the Jerry Sandusky scandal and its accompanying fallout. You want to know what Joe Paterno knew and when he knew it. That is the elephant in the room. I get that.

My father's life was big, complex, and principled, and he himself would tell you he was not perfect. But what the Freeh Report asserted is far from the truth.

Child sexual abuse is the witch trial topic of our time. I fully grasp the powerful emotions wrought by this issue. Calm discussion is difficult. It is outside our comfort zone, creating a lack of awareness that provides cover for perpetrators to operate in plain sight.

However, we must remember what Johns Hopkins University professor Dr. Fred Berlin stated in his report: "In our legitimate effort to protect innocent children, the fair treatment of adults should not become a collateral casualty."

After the Freeh Report, I understand why people are angry at the university and my father. But as FBI director, Freeh took Richard Jewell from hero to suspect in the 1996 Atlanta Olympic bombing. After the facts were uncovered, Jewell was indeed the good guy, but the damage was done.

Our world demands immediate reaction and analysis. Initial reporting is often inaccurate and lacks perspective. For my father and Penn State, almost three years later the truth is getting clearer. An in-depth investigation by former U.S. attorney general Dick Thornburgh, former FBI profiler Jim Clemente, and Dr. Berlin presented a record supported by facts and evidence.

Both Thornburgh and Clemente worked with Louis Freeh. Yet both studied the report he issued and found it deeply flawed. Both addressed Joe Paterno's role related to crimes committed by another.

My father did not commit a crime or even witness a crime.

I grew up a son to Joe Paterno and worked alongside him for 17 years. I know all too well that he was human, an imperfect being. But he always tried to do what he believed was the right thing. When he erred, he erred with the right intentions.

This book is not an attempt to include my father as a victim in the horrible Sandusky story. When my father was fired, he reiterated to me that being fired paled in comparison to what had happened to others.

Beyond the victims, others lost their jobs and reputations. Recognizing that does not detract from our concern for the direct survivors of a predator. It simply realizes this truth; the bomb that went off threw shrapnel all over the place.

But the immediate media focus was not on the crimes committed or even the victims. On November 12, 2011 on *Saturday Night Live*'s "Weekend Update," host Seth Meyers had a bit with actor Jason Sudeikis dressed up as the devil. The devil yells "JoePa, a cover-up? This is college football, not the Catholic church." In the entire skit, they referenced the Penn State scandal and Joe Paterno—but the man actually charged with the crimes not a single time. In an email to their subscribers in November of 2011, *The New York Times* recapped how they had covered the story. It concluded the email by saying this: "More than boys had been violated it seemed. A proud university's sense of superiority and privilege and arrogance had been blown up, too."

Using the specter of boys being violated was inappropriate. But in the headline and body of editor Joe Sexton's story, the name Penn State appeared six times, Paterno four times, and the man charged at the time, Jerry Sandusky, *zero times*.

Although Sandusky had not worked at Penn State in almost 12 years, the focus became the university. That the vast majority of the charges occurred at locations unconnected to Penn State did not matter.

The focus also fell on Joe Paterno, who did not witness a crime but when told of what *might* have been one, *a day after it happened*, reported it exactly as directed by university policy set by state law.

Joe Paterno has been pronounced by the media as "the most powerful man in the state," the foundation of an argument alleging he could and should have done more. His own words: "In hindsight I wish I had done more" have been used against him over and over again as a sign of guilt.

It never was an admission of guilt. It was a painful statement that if he had only known more, then he could have done more. Clemente's powerful report makes the point that Joe Paterno was but one of many, some infinitely more highly educated on this issue, who missed this.

One powerful element to come out of our family report was one that surprised me. If you had asked me three years ago what a pedophile looked like, I would have described a loner in a trench coat, cruising parks and elementary school parking lots in a white van.

We were totally unfamiliar with the nice guy offender. Most never suspect a predator could be a married, non-drinking churchgoer who'd spent his life building a charity to help young people. Yet as the experts in our report point out, these people set themselves up in ways that put them around children.

Why did we miss it? It is a societal problem, a lack of discussion and education on this issue. We have that image of the loner in the white van. We prefer not to talk about it or look in the shadows of ignorance where these criminals hide within plain sight.

Before you condemn Joe Paterno, I ask you to consider if you too would have seen into the darkness of another's heart when all signs pointed you to look the other way.

Before you condemn people at Penn State or in our community, consider this: in adopting Matt Sandusky, Jerry Sandusky went to court to fight for him. I recall him talking to us in the office about the setbacks and ultimate triumph in court.

In the end the presiding judge and the state of Pennsylvania ordered that Jerry be allowed to adopt Matt over the wishes of Matt's biological mother. They viewed Jerry and his home as the better place for Matt.

The State experts viewed him as a good person with a safe home, but we were to suspect something different? What would you have thought?

Given how little I knew about pedophilia at age 44 and given that my father in his 70s and 80s knew even less, I wonder how anyone could expect him to have known more than others who work every day in that field. By his own admission, he did not know how to handle such an accusation, so he took it to the required people. But for many that was not good enough because of some perceived power he held.

But how powerful was he? Did he have a police force? Did he have subpoena power? Could he bring charges? Was he capable of investigating what he'd been told a day after it happened?

The answers to all these is no.

On gameday facing a fourth down and 1 yard to go, he had all the power to make that decision. He decided who played and who did not play. Many people valued his opinion in politics, in business, and in society.

But when it came to criminal laws, he was like everyone else— a citizen equal under the eyes of the laws and governed by the rule of law. That's it.

These are the facts. Joe Paterno was made aware that Jerry Sandusky was in the shower with a young boy a day after a witness saw it. What that witness told him is subject to interpretation, but we do know that the witness *never* told him that he had seen a boy being raped. It was the first and only time Joe Paterno had ever been told by a witness that Jerry had been in the showers with a young boy.

I must reiterate that the witness never told Paterno he witnessed a rape and never told police that he had seen one. The grand jury presentment inaccurately stated that the witness stated he had seen an anal rape and had told Joe Paterno "what he saw." The perception that Joe Paterno had been told about an anal rape and did nothing took hold and cost him his job.

In early 2013 University of Arkansas law professor Brian Gallini made that point the centerpiece of a 64-page paper published in the *Tennessee Law Review*. On page seven of his paper, he wrote: "Paterno's downfall illustrates the importance of grand jury secrecy—both during and after its investigation. That secrecy, present in all federal grand jury proceedings, prevents collateral damage—like job loss—to unindicted criminally innocent third parties. The absence of that secrecy in Pennsylvania's investigative grand jury proceedings took Paterno's job, tarnished his legacy, and perhaps even shortened his life."

The presentment, combined with the state police commissioner's statement that Paterno had failed his moral obligation, doomed Paterno's career. The commissioner made that statement despite the attorney general's having stated that Joe had been wholly cooperative, followed the law, and was not a subject of the investigation.

I would counter that Joe Paterno fulfilled his legal obligation and his moral obligation. In this country we have due process and the rule of law to protect the accuser *and* the accused. Joe Paterno did not witness anything, and as such his *moral* obligation was to allow the proper authorities do *their* investigation. You cannot simply run out in public and declare a man is a child predator based on a story someone told you.

But the police commissioner's irresponsible characterization was allowed to stand unchallenged. The counter-narrative took hold. Even after the trial was over, Jerry Sandusky was never convicted of any rape on Penn State's campus.

The 2001 incident was one of two incidents at Penn State's campus that were brought to anyone's attention. A 1998 incident was investigated by the police, given to the county district attorney, and investigated by the state. The determination made was that no crime had been committed, and charges were never filed. The NCAA in handing down Penn State's sanctions stated that Penn State had failed to respond appropriately. The NCAA ignored the facts.

In his report Freeh alleged that Joe Paterno was not only made aware of the 1998 incident, but also "followed the investigation closely." He based this premise on an email from athletic director Tim Curley to university vice president Gary Schultz with the subject line "Joe Paterno" and the sentence "I have touched base with the coach." Not a word what he touched base about, nor the coach's identity.

What Freeh failed to consider are other 1998 factors. Jerry Sandusky was negotiating a retirement package. He was also talking with the university about starting a lower-division football program at Penn State's Altoona campus. There was also an investigation into a 1997 All-American running back's acceptance of improper benefits from a sports agent before the bowl game.

But Freeh's report made two assumptions about one sentence while ignoring the context, of which he was ignorant.

Several people testified under oath that Joe Paterno was never told of the 1998 incident. In the lengthy 1998 police report on the Sandusky incident, Joe Paterno's name was never mentioned. And Joe Paterno stated he had no recollection of being told. State law also required strict confidentiality in child sexual abuse investigations, so it would have been illegal for Joe Paterno to have been told.

All of this information was available to Freeh, but he chose to shape his interpretation to fit his unproven narrative in the face of a preponderance of evidence to the contrary.

In 2001 Sandusky no longer worked for Joe Paterno, and access to the facility had been granted to Sandusky by the administration and signed off by provost Rod Erickson (who would ascend to the presidency in the first days of the scandal). Paterno, not sure what he could do in this situation, reported it to his superiors as required by law and by university policy. ESPN writer and holder of multiple Pulitzer Prizes Don Van Natta said after reading all the reports: "Even if you believe he should have done more, it is a big leap to a cover-up, one unsupported by any evidence."

In a September 2013 interview with the CBS show *60 Minutes* Sandusky prosecutor Frank Fina was asked if he believed Joe Paterno had been involved in the alleged cover-up. "I do not," he said. "And I'm viewing this strictly on the evidence, not any kind of fealty to anybody. I did not find that evidence."

Critics contend that Joe Paterno should have called the police immediately. They forget he would have been calling the police with secondhand information. Joe Paterno did not even know for certain if the story was true. The witness did not perceive something that he thought needed immediate police attention, so how was Joe Paterno to interpret that? If Joe Paterno had made that call, any officer would've asked to talk to the actual witness.

As for those who say he should have closely tracked the investigation, he was not allowed to call police and follow up. He had reported it to his superiors, and they met with the witness. As far as Joe knew, the matter was resolved, and no wrongdoing was found. A decade later it resurfaced when he was made aware that Jerry was the subject of a grand jury investigation.

A few months after Joe Paterno's grand jury testimony in January 2011, the state police came to the Lasch Football Building to question all of the coaches. At that point Joe Paterno had already been to a grand jury session, requiring him to testify for a total of roughly seven minutes. Just before we were to be questioned individually, Joe had us all in a staff meeting. The story had already broken in *The* (Harrisburg) *Patriot-News*, so we were all aware Jerry was being investigated. Joe looked at us and told us that the state police were here to question us.

"You guys all know Cynthia Baldwin," he said. She was a former Pennsylvania State Supreme Court Justice before becoming Penn State's legal counsel. She would be in the interviews with all of us. "She is going to come in to talk to you. All I'll tell you is this: when you talk to the police, just tell them the truth. If you know anything, tell them. If you don't, you don't, but just be honest."

The honest truth in this is: no matter how much society wants to spread that blame to others, using perceptions fostered by false narratives in the media, the culprit is the one responsible. This problem involved one man with young people in his children's charity The Second Mile. Almost all the crimes he committed were in no way connected to Penn State or the football program.

Clemente stated on ESPN's *Outside the Lines* on February 10, 2013: "One man was responsible for this—Jerry Sandusky. This was not a football culture problem. This was not a Penn State problem."

There is a perception that Sandusky continued even after the 2001 incident to bring kids to Penn State practices, travel with the team to away games and bowl games, and even bring them to the sidelines for home games. There is a perception he kept showing up and showering with boys in our building. That is one reason why some people believe we knew and looked the other way.

None of that is true. After he retired Sandusky was no longer part of our program, and we did not see him except when he came in to work out alone early in the morning.

When I went to ESPN in February 2013 to discuss the results of our report, I found persistent misinformation. After I explained the 1998 situation to Mike Golic and finished our interview, he stated Joe Paterno had to have known when Sandusky was arrested. Sandusky was not arrested in 1998.

Later that morning, Colin Cowherd stated that Joe Paterno should have known that Sandusky had been to a grand jury in 1998. There was no grand jury at that time. Cowherd also asserted that Paterno should have fired Sandusky in 2001. That would have required Joe Paterno to have re-hired him, so that he could fire him. All those months later, the false narratives persisted.

But the university administration finds it convenient to let the false perceptions remain because they help justify actions they took against Joe Paterno and the Penn State football program.

The day the Freeh Report came out, I was the only person who went on television to defend Penn State, the truth, and Joe Paterno. The only one. The first satellite truck showed up at my house at 5:00 AM for the *TODAY Show* and the last one left at 8:15 PM after I was on CNN for *Erin Burnett OutFront*. During that long day, I did interviews with NBC, ESPN, ABC, CBS, CNN, and numerous state media outlets. At the same time while I was defending our school, the Penn State administration did nothing to defend our university. So how could people not come to believe a narrative the administration allowed to persist?

But the record is now clear, that narrative is *not* true.

It's human nature. We all have a tendency to assign the facts and perspective we have on a historical event and judge the actions of people at the time but forget that they did not have the information we have now. As I said on the air that day, we cannot judge the 2001 actions of people who weren't armed with the information we have over a decade later.

The morning after my father had been fired, I was seated at his desk, and he sat in his robe in another chair looking over at me. The pain, the sleepless nights of the previous days were visible in his face. But he had something he wanted me to know. "Jay, I never told you guys about Jerry because I didn't know if it was true," he said. "I certainly couldn't walk into the office and accuse a guy of something that I didn't witness or know to be true. I didn't know that he'd done all that stuff. I had no idea. I just didn't know."

As Dr. Berlin states in his report, any evaluation of someone's actions must take into account how he lived his life. For Berlin there is too much evidence in the way Joe Paterno lived his life to believe he would have acted to conceal this, especially without any evidence that he did.

I can tell you that I knew Jerry Sandusky from the time I was a kid. I coached with him and did charity events for The Second Mile. None of us knew. My own children were around him. My own daughter went to his house for a birthday party for his granddaughter in 2011.

Many believe coaches showered with Sandusky and young boys. During the Sandusky trial, Penn State assistant coach Dick Anderson was asked on the witness stand if "coaches often took showers with Jerry and young boys."

Anderson replied, "Yes".

That answer in court remains, but no other coaches were given a chance to answer. I know that in 17 years coaching at Penn State, I was never in the same shower with Sandusky and a young boy. The other Penn State assistant coaches I talked to said that same thing.

The subsequent use of Anderson's answer in the Freeh Report that "coaches often took showers with Jerry and young boys" was used by the NCAA to help sanction Penn State and damage the reputations of a lot of good men. It fed the perception that we all knew or should have known.

Perception too often becomes reality, but that doesn't make it truth. All Joe Paterno ever wanted was the truth. He had no fear of the truth.

Joe Paterno made the statement: "In hindsight I wish I had done more." But there is a more important statement he wrote on a pad just before he left the house to go to the hospital. It was the last thing he wrote in his own home: "Maybe the silver lining in this is that some good can come of this."

That is the story. Those are the words that we should focus on. Despite all that had happened to him, and more importantly all that had happened to Sandusky's victims, maybe new awareness and a new vigilance on these crimes can help prevent them in the future.

I am not writing to exonerate my father because he did not commit a crime that needs a pardon. If anything, he is guilty of failing to possess the God-like qualities ascribed to him by others, qualities that Joe was the first to insist he never had.

Sandusky was a man who'd adopted several children and had even more foster children placed in his home. The state evaluated him and his home many, many times. That is all we knew back then and we missed it. Can you blame us? Can you blame Joe Paterno? Can you blame our community?

Whether we like it or not, we live in a society where the presumption of innocence is one of, if not *the* most important foundation of our nation. Our system was designed to keep innocent people from being locked up for crimes they did not commit.

Even for the most revolting crimes, we must guard the presumption of innocence for those charged. And even more so for those who report the crimes. To vilify and demonize someone because they did not do more and they did not go outside the law is wrong. It also sends terrible shockwaves to others who may re-think whether they want to come forward.

Discouraging victims or those with knowledge of these crimes from coming forward would be the worst outcome of this scandal.

If all this can happen to Joe Paterno for reporting something that was brought to his attention, how safe is the guy who manages a Walmart, or a middle manager at GM, or a teacher?

There are a lot of lessons to be learned, and maybe good outcomes will emerge from this saga. But this good can come only with a fair reading of the facts. Then we can have some prevention of these crimes in the future.

I have said over and over as I think of my father's note and I think of the words I've spoken so many times since: "We must not sacrifice truth at the altar of expediency."

Chapter 2

First and Last Memories

Maybe I'm like everyone else who has lost a parent. In the void after my father died, I've thought about my first memories of him.

It is hard to pinpoint any one moment. With my parents it's a series of memories. With my mother it was a smile when she fed us a meal she'd prepared all afternoon. It was the panic she felt one afternoon when I went home on a friend's school bus and she couldn't find me. It was the calm with which she held blood-soaked towels on my brother Dave's head after he'd been bitten by a neighbor's Great Dane. It was her putting a Band-Aid and Bactine on a skinned knee while wiping away my tears. She always engaged her kids at their level, kneeling or sitting to talk eye to eye.

With my father my first memories were his presence. As a young child, I would walk into his den in the early morning. The whirring noise of the projector filled the air as he watched films of games and practices from his job as a football coach. I remember leaving my room still clad in footie pajamas. By the time Dave and I reached the kitchen, we'd hear the projector's hum through the dark pre-dawn house.

In the den I'd see the projector's light in his face as the small black-and-white images of 22 little men moved around the small screen and were reflected in his glasses. The men would move forward and backward as he clicked the control, studying each play over and over again so he wouldn't miss a single detail.

With toy cars in hand, I ungracefully waddled bleary-eyed into the den and sat on the carpet. Sometimes I sat in a chair, affording me a view of the magic monochromatic football world unfolding on the little desk-sized screen. Being near him was enough for me. There is an image in my head, a much younger image of my father, turning momentarily from his work and smiling at me.

That smile meant the world to me. For all my life I lived for it. Even as a coach on his staff, seeing him smile after a good joke or after a win was what I lived to see.

As a child I loved to hear him laugh. He'd get on the floor, and we'd attack him. He appointed himself as the resident monster. We jumped on him and when we started to rough him up he'd say, "Hold on, hold on, let me take off my glasses. I don't want to break them."

At three and a half, I have vague memories of driving to Florida before my brother, Scott, was born. It was a long trip, but I remember him at the helm of that Oldsmobile station wagon with the faux wood panel siding and a bubble skylight window midway down the back roof of the car. No one was in a car seat.

A few months after I turned six, Dave and I rode with our father in a private jet to Waco, Texas, for his visit to Baylor University. Penn State had beaten the Southwest Conference-champion Baylor Bears a few months earlier in the Cotton Bowl.

On the plane it was just the three of us. When my father fell asleep, the pilots helped us get all the Chiclets gum on the plane that he didn't want us chewing. When he woke up, we had mouths full of gum, but he didn't protest. He gave us the cowboy hat he had been given on the trip. I wore that hat to school for a week, making my mother cringe at the image of a little five-gallon pipsqueak walking around central Pennsylvania in a ten-gallon hat.

But with a demanding job, a measure of fame that restricted a lot of public activities, and five kids, his free time was limited. There were no hunting trips, no four-hour golf rounds away from us. The time he had was invested in his family.

What he lacked in quantity he did his best to make up for in quality. He was too impatient for fishing, but he gave it a try for his sons.

On a trip to Cape Cod, he took us deep sea fishing and barely survived sea sickness for us. When we returned to the house he smiled as he awarded me my $2 prize for catching the biggest fish—a flounder that we ate that night.

During another fishing day at a friend's farm, I got a fish on the line. Excitedly my father told me to pull the fish out of the water. I yanked with all my might, and the little sunfish flew out of the water over my head, off the hook, and 30 or 40 feet behind us, where it flopped helplessly in the dirt and grass. The fish was returned stunned but alive and swam away. My father smiled and laughed. Those are the things I recall—the joys of my early life.

The daily schedule of our lives revolved around my father's career. Coaching major college football is a demanding, time-consuming pursuit. The head coach assumes responsibility for more than 100 young men, and the practices and the meeting schedules have to fit around class time. Practices often ran until 6:30 or 6:45 at night after a day that started before dawn. My mother always held dinner until my father got home.

Early in life we'd wait until 7:00 PM or later to eat as a family. On Wednesday nights during the football season, my father taped a television show from 7 until 8:00 PM. We would wait until just after 8:00 to eat. By then we had our pajamas on, and as he walked in the door, we could see the first few minutes of *Little House on the Prairie*.

As little Laura Ingalls ran down the hill ahead of her two sisters, we usually saw my father walk around to the back door. The light from inside the big kitchen windows would illuminate him in the dark as he walked past. The television would get turned off, and the focus would be on family.

I remember that old television on a wheeled cart in the kitchen. On summer evenings my father sat on the screened-in porch just off the kitchen and watched reports on the Watergate hearings. I remember the evening news with images of helicopters and wounded soldiers in Vietnam. Most of my television viewing was the news I watched with my father, football, or Saturday morning cartoons.

My interest in politics and the news of the day was cemented one summer afternoon when I saw my father deliver a speech for John Heinz, who was making his first run for the United States senate. But my biggest interest in my life involved my father's job, coaching Penn State football. It was what he did, and as a kid I wanted to do it, too.

In 1973 the foundations were laid for my love for Penn State football. It was late September, and after two road games, Penn State opened the home schedule against Iowa. I had seen Penn State on television before, but finally I was allowed to go to a game in person. My mother was astonished because unlike most five-year-olds I sat still, transfixed by the game action.

I didn't miss a home game for 18 seasons.

My first memories of my father's job and the impact it had on my life are from the autumns of 1973 and 1974. The fall of 1973 was a magical run to an undefeated season and John Cappelletti's Heisman Trophy. That fall I drew pictures and wrote letters for No. 22, and my father delivered them to Penn State's star running back.

The next year started with a home game against Stanford and brought the Goodyear Blimp to town for a few days. In the late summer evenings, it flew around town with the lights on the side relaying messages about Goodyear tires. After several days of hearing my two-year-old brother Scott repeatedly saying, "See bimp, see bimp," we got to ride in the blimp. It was quite a thrill for all of us.

We got to do things that our friends would never get to do, but we were unaware of the things our friends did with their fathers that we could not do with ours. At that age I didn't understand that everything comes with a price.

From my first memories, I saw my father always try to do the best he could whether things were good or bad. He never complained about circumstances he could not control. "Play the cards you're dealt," he'd say to me.

As I recall the last memories of my father in my life, his philosophy carried me through.

First the Sandusky story broke, and then my father was fired. I had walked onto the practice field and carried on.

I tried to see my father every day after practice and meetings. Through everything he was rock solid. I felt an inner sense that I was carrying on when I shouldn't have been, but he remained supportive. In those last few games when I put on my headset before kickoff, I knew he was watching. I felt him there with me, and that enabled me to do my job.

The most lasting final memories were the walks. After he was diagnosed with cancer, the doctors told him to get outside and to walk to build his strength. The treatments were kicking the crap out of him, but the walks were uplifting. My sister Mary and I would take turns walking with him.

We took walks whenever my schedule allowed it. Often a news photographer would follow at a distance. We talked about football, about my kids, about how my wife, Kelley, was holding up through all this mounting pressure.

Each walk was the same, a chilly tromp across Sunset Park in our backyard. The late October snow that fell during his last game had vanished, leaving behind scattered leaves and twigs on the brown frost-scarred grass. He would bundle up in his blue toggle coat and put his hands into his pockets. We'd slip out undetected via the side garage door and across the small backyard. Ducking under evergreen branches, we made our way into the late fall sunlight shining through the tall oak trees in Sunset Park.

The circuit was short at first, but with each walk, he pushed farther. Walking a little more than he did the day before was a triumph, a sign that he was on the upswing. It was his old mantra: *"You either get better or you get worse. You never stay the same."*

Most of the time, the walks were quiet. As it had been on those early childhood mornings, it was enough just to be with him, to be alone in his presence with an occasional smile from him. Despite the cancer he never let his love of humor fade.

But it was on what would be our last walk that I decided to ask about things we had never talked about. Even now I have no idea why I asked about his brother, Franklin Delano Paterno, who'd died as a toddler. I guess when your father is in his 80s and battling cancer you realize if there is something you want know, you need to ask.

He looked straight ahead as he spoke of his mother when his kid brother died. He described her crying and wailing and as he finished telling the story he turned to me and slowed his pace. "You know, she never did get over that," he said.

"Dad, I don't think any parent ever really recovers from losing a child."

He nodded and continued. "I can still hear my mother. I can still hear her on the porch sobbing for him. I'll never forget that."

A tear was in his eye. Maybe he knew more than he was telling me about his own health, his own mortality. What did he know?

We walked another 10 minutes or so, but neither of us spoke except to say "let's keep going" or when we turned for home at the end of Ferguson Avenue.

"I'm getting cold, let's head back," he said.

It struck me that he never complained about being cold. That night he fell and broke his pelvis. He and I never walked together again.

All these years later, there was symmetry to his mood, his personality. As he had been jovial and laughing among a big group of children when we were young, he was that way for his 85th birthday and his last Christmas.

He looked around the room amid the chaotic din of 17 grandkids aged from 16 to the youngest at three years old. Despite the passage of time on his face, there was the same laughter and smile from my early childhood mornings in his den. He had a gleam in his eye as he watched his children trying to settle his grandchildren. "Look," he said, "look at all this. I've had a great life. I have you kids, all these grandkids, and thank God I have your mother. I'm 85 years old. I've already had a life of so much more than I probably ever deserved."

Maybe he knew, but no matter how dark the void seems it cannot eclipse my father's smile from that day.

Chapter 3

My Father at Home

When I was young, every night our family would get together for bedtime prayers. We started with a little prayer that mentioned Mommy and Daddy, Buttons (my parents' nickname for my oldest sister Diana), Mary Kay, Dave, Jay, and George. (My younger brother Scott's name is George Scott Paterno.)

Praying together was something we did nearly every night—five young kids, bathed, teeth brushed, dressed in pajamas with two parents kneeling together to pray. It was truly a Norman Rockwell Americana moment. But our parents were not infallible, and as kids we were far from perfect.

Being the child of a highly successful football coach in a college town is not easy. It comes with benefits but also with negatives. For the people who would help you, there were also some who resented you for the perceived easy life you got. My father always reminded us about the positives and negatives. "You never get anything for nothing," he'd say.

He was also always trying to be fair or appearing to be fair with his children. He hated counters, especially if we kept score of what he'd done for one kid versus what he'd done for another. "Quit worrying all the time about what someone else got," he'd say.

But my father was aware that the world around us was full of scorekeepers and counters and he was keenly aware of public perception. To that end he did everything he could to keep us out of the public eye. He didn't want to create any resentment, and as his fame grew, he did it so that we, as his children, could do our own growing up as privately as possible.

That was what he wanted us to do, to do our own growing in private to find our own paths. In college I was wandering academically, unsure of what I wanted to do. In high school I had been able to get through, to smile, and get by with A's and B's without a tremendous amount of effort; college would demand a higher effort level.

Having a parent in the public eye is a very different reality. Several years ago I caught a piece on television with actor Michael Douglas talking about being the son of Kirk Douglas. That caught my attention.

Michael Douglas stated that children of highly successful parents have people who treat them differently, and it does impact the children's growth. It made a lot of sense. As we grew up in State College, there were always those people who would ask, "Is Joe your father?" And then you could see their attitude and approach to you change.

Unfortunately as a kid I may have been aware of being treated differently, but I did not *understand*. If my homework was a little late, sometimes I wouldn't get points docked. If I was a little out of line, they'd let me slide. A kid subconsciously picks up on that, and then always expects expanded boundaries.

By the time I got to college, suddenly I was trying to figure out what it was that I wanted to do with my life. Without any direction I drifted, doing very well in some classes and poorly in others.

That was what drove my father crazy. One day he gave me an article from *The New York Times* about a son who finally released himself from what he perceived to be his father's expectations. It was written by Richard Lapchick, the son of former St John's and New York Knicks head basketball coach Joe Lapchick.

My father wrote a note on it for me with the lesson being that my life and my future were up to me. I did not have to try and be him or try to do what I thought he wanted me to do.

I still didn't get it, and my college academic career fell well short of what I was capable. That is a great regret of my life. There was so much more I could have and should have done. But I did learn from my father that you never stop learning. Many of my life's lessons have been what I've learned from the people around me and from a constant appetite for reading.

Through my ups and downs, there was a constant. I always knew he was there for his family. When big trauma struck, he was a rock, showing an even bigger sense of responsibility.

In 2004 we were in the midst of a bad night game at Wisconsin. Two quarterbacks I coached were hurt; one was taken off in an ambulance. With about two minutes to go in a 16–3 loss, Penn State president Graham Spanier and assistant athletic director Fran Ganter came into the coaches' box.

My sister's husband had sustained a bad injury in a bicycle accident. As soon as the game ended, we rushed to the airport where the university plane took us home. The flight was bumpy, and my father sat quietly for most of that flight, trying to sleep. I knew he couldn't. The loss didn't matter. We were leaving one player behind in a Madison hospital and headed to see a family member in another.

By the time I finally got my father back to his house, I had a moment to talk with him. His thoughts were immediately with his daughter and his grandchildren. He never talked as though he had no faith, but he was preparing for a future that would be different. In his mind he was worried about how his daughter would raise her family and take care of her children if her husband wasn't able to resume a normal life. "Jay," he said to me, "maybe it is time to get out."

"Why is that?" I asked.

"If he isn't okay, I can retire, and your mother and I will help take care of the kids. Your sister may need a lot of help."

That was the length he was willing to go. Football had always been important, but in that moment I knew where his priorities were. I don't know if I ever told my sister or her children how much their future meant to my father that night.

Twenty-seven years earlier he missed a Penn State game at Syracuse to be at Geisinger Medical Center. He and my mother knelt at the bedside of my brother, praying for his recovery while Dave lay motionless in a coma, fighting to stay alive. My father prayed to God to take him, if he'd just spare his son. He'd told Dr. Henry Hood that if he just gave Dave a chance he'd make it because he knew Dave was a fighter. He was right.

In 1998 he shared kind and wise words with me after my wife, Kelley, and I lost our first baby in the third month of pregnancy. My mother and father had suffered through a couple of miscarriages. It happened in January during recruiting, and I was anxious to get back on the road. He told me to take a couple of days off. "Jay, you don't know how hard this will be on Kelley. I underestimated how it would hurt your mother. I wasn't there for her and I regret that. Stay home."

It was never easy for my father to admit mistakes, but he shared this most personal admission to me so that I wouldn't make the same error. The next day I walked into a supermarket and saw a man holding his baby. Seeing what I'd lost brought me close to tears. Then I remembered my dad's advice and I thought how hard it would hit my wife.

When I finally became a parent, I was armed with the lessons he'd given me. He had been a great father, certainly not perfect, but great.

In my conversations with my father, I came to understand one thing. From the time his father died, he carried an incredible sense of responsibility to head his family then and his own family when he married a few years later.

Family pictures were always present in his office. To him it was a visible reminder of why he worked, to take care of his wife and his children. He knew how lucky he was to be able to do a job he loved that enabled us to have a good life.

After a long day at work, my father would come in the house and go to his den to relax, make notes on that day's practice. We avoided him and allowed him to decompress as he sipped a small glass of Old Grand-Dad bourbon on the rocks.

My mother kept us away, but through the crack of the slightly ajar door, we could see him in his chair, thinking and making notes on a yellow pad. As a kid it was tough to wait for him to finish. Like most kids, when Daddy came home, I wanted to run and jump on him and tell him all about my day.

If he was done making notes before dinner, he'd open the door a little and peek around and ask where the kids were. Whoever was near would run, crawl, or waddle into the den. Then he'd listen to our ceaseless chatter about our days.

Once dinner was ready, the mealtime turned into a class lecture on anything and everything. This was when he challenged us to think, to defend a position. If all of us agreed on something, he'd argue the other side just so we had to defend our position. This was where he thrived.

It also showed him how different each child was. My sister Mary argued passionately for her points. My brother, Dave, had his point and 20 other points he wanted to make. Diana was pretty concise. Once Scott started on a point, the challenge was getting the floor back from him.

We argued about anything and everything. My mother would grow tired of the arguing and get the encyclopedia to settle any factual disagreements. Then we'd start to clear the table and do the dishes while whoever would not let the argument rest was seated with my father arguing a last point.

Dave figured out that if you kept arguing you ended up with someone else clearing your plate and doing the dishes. There were many occasions when whoever was vacuuming the floor after dinner had to ask my father to lift his feet so they could vacuum under his chair.

The arguing was the bluster, the Socratic debating society, but there were lots of card games, too. My father and his brother, George, used to play pinochle. One night while at the Jersey Shore, Dave and I rigged the deck so that Dave would win every hand. I dealt the cards, so he wouldn't suspect us.

My dad knew what was up and watched as his brother got suckered by a 10-year-old and an eight-year-old. My uncle's expression changed, and disbelief grew with each hand my brother won. Finally about a half an hour after we'd fooled him, we fessed up, and my father laughed and laughed.

Like all fathers my dad had a soft spot for his daughters. They were spared the same types of punishment that the boys got, mostly because they actually stayed out of trouble.

That said, my sisters, Diana and Mary, as the oldest had the strictest rules and the most pressure. Diana rose to every academic challenge, and still my father pushed her to do better. To this day I think that drives her. By the time Mary was finishing in college, my father's constant pressure had moderated.

But the challenge of being a family remained and was more difficult because our father was highly recognizable.

In 1983 we went to Disneyland in California. We got to the park and headed to ride the Matterhorn. Within a minute in line, someone recognized my father. Then it happened again. Before we'd been in the park two hours, it was obvious to my father that his wife and five children were spending time waiting for him to talk to people he didn't even know.

He felt he was ruining our day so he decided to go back to the hotel rather than slow us down at the park. Now as a father myself, I know how different it is to be there and see the smiles on your child's face as opposed to just hearing about their day after they do something really fun and exciting.

My father did his best to work around his fame. But there was a void for us as kids. There were moments in life when you want to see your parents. Little League baseball, school plays, and games were moments where friends saw their mothers *and* their fathers in the audience or the crowd. He missed a lot, and as a child, I focused on his absence rather than on my mother's presence. That wasn't fair to my mother or to my father. We may have taken my mother for granted because she was always there.

But his absence was something that I, as a child, noticed. As a coach I missed many of those moments for my children and I now realize that it could not have been easy for him. Now that I have many of those moments to share with my kids, I realize how valuable that time is for them and for me.

He tried his best to be a good husband. He believed that being a good husband requires knowing what you don't know. That came in handy every Christmas, Mother's Day, or Valentine's Day—which also happens to be my mother's birthday. Once my sisters reached high school, my father figured out that they could pick out gifts for my mother far more effectively than he could.

He did shop for her in the early days. When we were young, he took the four oldest children to a store on Allen Street. We walked into the old Bostonian store and my father, with the help of Guy Kresge, one of the store's owners, picked some boots, a purse, and gloves. There were three boxes wrapped up for my mom.

But all four of us wanted to take a box home, and my father was stuck trying to get out of there without one child crying, so Kresge gave him an empty wrapped box for us to take home. My mom was excited to see four boxes under the tree. She was surprised to open an empty box and ultimately laughed at my father's attempt at shopping with the four kids.

Later in life my sister Mary Kay ran point on my father's gift shopping for my mother. In recalling her duty as a loving daughter she said, "Dad always thought about getting Mom something but could never get downtown to shop for it because he was hounded by people talking to him. I started asking him if he wanted me to shop for him. I showed him the gifts before they were wrapped, so he could at least pretend he'd picked them out. It was always a game—Mom would say, 'What is it?' before she opened it. But then after she did, he would always say, 'I thought you'd really like this.'" Actually in 2011 he walked downtown and purchased cards for their anniversary.

He always felt he owed my mother the best of everything he could do for her because she meant so much to him. Throughout his career he could focus on his job, knowing she had the home front secure. But there were times when he had to watch us, and most of the time no one got hurt. On occasion there were disastrous moments.

When we were very young, my mother went to Mass alone, leaving my father in charge of four young kids. Dave was about four years old. He cut his head. My father could not find the bandages, so my sisters, ages eight and six, looked for some in my mother's bathroom cabinet.

What they found were feminine hygiene products. So as my father pulled up outside the church, Dave was hanging out the window with a maxi pad on his head.

My mother was justifiably mortified. As she got into the car, she looked at my dad in disbelief. She asked why there was a maxi pad on her son's head, and my father replied that he couldn't find the Band-Aids. Then she asked why he didn't take the maxi pad off of their son's head. "I'm not touching those things," he replied.

It was part of who he was. There were just some things he couldn't and wouldn't deal with. That was one of the minor incidents. Dave broke his arm as a young kid after jumping off the fireplace ledge. There was my sister Mary's broken hip when she was just out of college.

There was a whole series of accidents that my mother had, and every time he was by her side through it all. The worst was when my mother broke her hip in Spain. My father was across the Atlantic and did not speak Spanish, so he called home to get help from his children.

Mary swung into action along with my father's staff assistants, Cheryl Norman and Sandi Segursky. They arranged to get a way home for my mother and father and even to get a Spanish speaker on the phone with the doctor.

As they were leaving Spain to get home to have the surgery done here, my father offered the doctor cash to pay for the help they'd given him. Through an interpreter the doctor told my father, "There is no charge here in this country. We may not have much money, but we are not poor."

Through that event we saw my father rely on his children and then remain by my mother's side after the surgery and through the recovery in Hershey, Pennsylvania, until she was ready to come home. Seeing my father by my mother's side in those days reminded me I had grown up in a home with two parents who loved each other.

As a kid I thought my father had one of the coolest jobs in the world even if I didn't know exactly what it was that he did as a coach, as evidenced by a letter sent to a colleague of my father.

LETTER TO PENN STATE ASSISTANT ATHLETIC DIRECTOR JIM TARMAN

May 13, 1976

Dear Jim,

My wife and I thoroughly enjoyed attending the Blue-White Game and the party at Stone Valley.

This event and the way it is handled has to be unusual for a big university, and I doubt that any other institution has members of the Department of Athletics cook steaks and serve the kind of dinner that you and your associates did. It was great.

We also enjoyed the view of the game from the Press Box. Perhaps you have not heard that Jay Paterno, the youngest son of Joe, when questioned as to what his father did said he had an office in Rec Hall. The questioner asked, "Well, what does your father do in his office?" The answer was "He writes." Then the question was posed, "What does he write?" Whereupon Jay answered, "He writes circles and x's."

Thanks again for a memorable weekend.

Sincerely,
Roy

I may not have fully comprehended everything in life, but he said something to me that I remember to this day. In second grade I was a student at Our Lady of Victory elementary school. Every lunch was from 11:30 to 12:30, and once we were done eating we went outside to play. That meant a 10-minute lunch followed by 50 minutes of football, kickball, dodgeball, or basketball.

My mother had the idea that I could spend two lunches a week taking piano lessons. At first I went along with it. Then I started to regularly forget my book or to practice, anything to get out of the lessons. The teacher suggested that I was wasting her time and my parents' money. I begged my parents to let me quit. "Jay," my father said, "when I was your age, I quit piano lessons and now I wish that I had never quit. You will regret this."

He was right. To this day I regret never having learned to play the piano or any other instrument. Football and kickball end, but a talent like playing the piano never leaves you.

There were other lessons, lessons on compassion and empathy and concern for our fellow man. One summer my father had received a letter from a family that was facing big challenges. All of their children had a disease that would eventually leave them blind. The oldest was already blind, and his younger siblings were starting down the same path.

My parents invited them to the house, and we took them to Sunset Park behind our home. It was something for us to see. We had to adapt to accommodate them and have compassion for the limitations they faced in their lives.

As we grew up, my mother became involved in Special Olympics, and we saw her commitment to the happiness of other people. Even now my own children have learned that compassion from my mother and father's dedication to serving others less fortunate.

But the involvement in the lives of others came with a price. We found our father being pulled away from us. We found that he was someone who we shared with many other people, and that was not easy.

He missed most of Mary's gymnastics meets and had a hard time coming to see Diana's high school cheerleading events. Most weekends he missed Scott's youth hockey games. Once he went camping on a scouting event with Dave. That was the first and last camping trip of his parental career.

In my senior year of high school, he missed my football banquet and all but one of my games. The one he came to see was one where I threw a costly interception while trying to avoid a sack. We lost the game 10–7 to Punxsutawney.

The toughest years were the years he was Penn State's athletic director as well as head football coach. In those years he never seemed to be home.

There was an upside in his years as athletic director for us and for him as well. My mother always suggested he take us along to Penn State athletic events. We saw a whole range of sports, both men's and women's sports, but mostly we just enjoyed sitting next to my dad.

My father also learned from the events. As athletic director he saw women in sports with the same drive and commitment to excellence that his own higher-profile football student-athletes had. That changed his outlook on women's sports and on all women for the rest of his life.

When he met my wife, Kelley, he was impressed by her poise and the fact that she'd been a college athlete at the University of Virginia. My father also found common ground with her parents, Arlene and Leon, who had both been college athletes when they went to Tufts University.

As time rolled on, I got engaged, and my wedding was set for the summer of 1992. My father had a great day at that wedding. You would be hard pressed to find anyone who was at a wedding with my parents that did not cite them as the life of the party.

But at their own children's weddings, there were real emotions.

I remember seeing my father wipe tears from his eyes as my oldest sister, Diana, the first in our family to get married, came to greet my parents during Mass after she and her husband, Gary, had taken their vows. By the reception the tears were gone, and my parents owned the dance floor.

It didn't even have to be a wedding. At my mother's 60th birthday party, he joined as we sang Rolling Stones songs with the band. During "Sympathy For The Devil," he was there singing the backup "Woo, Woo" with all of his kids. There was never a less talented singing group that covered the Stones.

Friends who'd invited my parents to Bar Mitzvahs reported how my mom and dad jazzed up the party. "Sue and Joe Paterno—they do weddings, Bar Mitzvahs, and birthday parties," they'd say.

Those moments were special for him and for the people around him. It was in those events that people saw my father as a man who wanted to be a part of everyday life despite his job and the fame that came with it.

It was that fame that created a conflict within him throughout his life. When I had left to coach, he had a couple of opportunities to come see the teams I coached play a game. In 1993 Connecticut played at Villanova when Penn State did not have a game. He planned to go, and it would have been an easy trip for him.

The day before the game, he called to tell me he couldn't make it. On the call he explained that with a game the following week he couldn't afford to have people see him taking a Saturday off to go see his son. Not wanting to hurt his feelings, I bottled up the fact that I was disappointed.

The next season while I was at James Madison University, Penn State had another off week while my team was home. We were playing William & Mary in a meeting of two highly ranked Division I-AA teams.

Again my father indicated that he would come down for the game. Sure enough, on Thursday I got the call that I knew would come, the one where he told me he couldn't come because he didn't want to be seen away from campus during the season.

I wanted to tell him that it was high time he stopped caring about others' opinions; my feelings should carry some weight with him. But I didn't and I suspect he knew how I truly felt. As my mother arrived on Friday, I was glad to see her but still sad that my father was not here. It was Little League all over again.

In all the years I lived away from Penn State, he never was able to come visit me or see where I lived. At the time it bothered me, and maybe it did for many years afterward, but we made up for lost time eventually.

Part of what eased the moments we lost as kids were some of the things we did get. There were people in and out of our house who were accomplished and fascinating. There were Corporate CEOs Bill Schreyer of Merrill Lynch, Phil Knight of Nike, William Weiss of Ameritech, and Quentin Wood of Quaker State; governors Tom Ridge and Milton Shapp; Steelers great Franco Harris; Pirates manager Chuck Tanner after the 1979 World Series; authors James Michener and Bill Blatty; Oscar winner and *Casablanca* co-writer Julius Epstein; and Grammy winner Mike Reid.

When people like them were in the house, I knew to shut up and listen. We knew that instinctively because my parents believed and explained that children were "to be seen and not heard." I made sure that while not being heard that I listened intently when given the chance to be around successful people.

It was a fascinating home to grow up in, and there were always lessons to be learned. After home football games, the house was always full of friends and guests eating and drinking and celebrating after a win or commiserating after a loss.

The lessons of how to conduct your life with grace and poise after success or failure were evident after every game. My parents smiled and welcomed people to their home with the same composure whether the game was a win or a loss.

That lesson carries me today. The things we learned from our parents, who tried their best to raise us in circumstances they probably never imagined, will always stay with their children. There was a dignity and class that was always the undercurrent of their life conduct.

In those moments we, their children, saw that while they made mistakes they never gave up that dignity nor did they give in on their values. They knew their place, and we, as their children, knew even if we strayed, there was always a guiding light of principle.

Maybe the best memory of all the postgame parties came after a tough 7–6 loss against Iowa in 1976. Sometime after dinner my brother Scott, then a little over a month from his fourth birthday, climbed on a chair. He held a plastic toy guitar and wore blue and white pom-poms as a wig.

Before my parents could stop him he started singing a song he'd made up. "When my Daddy *was* a coach..."

Everyone, family and dozens of friends, roared in laughter at the idea of Joe Paterno being a former coach, something that wouldn't come to be true for another 35 years. The truth was that he lived his entire parental life as a coach and a father; we all had to balance those demands.

The demands required sacrifices from us, and we lost a part of him. That will never change, but what we could not understand was how much it cost him and how much it hurt him as well.

Chapter 4

Crime and Punishment

Growing up as the child of Joe Paterno in State College had its challenges. But it was a smaller town back then, and people looked out for one another.

My parents were spoiled having two girls first, my well-behaved sisters, Diana and then Mary Kay. Then they had three boys, Dave, then me, followed by my brother Scott. My sisters were easier, a lot easier, and my father used to joke that they should've stopped after two kids. Boys tend to challenge mothers and fathers, and we were no different. My father's job kept him away from us quite a bit, so my mother was left to pick up the slack.

In October of 1977, Dave had a very serious accident on a trampoline at our elementary school, Our Lady of Victory. The accident left him in a coma for a week, and it was really an act of God that he survived. I'm not sure that week ever left my mom's psyche.

Given how her sons tested limits, my mother rightfully worried. On summer nights we'd sneak out of the house to a nearby Mr. Donut and steal the flour sacks of day-old donuts they'd normally throw away. We enjoyed the donuts, but far more exciting was the thrill of the chase and the fear of getting caught. At 2:00 AM there were usually police cars parked there with officers inside drinking coffee.

Dave and I never did get caught. As for Scott the police brought him and his friend home one night from Mr. Donut. My parents were out of town, and my sister Mary was in charge, so that ended the era of Donut raids.

In fifth grade I walked with a friend to a store called Boot's Dairyette to buy smoke bombs. My friend's mother caught us playing with lighter fluid, matches, and smoke bombs—a big no-no and not to mention more than a little stupid.

After she called my mother, I had to be punished, but not before my father relayed a story to me. It was about peer pressure, about having people respect me and not just like me. The story he told was from his childhood in Brooklyn. A group of friends had decided to steal money from the Chinese laundry and asked my father to go along. After thinking about it, he decided to go along with the group.

They didn't get caught, but even all these years later, his failure to do right still bothered him. He had followed in the wrong direction rather than lead the right way.

My father had high standards for all of us. But if he were a cop, my father would've had his badge taken away. With us he was a shoot-first, ask-questions-later guy. If we were roughhousing in the basement, he'd come down and yell at us to stop fighting. After he would yell, he'd realize there was no fighting, then apologize, and then tell us to go outside to run around.

What he lacked in patience he made up for in consistency. The same things he demanded from his team and coaches he demanded from his sons. As coaches we were to wear ties in the office every day that school was in session at Penn State. For the team he demanded punctuality; short, well-kept hair; no earrings; a clean-shaven look; no hats indoors; socks; and cussing was never to be tolerated.

To this day I stay clean-shaven, have short hair, remove my hat inside, and wear socks (even with flip-flops). When in doubt I wear a tie, better to have one and not need one than to show up without one and wish you'd worn one.

But as hard as we tried, there were always moments we'd fail to live up to our parents' standards. The missteps I made along the way were mostly a function of youth or stupidity but not out of malice.

There were small things. Being on time for dinner was a big one. My father felt it showed a lack of respect for my mother's hard work preparing dinner. In the 1970s and 1980s, it was the norm in our neighborhood that we left the house and played with other kids. No one set up playdates back then. We just walked to our friend's house whether we were invited or not.

We had a park in the backyard, acres of woods, ballfields, a basketball court, and kids our own age all within walking distance. As with most kids, paying attention to the time was not a strong suit. My mom had a solution. About 15 or 20 minutes before dinner, she had a distinctive London police whistle that she would blow. When you heard that whistle and you could hear it all over the neighborhood, you knew to get home.

At dinner my father insisted we eat *everything* my mother made. It was about respect. Even on the unfortunate nights when we could smell the liver and onions cooking from a block away, we knew we'd have to eat it. If we smelled liver before we came home, we tried to finagle an invitation to a friend's house.

Scott hated fish and almost threw it up. My father informed him that if he threw it up, he would still have to eat everything on his plate, including whatever he threw up. Scott did not throw up. Dave did not like clam chowder and tried to get away with it by spitting it into his cup of milk. After dinner my mother took his cup, put it in the refrigerator, and when Dave sat down for dinner the next night he found a cup of clam chowder waiting for him.

Almost everything my mother made was excellent, so eating everything on your plate was rarely a challenge. But being late was inexcusable. Woe to those unfortunate souls who did not hear the whistle and came to dinner late. Being late meant being grounded for a day, and being grounded meant you stayed home to do whatever Mom had for you to do. I believe it was Mary who once said to my mom during a day of labor: "You know I am not your slave." The comment was not well received.

For most of the transgressions, there was acceptance that by failing to live up to the standards the consequence was being grounded (atonement) and then absolution. The hardest part of failing was admitting it. When you got caught you had to appear before my father or mother and own up to what you'd done.

The vast majority of our problems were the same two-bit mischief most kids get into from time to time. Egging houses on Halloween was something we did once or twice. The great irony of that was the one time someone called my parents we were actually innocent. I knew who did it, but I did not commit the crime.

I'll never forget listening to my parents defend me. My mother argued on the phone with the neighbor who told her that she had smelled the "odor of egg" and looked outside to see me. My mother yelled from the kitchen to my dad's den. I was in the kitchen, listening to my mom going after the neighbor and loving it. "Joe," she yelled "get on the phone."

He was in the den working on game plans, but when my mom called out to him, he picked up the phone. I heard him start into the conversation and I was excited at this new development in the story. From the kitchen I could see him in there, and he grew quiet.

What I did not hear was the neighbor say to my father, "Joe, I know you're a good father, but I am not sure what kind of a mother Sue is." That was all he needed to hear. "Look, don't you dare question what kind of mother Sue is. Now you listen, my son says he did not do this, so I don't care what you think you saw. He did not do it. But above all don't ever say that about Sue ever again."

Boy, did I ever think that was cool. My father had defended me against a false accusation and had gotten mad at a neighbor for questioning my mom's ability to raise us.

Other phone calls were warranted.

One call that wasn't made would've been as bad as anything that ever got home to them. In fourth grade at the Our Lady of Victory Catholic Elementary School, we were using foul language. The entire fourth grade was called in to sit and explain who was behind the foul language epidemic and ask what we thought those words meant. Toward the end of the meeting, it got real interesting. When the principal, Sister Moya, yelled, "And what does F--- mean? I have heard of intercourse but never f---. I am going to call all your parents into school. You can tell them what f--- means."

We envisioned the roof of the school splitting open with lightning striking all of us, God's wrath upon us because we'd made a nun say a bad word. Then I thought about my parents coming to school and having to explain what I was saying. The lightning sounded like a much better option. The call never happened, but every day for over a month, I went to school, fearing that today would be the day. We didn't step out of line for a long, long time. That fear of facing my parents was all I needed.

Lunchtime in elementary school also meant throwing snowballs on snowy days. Our school principal issued a stern warning that anyone throwing snowballs would be paddled. We took that to mean we couldn't throw snowballs at other students or people, so we went out and invented a game. One kid would throw a snowball on the pavement, leaving a marker for us to aim at. The rest of us tried and get our snowball closest to that mark, like snowball bocce.

Some girls reported that the boys were throwing snowballs. We were rounded up and paddled without any chance to explain our side of the story.

When I went home to complain, my father was not sympathetic. Then he explained one of the reasons why we went to the Catholic school. Dave had acted up at the public school, and the principal called home. My father suggested that the principal might want to spank Dave if he was out of hand. The principal was taken aback. "Well, Mr. Paterno, we do not do that here at this school," the principal said.

The next year Dave and I were at a new school, one where we might get spanked. I had been spanked for a legitimate misunderstanding and got *zero* sympathy from my father. We live in a different time and place from those days. Not only do schools refrain from spankings but so do parents. My parents had a wooden paddle. The threat of it was actually scarier and more painful than the actual spanking. Dave was a genius. When he knew he was in trouble he'd wear an extra pair or two of underwear so the spanking would be deadened through his pants and multiple sets of underwear.

If you really did something horribly wrong, there was the threat of a belt across your butt. One time I showed complete disrespect for my mother, one of the things that made my father angriest. He decided that I had committed a belt-worthy offense and ordered me to go get his belt. I wasn't the smartest kid, but I wasn't dumb either. Given the option to select from an entire rack of belts for my own punishment, I selected a thin preppy cotton belt with sailboats on it, the kind of belt that my father never actually wore.

In the kitchen I handed him "his belt". Needless to say he didn't find it as funny as I did and he sent me back for another belt. By the time I returned, I was already so scared that he gave me one lame swat with the belt and sent me on my way.

I wasn't the only one to step out of line in our house, in fact far from it. We all had our moments. But we knew what the standard was. We knew he expected more from us than we even expected from ourselves.

There were difficult years when I was a teenager. The summer before I started college, a number of friends had started classes in the summer. Through my friends I met girls who were new in town. Since I hadn't started college, I was living at home. My friends, both old and new, had no curfew in the dorms, and I wanted to stay out later than my midnight deadline.

I headed home at 11:30 and waited for my parents to go to bed. Then I headed right back out and returned at 2:17. Successfully, I slipped back into the house unnoticed and went to bed.

The next morning my mother woke me up at 7:00 AM to do housework, weeding and cleaning gutters. Around lunchtime my father returned from the office and stopped to ask me what time I had gotten in. I admitted that I had gone back out for a little bit but wasn't sure what time I'd gotten in. "That's horse manure," he barked. "You got in at 2:17 and you know it. I saw you look at your watch when you came back in the house. I heard you leave and I waited up."

"Sorry Dad."

"I just can't stand a sneak."

"I did own up to going back out. If you knew what time I got in, why did you ask? Isn't that entrapment?"

"Entrapment? This isn't a courtroom. You're grounded for two days. If you'd have been straight with me, it would have only been for a day."

The punishment was always worse if you lied or offered a lame excuse. But for me that story wasn't the worst of it.

In November of 1986, Penn State was undefeated, ranked No. 3 in the country, and headed to Notre Dame for a big game. I was a freshman in college and, like the other guys on the team who were not on the travel squad, stayed behind. My mother was going to the game, so there would be no parents in town.

On Thursday I decided to go ahead and have people over for a party. We made a couple of calls and found a 21-year-old willing to buy the beer for the party. I myself did not drink, but I knew that everyone else at the party would want beer. The expectations were for a manageable number of people to come over to the house and have a good time. Growing up in State College, I knew most of the people I had gone to school with, and no one made a big deal about coming over to my house.

Well, plenty of college kids felt that it would be a big deal to be at that party and they showed up. Ultimately we kicked everyone out and spent the rest of the time cleaning up. We vacuumed the carpets with Carpet Fresh and then walked around on them so it wouldn't look like we'd cleaned the house and arouse any suspicions. Despite our best efforts I got caught and faced a lengthy atonement period. For a few weeks when my father spoke to my mom about me he acted like I wasn't in the room. "If he doesn't like what you're telling him to do, Sue, tell him he can move out."

I was standing five feet from him.

It went on like that for a while. But over time, a long time, it was eventually forgiven.

Forgiveness often took some time, even after the threat of even greater punishments. At one point he told Scott that the way he was living his life, the house wasn't big enough for the both of them. "If you keep it up, one of us is going to have to find somewhere else to live, and since my name is on the mortgage, I guess we know who is staying."

During college I was so inconsistent academically, and that drove my father crazy. This was a man who preached discipline and consistent effort as the keys to excellence. I couldn't grasp it.

There was a time when I was convinced he didn't really like me much, and I walked on eggshells around him. I was acting like a jerk in college and in a file I found after he died I found some difficult notes in there from that time.

VERY DIFFICULT RELATIONSHIP

Maybe it is my fault that I didn't let you in when you were very young—wanted to watch films and talk football—It always seemed you were too young and I didn't have time. Because of the intensity to have good football teams I gave up so many joys I might have shared with all my children.

As a father I can understand your shortcomings—your youth—your immaturity—your indecision as to what is important to you day to day—your commitment to studies or lack of commitment.

I have no care for you to be a football player or a coach—although it would be wonderful to have you succeed. I want you to be happy, to be successful in whatever way you define success.

I feel that I am either about to lose a Son whom I love deeply or that I can keep a son who will hate me someday because I allow him to do foolish youthful things which will impair his character and purpose all his life.

As a father I can comprehend how difficult those words had to be for him to write. His concerns were warranted. But he was unyielding in his deep belief in his responsibility to prepare us for life. That came through in the way he dealt with crime and punishment.

Joe Paterno's way requires us to set standards, to challenge our children to understand consequences for all of their actions. That's how children ultimately grow to be adults and that's how I learned to be a better person, even if it did take some time.

Chapter 5

The Three Things We Didn't Talk About at Home

In Joe Paterno's house there were three things that we didn't talk about. One was office business. Another was money. The third was anything related to or that might allude to anything sexual.

Being a college football coach in a college town obsessed with the game, inside information is valuable. Fans, journalists, bookies, and gamblers are curious about game plans, practice information, or injuries. My father didn't share information at home. I coached with him for 17 seasons, and when our family got together, if office business would come up, he'd change the subject.

The other two subjects that were treated as though they didn't exist were money and sex. We had old-school parents, old-school *Catholic* parents.

We never knew how much my father made until a Freedom of Information Act request was made, and after some time in the courts, his salary was released. People were genuinely surprised how low it was—somewhere around $1 million a year.

People who do not know college football may think $1 million a year to coach football sounds good, but understand that it is low for a coach at this level. In 2013 just two years after Joe Paterno's career ended, the *average* salary for a Big Ten head coach was more than $2.6 million.

The popular portrayal was of a Penn State conspiracy trying to keep Joe's salary a big secret. Joe told the administration to go ahead and release it and not waste the court's time with it.

Coaching wasn't the profession he chose because he thought he'd get rich. In the 1950s coaches weren't paid a lot of money. In 1966 he took the head coaching job with a handshake and the promise of a $20,000 annual salary—no agent, lawyers, buy-out clauses, shoe deals, negotiations over facilities, or exceptions to admission rules. Today you don't even step in that room without all those things either settled or present.

But as bad as the topic of money was, talking about sex was something that he really avoided. Both as a parent and coach when he was cornered and had to talk about it, he danced on the edges of it. My mother was the same way.

There were really only two talks on the subject of sex that I ever got from my parents. One included the time I got "the talk."

On Thursday, July 9, 1992, I was packed up and getting ready to head to Pittsburgh, where I was going to get married two days later. It was around one o'clock in the afternoon, my car was packed and in the driveway. Before I started on the drive, I ran into the house to grab a Diet Pepsi and jogged past my mom in the kitchen. "See you tomorrow, Mom," I said.

"Drive safely," she said.

At the door into the garage, I opened it and started down the stairs. Heading up the driveway was my dad coming in from a lunchtime walk. I saw him stop to look into the back of my car and see my bags in there.

Halfway through the garage, we crossed paths. His face was covered in sweat, and his white Nike golf shirt was soaked through. He was still puffing from his power walk that had lasted for several miles. He hesitated and said, "Are you leaving now?"

"Yes, I'm going now," I said.

I had walked slightly past him as I spoke, but I stopped and looked back. He was still headed toward the steps, but he paused and turned back to me. "Hey," he began, "drive safely."

"I will."

There was a sense that he had something else he wanted to say, but I wasn't sure what it could be. "Um..." he said hesitantly, "do you need me to talk to you about anything?"

At first I didn't have the slightest idea what he could possibly be talking about. Then it hit me. He wanted to talk about *that*. I was the first of his sons to get married, and this was "the talk."

"Oh? It's okay. I'll figure it out," I said.

A look of relief overcame his face that I've rarely ever seen. I'd let him off the hook. To this day I'm not sure who was more relieved—my father for not having to talk to me or me for not having to hear it or witness him telling me. "Okay," he said, "We'll see you tomorrow."

I was on my way, but that moment still makes me smile.

The other time we talked about it came after I had left the house to help a female friend move into her college apartment. I had left the house right after dinner and did not return until nearly midnight. We moved her stuff in and then hung out with another one of her friends and her brother.

As far as my father knew, I was alone with her in her apartment for five hours. The next day he stopped me. "What time did you get back last night?" he asked.

"Around midnight," I replied.

"You were at her apartment for five hours?"

"Yeah."

"What did you do all that time?"

"We moved her in and then hung out," I answered.

"Five hours? No *shenanigans*?"

It took me a minute to realize the word "shenanigans" was code for something else. I assured him that there was no funny business by letting him know that her brother had helped move her in.

That was the extent of my discussions about sex with my father at home, but as college coaches, there were times where it could not be avoided. Having spent his entire life on a college campus, he brought a slightly more enlightened perspective on the subject to his players than he had at home.

Times had changed from the days when a number of his players had gotten married in college. A few had fathered children in college or even high school. When those issues presented themselves, he wanted the player to be aware of and own up to the huge responsibility he was now facing. The directive was to ensure the player received all the financial aid, grants, and benefits so that they could finish their education.

But sex on campus isn't limited to having to talk to players about it or help them adjust to life with an unplanned pregnancy. There were legal issues, sexual assault and rape allegations, that arose.

The topics were tough for him. As a head coach, he'd be sure that our players would hear talks from people on campus about the dangers of drugs, alcohol, gambling, agents, and sexual assault. Date rape was and is still an issue on college campuses.

In big-time college football, where players are seen as potential pro prospects with lucrative future contracts on the horizon, women can be drawn to them. Some approach them for the young man they truly are, while others are drawn to the excitement of being around a star.

Inject alcohol and some predictably bad late-night judgment, and the potential exists for miscommunication and lust to explode into something that is not wanted by one or both parties with potentially life-altering consequences.

As much as Joe Paterno did not want to talk about sex, he knew the dynamic of the issues his student-athletes faced. In team meetings he'd bring up the subject and remind players. "How many of you have sisters?" he'd ask. "When you are around girls, remember they are someone's sister or daughter, and someday may be someone's mother. Respect them like you'd like someone to respect your sister or mother."

But he wasn't one to break down the possible scenarios and situations his players might face. To his credit he knew he wasn't the most well-informed person to talk to them about it, so he brought in more qualified people.

In a staff meeting, one of the coaches suggested that the message might be more effective coming from him. "You think they want to hear a guy in his mid-70s talk to them about that stuff?" Joe said. "I'm not even sure I remember exactly what happens anymore." He laughed.

So we stuck to bringing in campus resources to help them understand the areas and situations where a fun night can become something that ruins lives. Through all the attempts to educate players, ultimately they are human and would make mistakes.

The most awkward was a sexual assault allegation involving a female student and two of our players that was later dropped. Our two players had engaged in sex with her at the same time. She alleged that she consented to have sex with one of them but not both.

When it came up in a staff meeting, Joe read the report and a puzzled look came across his face. He paused, leaned back in his chair, and thought for a minute. "So about this incident..." Joe said in a confused tone. "It says she had sex with the two of them...*at the same time? How is that possible?"

The room went silent. Every coach tried to avoid eye contact with Joe. *No one* wanted to get caught looking at Joe and get asked directly for an answer. *No one* wanted to have to draw him a picture, so to speak. It was a concept so foreign to Joe's nature and his era that it was hard for him to grasp.

On a walk in the park, he got the same puzzled look on his face as we discussed the Jerry Sandusky case in the last months of his life. What happened was hard for him to process. The people of 1930s Brooklyn did not talk about this stuff, as he explained when we were talking about this case. "Look Jay," he said, "if this was going on back then, I certainly never knew about it. If something like this had happened where I grew up, that person would have been beaten to within an inch of his life. No one would talk about it or know why. It was a different time and place. Maybe it was better, maybe it wasn't. I don't know."

"Who knows, Dad?"

"But how could this happen here?"

"Dad, this happens in every town in America."

He looked through the low sunlight of early December in Sunset Park and frowned. The lines on his face and forehead seemed to have grown in the weeks of the scandal. The park had been a place of childhood play, of dreams of tossing footballs, of bank shots on the basketball court, and neighborhood kickball games.

Now it was a place to unburden a soul of regret.

"Jay, he fooled me."

"Dad, he fooled me, too, he fooled *everyone.*"

That didn't ease his mind. There was a feeling there that either his age or being unaware had allowed something like this to happen.

After my father died, I received a letter from a woman who shared her father's story with me. In her father's childhood in the 1930s, he had been raped by a man in a small town in Pennsylvania. She shared the story with me to help me understand the era that her father and my father had grown up in, an era where these things were not talked about.

The letter pointed out that only 70 years after it happened could her father tell his own family. Her hope in sending the letter was that it would help me understand my own father's lack of understanding. After getting the letter, I wrote back to her, and she knows how much that letter helped me.

Sex was something that people of that era did not talk about. To my mind maybe it made them more moral and more refined. But maybe it made them more vulnerable to the happenings around them in a world obsessed with the topic.

Chapter 6

A GRANDfather

In October of 1995, I rode across the aisle from my father while flying to a game at Purdue. My sister Diana was in labor, and my father was anxious to land so he could hear that both mother and baby were doing well. Just two months shy of his 69th birthday, he'd waited a long time for his first grandchild.

Both my father and mother loved children. They were intrigued by the little minds willing to learn and ready to absorb everything around them with such innocence.

In January 1998 we were recruiting a player in Illinois whose mother was a grade school teacher. I thought it would help win over the mother if Joe were to go in and read to her class. As he sat down he was handed the classic children's book *Where the Wild Things Are.*

In the back of the room, I watched him eat up the moment with all the right sound effects and making silly faces as he recounted how the Wild Things "gnashed their terrible teeth or growled their terrible growls." He ended with Max waking up in his room with the dinner his mom had brought up and noted, "It was still hot."

There was just a natural affinity he had for children, and it came through in that moment. The kids were riveted because Joe showed such enthusiasm for the material. I knew he'd be a great grandfather when I had children.

After Diana's son, Brian, was born in 1995, the floodgates opened. Within a decade and a half, there'd be 17 grandchildren. Despite the vast number, my parents always had enough love to go around. Nothing made them happier than to see "the little people" walking up the front walk like a line of ducklings behind one of their parents.

The grandkids loved visiting "Candyland." Grandchildren could find Grandma's M&M's stash or Granddad's big jar of gummy bears. The children would ask, and the answer was always a smile and a yes. "I love being a grand-parent," my dad joked to me once. "It means never having to say no."

The answer wasn't always yes. There were occasional standoffs on eating vegetables at dinner or about bedtimes. My sister once reported how funny it was seeing her daughter resist my father's demand that she go to bed at the appointed time. It was a standoff. My father tried to be stern, but the young girl's insistence and stubborn refusal was too much for him to take without laughing. Ultimately he prevailed, and she went to bed.

My story about my father as grandfather to my children began seven and a half years after my wife Kelley and I were married. On December 31, 1999, my parents and my in-laws gathered at my house to celebrate the New Year and the dawn of a new century.

My wife and I were expecting twins any day. She had been ordered to bed rest by the doctors who hoped that she'd be able to carry the two babies to full term. A month earlier we'd learned that we were having a boy and a girl, and I decided to name my son Joseph Vincent Paterno, passing down my father's name.

My father called after my mother told him we were naming the expected son Joe. He called to thank me for honoring him. "Dad," I said, "I named him after myself. Remember that I'm named Joseph, too."

He apologized until I laughed and told him that indeed the name was to honor him.

My first children arrived in January, and in the hospital, I saw pride in my father's eyes as he saw me as a father. But it was the first of many mo-ments shared with my children and my father.

His life was full of grandchildren. Eleven of them lived within five miles of his home, so he got to see them around his work schedule and made time to see the grandchildren who lived out of town.

The time he spent with them, he was in the moment and completely focused on them. He played games with them, he read to them, he taught them things, he encouraged them, and he mostly laughed with them. Then he would excuse himself to go work on the next game or on recruiting or whatever was on his day's agenda.

My son would come over to watch football tapes in his den. My daughters shared pictures and poems they had created for him. There was a great moment when my oldest twin informed him she had made the honor roll. "What's the honor roll?" her twin brother asked.

"Well, I guess we know you're not on it," my father quipped.

After the laugh my father asked what was keeping my son from the honor roll. My son heard from his grandfather that it wasn't a lack of ability but rather a lack of effort. For my father he must have felt like he was looking at me all over again.

Mostly what seeing him as a grandfather did for his children was allow us to relive the moments we'd forgotten. I'd forgotten how much he loved the smiles and hugs from little children or how horribly off-key he'd sung the itsy-bitsy spider song to us.

Through our children we got to see it all over again.

Diana and her kids spent a lot of time with them at the shore in Avalon, New Jersey. Many evenings my father and mother would gather the children together and walk to get ice cream.

My father attended Baptisms and First Communions, many of them scheduled so he could be there. He relished the moments. Almost always he'd find a moment to relay to the parents how special he felt being there and how proud he was that they'd honored the religious traditions of our family.

At my daughter Lizzie's First Communion, my father sat next to me and wiped a tear away from his eye as Lizzie walked by in her white dress. She gave him a big smile and a small wave. "She looks like your sister Diana did at that age," he said, smiling.

There were moments when he was able to attend youth sporting events. It wasn't always easy to do, as other parents or relatives of teammates would approach him for autographs or pictures. Even at Communions or Christmas or Easter Mass, people would take pictures of him in church. But he endured the requests so that his grandchild at some point in the game or event would look in the crowd and see his or her grandparents there together.

When my son Joey was playing an elementary school basketball game against a team that included his cousin Christopher, my mother and father attended the game. The day before my father had told me that he was going to go to the game. "Dad," I said, "you don't have to. I know people may bother you."

"Jay, I want to go. It's important to me and it may mean something to them."

From where I sat during the game, I could see both Joey and Christopher look over at their grandparents seated watching the game. It was evident the boys made extra effort because they were there.

My father, as usual, was right.

There was one game after my father was gone that really showed me the impact he'd had on my son. Six days after my father died, my son Joey had a youth basketball game. He was a solid player and he would get two or three baskets a game.

That day Joey wrote on one hand "JVP" and on the other hand "ALWAYS". Before we left the house, I saw what he'd written and left the room, so he wouldn't see the tears in my eyes. That day he played the best game he'd ever played. By the time the game was over, Joey had netted 13 points and lifted my soul as I saw his grandfather had inspired him.

The rest of the school year would be a struggle for my son. My son always believed in my father. Granddad was his idol. Now the world stood in accusation of his grandfather. I should have seen it coming and headed the problems off at the pass. Maybe I was too busy dealing with the fallout in my own life to notice.

His schoolwork suffered tremendously, and there were tests he did not do well on. I wish I could tell you that as a father that I swooped in and caught it in time and I made everything okay.

My wife was the one who saved the year. It was Kelley who helped lift him up again. She reminded him that his grandfather wanted him to do his best and give every effort to excel in school. The memory helped spark him from his funk.

In talking with my mother, I realized my siblings' children were having some troubles, too. I wrote to two of my nephews, hoping to provide words that would help them get through. The impact of all the turmoil was not absorbed only by the adults, and we as parents had to understand and adjust.

My father's life ended, but the memories of the moments will never fade from the minds and hearts of the grandchildren who loved him.

In 2006 we had a family reunion in State College. There was a family hike up Mount Nittany, which brought back memories of walks in the woods with my father when we were kids. Much of the reunion weekend was spent on the back patio of my parents' home, watching the grandchildren running around the yard and into the park.

Amid the tall oaks that towered over the park, the children ran to swing sets and slides and merry-go-rounds. They ran to parts of the park beyond our sightlines and as parents do, we worried.

On the patio tables were trays of pizzas, pasta, salads, and peppers that we were slowly eating. Some adults drank wine; others drank beer or soda. My brother Dave asked if anyone could see all the kids.

My father laughed and said, "They'll be fine. You guys worry too much. We didn't think twice about you kids going down to the park."

"You hoped that we wouldn't come back," Diana quipped.

"That's not entirely true," my father retorted. "We hoped that you and your sister would come back."

As the kids ran around, getting louder and yelling and making a lot of noise, the parents tried to quiet them. My father reminded us that they were kids and that we shouldn't stifle their enthusiasm. It went back to what he'd said so many times about never having to say no to any of his grandchildren.

For the most part, my father kept his grandchildren from the public eye, just as he'd done with his own children. There were a couple of notable exceptions.

One of the great pictures ever taken of my father occurred in the media room after he'd won his 300th game. My nephew Matthew, just a toddler, waddled up the steps holding the game ball and over to his grandfather seated on the stage in front of the media.

My father's smile lit up the large media room.

"What are you doing here?" he laughed as he hoisted Matthew up on his lap and continued the media interview.

A few years later, after he'd broken the NCAA Division I-A wins record, he was ambushed in the media room by my 21-month old son, Joey, along with his cousins Brian and Olivia, who were six and five years old. My father couldn't do much more than laugh.

Finally, in 2010 after the 400th win, my father was overwhelmed by the emotion poured forth by the fans, but also the love he felt with all 17 of his grandchildren down on the field with him. It made my heart soar to know that the grandchildren would have this moment in their hearts and minds to remember all of their lives.

But it wasn't the public memories that will last.

It was a lecture on schoolwork that he gave to his grandkids. It was him seated on a kitchen step, listening to two three-year olds reading the children's book *Blue Hat, Green Hat* and yelling "Ooops!" when the turkey in the book just can't seem to get his wardrobe right.

It was his voice from the den calling out, "Who goes there?" when he heard the footsteps of grandchildren hustling up the steps from the garage into the house. It was in his genuine interest and attention when any one of his grandchildren would tell him a story from school or a game or field trip.

It was the annual visit by Santa Claus to grandma's house. Lou Gatto, a friend from Scranton, Pennsylvania, would come every year with Santa Claus. Santa was played by Jerry Kowalski, who has one of the very best Santa suits on the planet.

When he came in, my father hammed it up with Santa to make sure that all the kids felt the magic of the season. Everyone would tell Santa what they wanted for Christmas, including my mother and father.

Usually my father asked for "Good grandkids and a bowl win."

Most of the time, Santa delivered on the bowl win. More importantly, my father and mother had delivered priceless Christmas memories. As I fidgeted during one of Santa's visits, my father looked at me. "What's bugging you?" He asked.

"I have some stuff to do, to work on the game plan."

"Calm down. Just enjoy these moments. I wished I'd taken more time with you kids when you were young."

In the end, that was what it was all about; he'd blamed himself for missing important moments in our young lives. Now 40 years later, he was determined not to miss the moments in his grandchildren's lives, and more importantly he urged me to avoid mistakes he thought he'd made.

Maybe that is what pushed me to Avalon in July of 2011. I hadn't been to the house there in nine years. On a Wednesday afternoon, I picked up the phone and called my parents at the shore. My mother answered. "Mom, we're thinking about bringing the kids down. Is that okay?" I asked.

"We'd love that," she said.

There was no plan to go that summer, but something pushed me to jump in the car with my family and go. I didn't know that within six months my father would be gone.

Late in the afternoon, my father came down and sat on a beach chair watching my kids play. They ran up to share stories with him about big waves or seashells or sea gulls. His smile told them their stories were the most important things in the world.

At that moment I am quite sure that they were all that mattered to him.

The late afternoon sun in the west cast a glow as the light shone on the ocean water and on my five children running all over the beach. As I sat I looked at my father watching my children with a smile of contentment, of appreciation for the gifts God had given him in his life.

Mine were but five of the 17 grandchildren he'd seen on this beach. Those grandchildren were the children of the five children he'd raised and watched play on this same beach.

If you really pay attention during certain moments in life, you can grasp time, the meeting of past and present as it flows from one generation to the next. That day I saw my father gazing upon young people he knew would carry on in this world long after he was gone.

He looked at those children as he sat with the sound of waves crashing and a light breeze blowing in from the Atlantic. He was healthier and happier than he'd been in a while.

At that time, I thought he'd be with us forever.

But still I watched him as he took in the noisy chaos of grandchildren running on the beach. In his heart he knew that no matter how long he remained on this planet these children were grand.

In my heart I knew that my father was indeed a Grandfather and a grand father.

Chapter 7

The Asterisk

"You're only as good as your last worst act."

—Penn State Football All-American
Charlie Pittman, then the editor
of the South Bend Tribune,
at a Penn State football banquet

Charlie spoke those words as he was being honored by the State College Quarterback Club as an outstanding Penn State Football Alumnus. He mentioned Bill Clinton, O.J. Simpson, and Michael Jackson—names forever linked to their last worst act.

Since that time we've repeatedly seen lives of good works overshadowed by a moment or two that place an asterisk alongside the poetry of their lives. My father lived with the knowledge that one weak moment could destroy a life of good works and honorable conduct. He preached that to his children and his players.

But the poetry of my father's life does carry an asterisk—for now. When the name Paterno is spoken, there's a connection to something other than the stellar academic and athletic success of his student-athletes. One book reviewer commented that a book about him covered "perhaps the most controversial figure in sports today."

In this country we want our news stories, our explanations broken down into one or two simple bullet points or 140 characters. The truth is never that easy.

I know this truth: far more often than most, Joe Paterno got things right.

But Joe Paterno was disparaged by the baseless conclusions of the Freeh Report and resulting NCAA sanctions against the football program he'd led. That program's foundation was set on a bedrock of core beliefs and values, values that never wavered and were never compromised.

The Freeh commission asserted that Joe Paterno wanted to avoid bad publicity for the program.

Joe Paterno never feared weathering bad publicity. In my first year as quarterbacks coach, our starter, Rashard Casey, a black student-athlete from Hoboken, New Jersey, was wrongly accused of assaulting an off-duty white police officer. The race-heavy incident exploded in May, and Joe Paterno stood by his quarterback. The media rained down recriminations and condemnations.

Over the next several months, I received threatening emails and anonymous letters calling Rashard a "nigger" and me a "nigger-lover" and referring to my "nigger-loving daddy." Joe Paterno stood firm against blistering bad publicity. Ultimately, when Rashard was cleared, Joe was just happy that the truth emerged even if it cost him some bad publicity.

But that is not how Freeh's report wants you to remember the name Paterno. Even after their investigation, the report found no NCAA violations, no academic fraud, and no crimes committed by Joe Paterno. Yet they falsely described a flawed football culture at Penn State, an insult to the values of the NCAA's member institutions.

Truthfully, *their* lack of values are an insult to the values that Penn State athletics has stood for in *everything* we have done for over a century.

A century of positive living between my father and his father created a respect to the name Paterno. For now it will be tinged by the actions of another. For years to come, that asterisk will reside in the memory of people when they hear his name or see his image.

SENT: Sunday November 20, 2011 2:44 PM
TO: Jay Paterno
SUBJECT: Your Resignation

It is not important who I am, but I will tell you that my name is Lisa and my family and I are very big fans of

Penn State. Our family is alumni from 30 years. I am writing to tell you that your time at Penn State is over.

Please tender your resignation. Your name is now synonymous with omission, guilt and shame. Joe Paterno did nothing. He cared too much about his precious career than to stand up for what is right and stop a monster. Your last name is your cross to bear. And, I am glad that it will follow you for the rest of your life. Please remind Joe Paterno that every child that was raped by Sandusky is still out there waiting for justice. Paterno could have been their savior. Instead he worried only about himself and his paycheck. We have lost all respect for your family, your school, and the staff.

If you are a Man, you will do the right thing. But, then again, you are a paterno. So, we don't expect much.

My Response:

Lisa,

I am sorry that I am late getting back to you on this. But I do want to make one or two things clear to you. I am responding to you not in anger as you might suspect—I am responding just to help you understand this. It is a difficult time, and these are extremely difficult issues involved. I understand and completely respect that and your feeling in writing this e-mail.

There should be no doubt that we are all horrified by the recent allegations. As for what you have judged to be Joe Paterno's actions as reported in the media I urge you to stop and re-examine what he did. When the facts come out in the future you will see Joe in a different light than when you sent me this e-mail. Read what the state attorney general has to say.

No one wants to see the truth come out and justice be done more than Joe does.

As for what you assert the name Paterno to mean—
My grandfather Angelo Lafayette Paterno dropped out of high school and fought with Pershing in WW I. He raised a family worked two jobs and went to night school to finish high school, college and law school. My father served in the Army and thanks to the G.I. Bill went to college and then gave over 60 years of his life to Penn State.

Both of them conducted their lives as honorable men in a time when having an Italian last name was an indictment in and of itself. Regardless of how Joe has been smeared (keep in mind he didn't commit the crimes, he didn't even witness a crime—but he did report a crime) ultimately history will judge him differently.

I thank you for taking the time to read this.

My grandfather dropped out of high school and returned to Brooklyn, New York. At that time Italians in Brooklyn with no high school degree didn't have a lot of good options, but he chose to make the name Paterno something special. His father, Vincent Paterno, worked hard every day as a barber.

Education and integrity would be my grandfather's path. In so doing, he created a clean legacy for the name Paterno, a name future generations could proudly carry.

I was there for 17 years working and coaching for Joe Paterno through great years and through his worst seasons. The pressure to win was immense, and some suggested we cut corners.

He stuck to his guns. We recruited Terrelle Pryor, and some alums hinted that they could help get him to Penn State. There were few, if any, recruits we were under more pressure to get than Pryor, but Joe Paterno remained true to his beliefs, and Pryor signed with Ohio State.

For decades he refused unethical shortcuts. It meant late nights and early mornings, time lost with families, having to do things the hard way. It meant sleepless nights, working to near exhaustion, and ignoring personal health issues. It meant sacrifice while competitors cut corners.

Yes, it took more effort, made for higher hurdles, but it was the only way he'd compete with high standards of integrity. There is comfort in knowing that history will eventually judge Joe Paterno and Penn State fairly, but for now the story of his life's last few months will be a part of that discussion.

I visit his grave and I see the letters "PATERNO" carved in black granite. I cannot help but think of how *my* grandchildren will see that name when they walk the grounds of that quiet hillside. In the distance Mount Nittany looms as a constant presence over this valley.

Ultimately that name will be rightfully thought of in the manner in which Joe Paterno lived his life. It will be the truth about his life, not the fiction that so many driven by panic or, worse yet, agendas of power and ambition chose to create.

It is coming. The day when the light of truth will once again shine favorably, the early dawn's rays across those letters carved in black granite on a quiet Pennsylvania hillside.

Chapter 8

My Father, My Coach

In the fall of 1986 when I joined the Penn State football team, I did so under no delusions that I had a great playing future ahead of me. These guys were the best, but knowing I wanted to coach, it was a great way to learn the game.

All my life I'd watched these guys play. I'd admired and looked up to these guys and now I was on the same practice field with them. It was a great way to start my college experience. As I walked onto that field I could see my father across the way.

The first few days of practice were fine. We had no contact, so I, along with the other quarterbacks, practiced plays, and it seemed pretty easy. Then the first day of full contact arrived.

I didn't realize there were so many guys who would have loved to tackle their coach, so the next best thing was to take their shots on his son. Early in the first full pad practice, I had the ball and was blasted by All-American defensive tackle Tim Johnson.

That got my attention.

A few minutes later, it was linebacker Quintus McDonald (a future NFL player) who absolutely blindsided me. I never saw it coming, but I felt the violent collision through the back of my skull and found myself lifted off my feet and flying through the air. I landed head first on the grass and as I got up I was very unsure of where I was. My brain was scrambled as I pulled a grass clump from my facemask. I kept on practicing.

It was a different time. You had a headache and just practiced the next day, so that was exactly what I did. The fact that I kept coming back from all the hits helped me gain some respect from my teammates.

If I thought my coach and my father would be protective of his son on the practice field, that idea disappeared quickly. After particularly hard hits on me, I'd hear him laugh or see him smile. He relished seeing me thrown onto the savanna to run with the lions and have to toughen up.

As I settled in to be part of the team, I gained new respect for what coaching was all about. Now I really saw all the detail. Every practice minute was allocated to a specific purpose, every drill scripted for maximum return on time invested on the field.

If we had a segment to teach inside running plays for 16 minutes, every minute was utilized. Each day we had a purpose on that field that demanded focus on that practice only.

Joe Paterno—who I referred to as "Coach" when I spoke to him during football hours—demanded complete focus.

The 1986 team was blessed with great senior leadership, and they preached it to the younger guys. Leaders we all respected like quarterback John Shaffer, defensive lineman Bob White, linebacker Shane Conlan, and safety Ray Isom were just a few on a team full of strong seniors. It ranks as one of the greatest groups of leaders any Penn State team ever had.

As 1986 rolled on, we continued to win. By the time the regular season ended, we were 11–0 and waiting to learn our bowl destination. Both Penn State and Miami completed the regular season with perfect records. Neither team belonged to a conference, thereby allowing them to go to any bowl they wanted.

At that time all the major bowl games were played on New Year's Day and all had at least one tie-in that required them to take a conference champion. The only bowl that could take both Penn State and Miami was the Sunkist Fiesta Bowl.

NBC Sports and Sunkist pitched in more money, and NBC agreed to move the game from Thursday, January 1 to Friday, January 2, pre-empting *Miami Vice*, the hottest show on television.

Miami was a heavy favorite, talking with a lot of confidence and with a lot of swagger. In our team meetings, Joe Paterno let us in on his secret. He was going to continue to build Miami's confidence in the media. He stated Miami was the best team Penn State had ever played, maybe the best team he'd ever seen. He kept it up, knowing the Miami players might be listening.

In our team meetings, he warned us. "Now look, don't pay attention to anything I say in the media," he said. "I'm going to continue to tell them how great they are. I'm going to keep saying how little chance we have. When you guys talk to the press, you say the same things."

He'd set up a false opponent, the opponent was Miami's rendezvous with destiny to prove they were the greatest team of all time. Pretty soon the discussion wasn't whether or not Miami would win, but what they'd have to do to be considered the greatest team of all time.

The plan from our side was to slow down their offense, hit them, challenge them, make them win a low-scoring game. Joe told us that Miami was a front-running team. "Front-runners expect to score early and often, and they get frustrated when things don't go their way," he said. "They haven't played anyone yet that has tried to slow them down and has really hit them in the mouth."

By game time we were in the most electric environment I have ever seen on a football field. After a week listening to Miami players talk, our team was focused and angry, and there was malicious intent in the eyes of guys like linebackers Conlan and Trey Bauer, defensive tackle Johnson, and safety Isom. It was chilling to behold.

By late in the Arizona desert evening on January 2, 1987, the plan had worked. Penn State's defense had continued to hit them in the mouth and had slowed them down, and across the field we could see the frustration mount. Our defense had imposed their will through physical intimidation.

As the final seconds ran off the clock, the most-watched and highest-rated college football game in history resulted in a surprising 14–10 win and a national championship for Penn State.

The rest of my time in college on the team I made my way through practices, taking my lumps but also standing up for myself. One day linebacker Mark D'Onofrio, a good guy but a really emotional football player, gave me one cheap shot too many. As I got up, I zipped the football as hard as I could at him, resulting in a scuffle between the scout team and the first-team defense.

Linebacker coach Joe Sarra jumped in and gave Mark the business. "Hey, Buddy," he said to Mark, "don't hit him late. That's gonna cost us a penalty in a game. They're just trying to make you better."

Sarra sticking up for me meant a lot. He was a coach who took a genuine interest in me. There were a few times when he'd grab lunch with me or meet with me to make sure I was doing okay.

Off the field I had some trouble adjusting to college life. I didn't turn 18 until late October of my freshman year, and my youthful immaturity showed through. Being from State College and going to Penn State can also inhibit your college growth. You arrive on campus with friends you carry with you from high school. If you're not careful, you never branch out and expand your horizons.

As a result I was distant with some teammates. They were all thrown here together without a support system like I had. They bonded together while I already had friends to lean on.

But being the coach's son also made it tough to make friends. There was a fear that I was a snitch just waiting to run back to my father and tell him what was going on. It took a while for that to dissipate, but some guys were more willing to accept me than others. I also found that some students on campus harbored resentment as well.

In an early fall fraternity party, a member of the fraternity told me he knew who I was and would kick my ass. I hadn't really done anything at that time and I laughed. I assumed he had to be joking since he only came up to my chest in height. He got louder, and people started to look. "*We're* gonna kick your ass," he growled.

"We?" I laughed as I asked.

"Yeah, me and all my brothers."

Then he pushed me, and it was on. His fraternity brothers came to his aid. I had made a critical mistake of going in and being alone. My plan was a slow retreat toward the door. Soon I found teammate Ray Tarasi, a kicker from Pittsburgh, had jumped in to help my cause.

We got out of the door, and I was still in one piece. Ray and I had only known each other for a few weeks, but there was an understanding. I learned right away that teammates helped each other out.

It was still not easy to overcome some teammates' suspicions. One night I ran into a couple of teammates at a party, and one of them voiced what I am sure many other guys felt. "Hey Paterno," he said, "don't go telling your old man you saw us here."

"I'd have to be pretty stupid to tell him I saw you at a party." I laughed.

"Why's that?" he asked.

"If I told him I saw you at this party, wouldn't I essentially be telling him that I was here, too?"

"Yeah, I guess you're right."

That teammate never gave me any trouble from that point forward, and the other guys warmed up to me.

There was one time when I was asked to keep an eye on someone. It was a player who'd had some trouble and there were rumors that he was involved with drugs. In 1986 there were a lot of drugs on college campuses. At Penn State there was marijuana and cocaine, but I never saw my teammates doing it. Now, I am not naïve. There were a few guys I'm sure who smoked weed, but I never heard of anyone messing with anything beyond that.

Joe Paterno only asked me to see if there was any truth to what he was being told about this teammate. But he did couch his request. "Jay, I am only asking you to let me know so I can help him. I am not trying to eliminate anyone, but if he has a legitimate problem he needs help."

"I got you," I said hesitantly.

"Jay, if you do not want to help, that is okay. I just want to reach this guy if he needs help."

As it turned out, the teammate did not have a drug problem, which I happily reported. To inform him I stopped by the house. He sat at the round kitchen table and looked at me.

"Coach," I said, "there is no problem."

"Are you sure?" He asked. "I don't want you to just tell me that to get off the hook. If you don't know, that is okay. I just don't want to be lulled into a false sense of security."

"No, I'm pretty sure."

"Okay. I appreciate it and I will not ask you ever again. It is just that I know you have a pretty good relationship with this guy and could help me to help him for his life. It's hard enough being my son on this team."

"It's okay."

It was okay. I knew why he asked and I knew it bothered him to do so.

If anyone on the team had any doubts, they soon found I was able to get into Joe Paterno's doghouse as easily as they could. Away from the football field and the classroom, I grew up awkwardly in college.

During my freshman year, I invited a girl to my house for my birthday dinner with my family. On the way over, she reported to me that her sorority sisters helped her pick out her clothes to "go to Joe's house."

Another time I was sitting in a high school friend's dorm room, and her new roommate got a call from her father. She then proceeded to mention school was going well. Then she had other news for her father. "Dad, you'll never guess who is in my room right now," she said.

There was a pause as she listened to her father. Then she looked at me, gave me a sly smile, and spilled her news: "Joe Paterno's son, Jay, is sitting here with me."

I started to realize that my last name was a benefit as it pertained to some females. She and I hung out, but ultimately nothing could have made up for my stunted emotional growth. I realized that you can't be boring so I made up my mind, if nothing else, to be entertaining.

Being entertaining meant I attended parties on Wednesdays, Thursdays, and on the weekends. I didn't drink until I was 21 because I really feared getting caught. Surprisingly I found that some girls found my sobriety interesting.

But my time on the party circuit meant being sober and dealing with ridiculously drunk people talking smack. Occasionally there would be minor fisticuffs or shoving matches. Eventually I grew up and behaved. I steered teammates to parties where I knew people would watch our backs.

Good friends had become officers at fraternities, and I got to know a lot of the brothers. I stuck to those places. It was advice my father had given me about going to places where I had already made friends. Surprisingly, I even grew into the role of peacemaker. Joe had always told us that instead of jumping in to help a teammate fight, we should pull them out of trouble.

One night at the Fiji house, a huge brawl broke out between people who were not football players. Unfortunately, one of the guys involved was visiting his brother on the team, and so that drew my teammates into the fight. Total chaos ensued, so I just helped pull our players out of the front door.

By the time things settled, police cars were outside Fiji. All of us were worried as we emerged into the chilly late fall night. Fiji sat on a corner lot on campus, and the cop cars were both to our right and left. They had the area cornered.

But times were different back then. As dozens of people, most of them heavily drunk, stumbled out onto the grass outside the old brick fraternity under a corner streetlight and the light emanating from the house windows, I heard a stern voice speak up.

The officers rounded up people by the dorm areas they lived in. They were making sure everyone was okay and then helping everyone back to where they lived.

In my senior year of college, I had become pretty good friends with teammates O.J. McDuffie, Rickie Sayles, and Corey Jett. The four of us would go to fraternities where I knew people. Sometimes we'd go to a party at the Paul Robeson Center, the black student cultural center on campus. The place was packed, people were dancing, and the music was good.

One late night we ended up eating at McDonald's across from campus. I was seated with those three guys, and a drunk girl at the next table decided to start a commotion. She made a comment to Rickie about her boyfriend's "superiority" that she asserted he could back up.

We all laughed because we thought she was just kidding around. She mistook that for some kind of insult. As her boyfriend looked at us, I could see he just wanted her to let it go. The sentiment was unanimous. But she kept it up.

Finally Rickie laughed and said something to the effect that there was really only one way to prove or disprove what she was saying. Her boyfriend rounded her up and left.

Thinking the night was over, we took our time eating before heading to the car parked across the street. I stopped to talk to a friend for a minute, but Rickie, O.J., and Corey were outside when a police car pulled up. The officer hopped out and approached the three guys, all of whom were black.

I realized I'd better get out there and I could hear the officer saying something about a girl. He'd gotten a call from a girl, telling him about three black men harassing her in McDonald's.

I jumped in and interrupted the officer who looked at me. "Officer," I said, "she didn't mention that there was a white guy there, too?"

"No she didn't," he said.

"Well I was there, and if you want to go back in and ask anyone in there, they will all tell you that she started a debate about genital size, and she got loud. I think she got pissed because her boyfriend didn't back her up."

The officer was a little skeptical and then asked for everyone's identification. He realized that we were all teammates and that it was pretty likely that

I had been in McDonald's with these guys. I sensed that those three guys might have had a much longer night had I not been there. It was a learning experience for me.

By the time I was finishing up my time on the team, I was fortunate to have learned a lot about football and a lot about life. My father and I benefitted from the time together, and when I left Penn State I had a much better understanding of what he was all about.

In the first weeks when I was on the team, a lesson forced me to understand the reality of playing for my father. The two freshmen in the room next to mine in preseason camp would stay up almost every night and argue about religion. Finally one night it came to a head, and one of the players was going to ambush the other player with a big can of water.

The other player was at the end of the hall with a fire extinguisher waiting for the attack. I tried to get them both to go to bed as it was after curfew. Sure enough, as the player with the water attacked, the fire extinguisher went off, and that chemical fire extinguisher threw a cloud of dusty fire retardant all over the dorm hallway.

Although I had tried to stop the exchange, I had been up after curfew so I was guilty by association. The next afternoon I appealed to team captain Bob White. Joe told him that there was no way I couldn't be punished. It wasn't fair, but that was just the way it had to be. Joe knew the team would be watching to see how he handled me.

The next morning as I ran hills I had to swallow a difficult lesson, but I ran my hills despite my bitterness toward this reality. Long after college I would find that being the son of Joe Paterno put other hills in my way, and that the only way out was to run up them.

Chapter 9

Working for a Father

I n late February of 1995, I returned to Penn State to coach at my alma mater. That was the easy part. It also meant I was returning to coach for my father, a man viewed as a legend in the profession. It would be difficult to live under the radar.

It was a unique situation but also a lot like other sons or daughters who work for a parent. It can be difficult on the parent or their son or daughter, but it also presents challenges to the people around them.

After college I began my coaching career as a graduate assistant at the University of Virginia. It was an honor to work for a future Hall of Fame coach in George Welsh. He remains one of the most underrated coaches in the history of the game.

I learned the game from a number of men who had been head coaches or would become ones. On those staffs were former LSU head coach Mike Archer, future North Carolina State head coach Tom O'Brien, and future Boston College coach Frank Spaziani.

When I would see new things we were doing on or off the field at Virginia, I would write to my father. Much of what I sent probably went in the trash. In Penn State's Fiesta Bowl rout of Tennessee following the 1991 season, Penn State ran a pick play I'd sent my dad for a score. After the game Penn State quarterbacks coach Jim Caldwell asked if I'd seen the play. Of course I'd seen it.

After Virginia I was hired to coach at the University of Connecticut with Tom Jackson. We had an up and down season with a young team on the cusp of better days. Just prior to our homecoming game against UMass, a writer in the *Hartford Courant* wrote that if things did not pick up it was time for a new head coach at UConn.

We lost that game and then went on a streak, winning to reach a 6–4 record before our final game against undefeated and top five Boston University. A few days after a hard-fought loss, our head coach Jackson resigned. After a few weeks under the interim head coach, we were all cut loose.

I called my father to tell him the news. He reminded me of what he had told me when I first wanted to get into coaching. "Jay, don't expect the kind of career I've had," he said. "No one stays in the same place very long anymore."

In a few weeks, I was headed to James Madison University to coach quarterbacks. In just three seasons, I'd been at three schools, already two more schools than my father had coached in his career.

The time at Virginia and James Madison influenced the way I envisioned an offensive attack. The best offenses I'd been around utilized dual-threat quarterbacks. Mike Cawley, whom I'd coached at James Madison, became the sixth quarterback taken in the draft. His ability to make plays running and throwing impacted my opinion on college quarterbacks.

After serving at those other schools, an opportunity arose at Penn State. The coaching staff advocated bringing me back. But Joe understood that you never get anything for nothing; this was not a risk-free decision for him or for me.

Ultimately, I decided to come back to Penn State over offers to stay at James Madison, an offer at the University of Buffalo, and an offer from the University of Memphis for significantly more money than Penn State was offering. The new head coach at Memphis was Rip Scherer, whom I had worked for at James Madison.

Ultimately the call to come home won out over money.

In my first week, wide receivers coach Kenny Jackson called me into his office. He wanted to make sure I understood something. It was a lesson I have always carried with me. "Jay, understand that you have to be twice as good as anyone else for people to accept you," he said. "You hear what I'm saying? You have to be twice as good."

The message got through, and throughout my career, I've always tried to live to a higher standard. I gave up drinking in 1997 when I challenged a player I coached to do the same. I wore a tie to work year round, even on days when we didn't have to wear them.

In every report or game plan, I spent extra time to make sure it was professional and at a standard beyond reproach. I didn't always succeed, but I knew that co-workers were looking for favoritism, and people outside the program were looking for flaws. It wasn't always easy, but it was my reality.

One of my first practices, I walked out on the practice field wearing sweatpants. Then I heard a familiar voice call me over before we got started. "Hey," Joe said, "don't come out here looking like that again."

"Looking like what?" I asked.

"Wearing sweats. Get pants or slacks on, but I don't want to ever see you coaching in sweatpants again."

As I took in his message, I looked around to see another coach or two wearing sweatpants, but I knew better than to bring it up. One advantage to working for your father is you come to work on Day One already knowing what will set him off. Complaining about other people was a surefire way to set him off.

What started almost immediately was me calling my new boss by his first name. Over the years I got asked why I called him "Joe" by media members and fans for years.

I started calling him "Coach" when I was on the team. It was an audible reminder to distinguish the business from the personal side. When I joined the staff, it was to keep it businesslike but also to remind everyone else from the staff to the team that I was there as a professional.

In coaching there are a lot of arguments and discussions in staff meetings where many of us argue our points to the head coach. There was no way I wanted to make a point in an argument with the words "But Dad…"

That wouldn't be fair to my co-workers or to my boss.

As he said many times: "It's not enough to *be* fair. You have to *appear* to be fair."

From that first week of coaching through the night he was fired, my trip alongside him was a thrill ride of triumphs and setbacks.

Coaching with my father gave me tremendous insight into his life. The game was just part of what this was all about. We had staff meetings about players' academics and not just current players. He'd ask about guys who went to the NFL and were one or two classes from graduating and ask if anyone was working to get them to finish.

Many staff meetings were completely devoted to personnel; the evaluation of every player did not just encompass what they could do or not do on the field. "Who recruited him?" Joe would ask. "Why is he not doing well in school? Has anyone talked to his parents or high school coach? Who is his roommate? Who on the team is close to him? Should I get him in to see me? Should I call his parents?"

It was always a search to reach that player who was not fulfilling his potential in school, on the field, or in any aspect of his life. It was an attitude that we should leave no stone unturned when it came to helping these young men make full use of their God-given gifts.

He was demanding as a boss, but he was fair. He never asked you to do more than he himself was willing to do.

He demanded that his players maintain certain weights. He himself always fought to keep his weight down and did not want to be a hypocrite. He'd walk five, six, or seven miles to stay in shape. In 2005 just before his 79th birthday, he would run some of the conditioning drills at the end of practice, usually alongside an offensive lineman he was trying to motivate.

In a true mark of his greatness as a leader, he was never harder on anyone than himself. He possessed the confidence to own the mistakes he made. Usually he publicly took blame for things that he didn't deserve while being quick to credit others even if it was rightly due to him.

After the 1997 season, a year when we started ranked No. 1 until we were throttled by eventual national champion Michigan, Joe Paterno re-evaluated everything in his program. Even after losing to Michigan, we routed No. 19-ranked Purdue and Wisconsin to move to 9–1 on the season.

When we got to East Lansing to play Michigan State, we were No. 4 in the country and in a tight game deep into the third quarter. Then all hell broke loose as they took the ball and ran it down our throats, setting an NCAA record with *two* running backs rushing for over 200 yards each.

By the time we lost to Florida in the bowl game, another running back gained 200 yards. Joe had seen enough. Sensing complacency he felt it was time to re-evaluate everything. He looked at the best defenses in the country and instructed the defensive staff to study tapes of Nebraska, Florida State, and Kansas State, among others. He demanded changes.

Also that offseason he received a gift in the mail. Bill Walsh, the great coach of the San Francisco 49ers, sent Joe a copy of his new book. In the front page, Bill wrote:

"For Joe—
The GREATEST of OUR TIME—
Bill Walsh"

Joe Paterno jumped into that book with both feet. Much of it reaffirmed what Joe already knew to be true, but he used it to challenge his thinking about his staff and himself.

In August of 1998, he sent a memo to his staff that outlined a lot of his thinking for the upcoming season. His new approach on the defensive side of the ball resulted in a great improvement in the performance of that unit. They returned to their usual place among the top defensive units in the country.

I pass written material on to you in order to save time when we meet. But I expect you to read everything and if any of it bothers you, you will bring it up at a staff meeting or privately with me.

I continue to examine the way we have done things in the past and I agree with what Walsh says about change "Sometimes it is appropriate to change for the sake of seeing matters and doing things in an entirely different, revitalized way."

I intend to be involved in the key decisions that we make—what we teach, how we teach, and what approach we will take to practice or to a game. It also has to be my responsibility to assure that our staff can be open in arguing for their point and have confidence that I am on board and I know exactly what the problems are as you go about working to come up with the best solutions. Having said that we should all be aware of the potential problems:

1. Any philosophical differences between you and me has to be addressed and resolved either at a private or staff meeting.

2. We will not always agree on philosophy, techniques, or coaching style but when the decision is made you will be expected to "go along" and with "enthusiasm and passion" when you work with your position people.

3. It is my responsibility to monitor what we teach, how etc. So that there is no misunderstanding as to what was agreed and that we progress as we intended to do, I intend to sit in on many of your meetings with your players and in fact to address your groups occasionally.

We have to stick together as a staff. It becomes very divisive if assistant coaches or the Head Coach chip away at each other behind their backs to players, other coaches or anybody else. We have to believe—as the team must believe—that what is good for the program is good for us.

FOR THE STAFF

I. Teaching

   A. "See it-Hear it-Do it"

   B. Players want to know— When, Where, How and Why

   C. Think about specific skills your players have to have to be able to do what is required in our plans

   D. How do we plan to develop these skills

   E. Every player must be made to understand how his skills and responsibilities dovetail with the other positions on the team with which he must interact.

Top: Joe Paterno holds Diana, my oldest sister, in 1965.

Middle: From left to right in back row: Dave, Diana, Mary Kay, and I wear our Sunday best during Easter of 1972.

Bottom: The family poses at the Penn State spring game in May of 1971.

Top: From left to right: Joe Paterno shepherds my brother Dave, sister Mary Kay, and sister Diana around Disney World during the summer of 1972.

Middle: From left to right: my brother Dave, sister Mary Kay, sister Diana, and I play with Joe Paterno.

Bottom: Dave, Joe Paterno, Scott, and I clown around before fishing at a family friend's farm in 1974.

Sue and Joe Paterno stroll through New Orleans while Penn State was in town to play Oklahoma in the Sugar Bowl.

Sue and Joe Paterno play with two of their grandchildren during Halloween of 2001.

Joe Paterno poses with his grandchildren in May of 2006 before climbing Mount Nittany.

Top: Joe Paterno, Joe Paterno III, and I celebrate, following Joe's 324th win, a 29–27 defeat of Ohio State on October 27, 2001.

Middle: Joe, Sue Paterno, and the family enjoy a Penn State reception in December of 2007, honoring Joe's College Football Hall of Fame induction.

Bottom: I learned lessons from my father off the field and on it, where I coached under him from 1995–2011.

SCRIPT

1. (B) I Rt 32 Base (on Quick)
2. (S) I Rt Buzz 46 Toss Crack
3. (S) I Rt Zig Hot Red 40 X Corner
4. (A) Trap Rt Spy 2 Bat
5. (B) bdy Lite Rt Zig 12 Naked Lt B Delay
6. (S-A) Ralph Pistol Red 90 Scud Lt
7. (S) I Rt 46 Slant
8. (B) Dbl Rt 42 Pitch Sally
9. (A) Rocky Up Hot Fit 91 Y Hook
10. (A) Rocky Pistol Shift 7 Power
11. (B) Dbl Rt 43 Iso
12. © Triple Rt Flight 12 Special Buff Rt

Joe, we'll always be with you — and you'll always be Penn State's Coach!

*Coach—
Like I have said—
You did everything
for Me Forever.
W. L. Dwezy*

*Coach—
It has been an
Honor to work
for you to
learn from
You. You
will be missed.
Love,
Jay & Bill*

*I can never
thank you
enough for the
life you gave me
and My Family.
Always True!*

*Joe,
Thanks for
everything.
Galen*

*Joe! Thank you
Forever
Dick*

*Joe,
you gave me
a chance to really
be something in life.
I'm forever grateful
Terrell*

Every coach signed the play call sheet from the 2011 game versus Nebraska, Penn State's first contest since 1949 without its legendary coach.

Barack Obama greets Joe and Sue Paterno in 2011. The President called to express his condolences after Joe's passing. (White House Photo Office)

The iconic Joe Paterno black shoes along with the game ball rest on the steps of his garage immediately following win No. 400, a 35–21 defeat of Northwestern on November 6, 2010.

II. How Much do we teach

   A. Walsh says, "Our job is the reduction of
        uncertainty."

   B. Chuck Knox says: "Don't Coach caution into
        them."

   C. Walsh goes on to say: "Do not give them something
        that in some measurable way increases their level
        of uncertainty or hesitation."

That spring we also had a major recruiting issue. We were chasing two high-profile quarterbacks: Chris Simms from New Jersey, son of NFL quarterback Phil Simms, and Eli Manning from Louisiana, the son of NFL quarterback Archie Manning.

There were some other guys, but we felt these two were a cut above everyone else. I was still coaching the tight ends but served as the recruiting coordinator. We would be graduating our top two quarterbacks in the next two years, so it was imperative that we get a big-time guy.

Chris Simms had been to our camp the previous summer. After I visited Eli Manning's school in May and watched him practice, I was sold on his ability to be a big-time quarterback. His father, Archie, called me to ask how seriously we were interested in Eli. After the phone call, Archie sent Eli to our camp.

Eli had a great week of camp and as he left he indicated that he had a lot of interest in Penn State. I was thrilled we were in the hunt.

Archie and my father went back several years. After Archie's senior year in college, Joe was coaching the Hula Bowl. Archie's mother was on the trip, and Joe and my mother spent time talking with her and with Archie. Archie understood what Joe Paterno and Penn State were all about.

Shortly after camp, trouble started. Fran Ganter, who was recruiting Chris Simms for us, wanted to sign him. He was worried that if we recruited Eli it might impact Chris' decision. As a result Joe was convinced to tell me to back off Eli Manning.

We backed away from Eli and told Archie that Chris Simms appeared to be a lock for us.

We had lost what had made us dominant in recruiting. In the 1994 recruiting cycle, Joe Paterno changed the way recruiting was done nationally. Because Penn State regularly had camps loaded with prospects, the staff was more familiar with the potential student-athletes.

In the 1992 recruiting cycle, Penn State lost a couple of kids late when Notre Dame came in and offered them late and got them. "These kids were waiting around for Notre Dame and stringing us along," Joe said. "We did all the leg work evaluating these kids in camp. They come along and take ones *we've* identified. Those days are over."

The next year he decided that with more access to video and with Penn State's camp advantage, he'd be in position to offer kids in their junior year and then ask for answers in the summer. When I became recruiting coordinator, Joe Paterno kept us on the same path. In my nine years as recruiting coordinator, our staff's lightning fast approach to recruiting produced eight national top 20 classes, including five top 10 finishes and two classes ranked No. 1 in the nation.

The approach was recruiting with swagger, making high school players believe this was the place for them. We created early momentum and built on it. With Chris Simms we went the other way.

As fall rolled on, I was getting calls from Penn Staters in New Jersey who were hearing that we weren't even in the ballpark with Simms. I tried again to see if I should contact the Mannings but was told to back down because Fran knew Simms was all set for us.

Joe was loyal to his older coaches. The young guys lost the battle, and we were out of it with Manning, who'd committed to Ole Miss, where his father had played. Sure enough, in December, Chris Simms went on television to announce live that he was going to Tennessee. (He would later flip to Texas.)

My argument had been all along that we needed other options to put the pressure on Simms. The truth in recruiting was that there are always several people at every position who are good enough. The key was to identify them, go after a few, and let them know that the number of scholarship opportunities was limited.

A few months later, Joe's great friend, Bill Schreyer, a former CEO of Merrill Lynch, asked Joe a theoretical question. He wanted to know why Joe let an 18-year-old kid drive the decision process. Joe came back with the idea that we would not go through that process again, but it had taken someone in his peer group, unafraid to be honest, to convince Joe of the point.

The next year we were chasing one of the top athletes in the country. Adam Taliaferro, possessing explosive skills on offense and defense, was being chased by everyone. He'd been to campus several times, and we felt we were pretty close to getting him.

By early August, Joe wanted to know what was taking him so long, so we went to the new aggressive model. We sent Adam an email, telling him that he was our first choice but that we had other guys we'd offer if he didn't commit. He would still have an offer, but we just couldn't guarantee him that there would be a scholarship available if he waited.

I called Joe on the phone and read him the email before I sent it. He approved the language, and we sent it. Almost immediately Adam's father, Andre, called Kenny Jackson. A couple of days later, Adam was on campus and committed to us.

Sometimes I was right, more often he was right, but most serious issues involved discussions in staff meetings. Joe loved to argue and discuss issues, hoping spirited debate would draw out new thinking and perhaps new solutions. When I first came back to Penn State, the arguments were lively with lots of people willing to weigh in.

Joe would set off the fuse and watch the fireworks. He'd sit in his chair and watch the back and forth with a smile. On occasion he would get angry, and you would see the expression change. He'd kind of glare at you over his glasses, so you could see his eyes.

If you won the argument and kept making follow-up points, he had a stock response. "You made the sale," he said. "There's no need to keep going."

If you didn't win the argument and kept after him once a decision was made, that got him angry. "Look, the decision's been made," he said. "I get paid to make these decisions. This is the way we're going to do things, so get on board and teach it."

Then he would go out to practice and pay close attention to the guys that disagreed with him. If they weren't teaching things to the players exactly as he wanted, Joe would subtly step in to coach the technique or the play the way he wanted it done. He didn't embarrass a coach on the field; he did it delicately and then he'd bring it up in the next staff meeting. "Hey," he would say, "the steps we were teaching to the running backs on the draw play, make sure they look the way we decided to run them, okay?"

He criticized in a way that was inclusive, using plural pronouns rather than individual.

It is important to understand this about Joe Paterno's leadership style; he was truly a team player, knowing he could not do it alone. Even if he had his mind made up, he would listen to counter arguments. Often he'd say he wanted to think on it and the next day readdress issues of dissenting voices, so they understood he'd listened to them.

Later in his career, the arguments became less passionate. As any CEO or coach approaches retirement age, the people closest to them often are trying to build their case to be an heir apparent. Those people stop disagreeing with the leader of the organization, telling them only what they think their boss wants to hear. The truth stops flowing to the head of the organization.

All through his career, Joe Paterno had people who were unafraid to tell him the truth. His brother George was one of those guys. Even though he was not coaching for Joe, he'd challenge his brother all the time. Budd Thalmann, who handled the public relations side of the athletic department, was a trusted voice.

After Budd retired and then George died, I believe he lost critical voices from his peer group. My mother always told him the truth, but she stayed out of football matters. Through my entire career, I always told him what I believed, but no matter how professional the relationship, it is not easy to hear your own son argue with you.

As he got older, some people he trusted just told him what he wanted to hear to his face while grousing behind his back. As early as the 2002 season, I warned him about the shifting loyalties of some trustees.

One of them pulled me aside at my parents' home after a game that season. He had the audacity to ask if in my opinion: "Is Joe still all there mentally?"

"Ed," I said, "he's all there."

The concern was after a game against Iowa that Joe had run after an official to argue a call. Joe was right on his point, and the only way to get to the official was to chase him. At a spry 75, Joe's sprinting was a sight to see. He was really flying.

That was the incident that helped spark this particular trustee's concerns, but the entire conversation betrayed his true feelings about my father. I was too respectful of his position to say to him that he should mind his own business.

As his career wound down, Joe gained grudging respect for me and listened but did not always agree. Guido D'Elia, the man in charge of communications and brand management for football, became a respected and honest critic in off-field matters. Tom Venturino would get things done and he kept us within what was allowed and what could be done within the NCAA rules and budgetary constraints.

On the medical front, Joe trusted Dr. Wayne Sebastianelli and trainer George Salvaterra with his own health as well as the health of the student-athletes. Our strength coach, John Thomas, had Joe's respect as well because Joe knew what a tough job that was.

He trusted us yet he'd challenge us to defend our assertions to test how strongly we felt.

The road we traveled was not easy. Across the 17 seasons we worked together, our relationship as father and son was strained by working together. Most of the time we were able to compartmentalize the personal from the professional, but it wasn't always perfect.

There were days when I'd come home with my mind made up that I would work for him but do nothing socially with him, but within a day or two I'd calm down. When I got angry, I tried not to betray how I was feeling and I would stay distant just to keep him from seeing how upset I was.

There were some difficult days we shared, but always when I needed his support, I got it.

In 1999 we went to the Alamo Bowl in San Antonio, and rumors later surfaced—some spread by people within our organization—that two other coaches and I had been out drinking with players. The rumors swelled to the point where I had allegedly beaten up our starting quarterback.

I got a call from Tom Bradley, who wanted me to know what was being said about me behind my back. Then I went to Joe to tell him about the false rumors and explain that *none* of it was true. I didn't even drink at the time so I am not sure how I could have been so drunk.

I knew who started some of the rumors, but I never confronted them because of the advice my father had given me. "Don't worry about the lies people spread about you," he had said. "The people who know you know the truth. The rest of 'em aren't worth your time. People are going to take shots at you as a way to get at me. It's not fair, and I feel bad for you, but that is just how it is."

That advice carried me through stormy times over and over.

There were funny moments too. The 2006 Homecoming win over Illinois fell on my birthday. After the game my wife invited people, including my parents, over to our home. We had one of those evenings that you never forget. Every time I saw my parents seated on the couch, they were smiling no matter who they were talking to.

The next Tuesday my father was asked if he had any Homecoming traditions he followed after the game. He mentioned that he didn't have any tradition, but that he'd been at my house for my birthday.

The reporter followed up by asking how old I had turned. "I haven't the slightest idea of how old Jay is," Joe said. "Do you want me to be honest? I don't know how old he is. When you have as many kids and grandkids I got running around the house, you don't really know how old any of them are."

Another reporter mentioned, "He's 38, Coach."

We had some fun with it, as I took the quote and sent it to my siblings in an email titled "Father of the Year."

My older sister, Mary, replied in an email, "I'm *glad* he can't tell anyone how old I am."

But the greatest lessons we saw as coaches were in his toughest seasons in 2003 and 2004. As the losses piled up, there were members of the staff, and certainly people outside the program, who advocated changes or firing coaches. There was even a letter from a fan, telling me that we graduated "too many" of our players and that we should run off guys who couldn't play.

Through it all, the temptation to change the team rules or recruit bad students or change what we were all about was indeed great. But he stood fast.

He even learned to adjust to the new realities of lost privacy. That was driven home when I received a fan's email, naming a couple of players that the fan had heard had failed our internal drug tests. He wasn't 100 percent accurate but he did get some correct.

I took the email to Joe's house. This was not a conversation that could be had in the football office if someone was in fact leaking information. In my hand I held the printed email and handed it to him. As he read the words, a look of concern came across his face. "Where did you get this?" he asked.

"It was emailed to me."

"How would this guy get this?"

"Maybe the kids who failed the tests told their friends," I suggested, "and one of them told someone."

"Jay...we haven't even told these kids yet. They don't know. I hope we don't have someone with an agenda in our program. Keep your ear to the ground."

It wasn't that Joe wanted to cover the drug tests up. The drug testing program was administered by the athletic department. The results were given to them, and the punishments were automatic. Joe felt the department should handle it within the set policy and without people shooting their mouths off.

He changed the way he handled a lot of information after that, but it was always a challenge. If there was one constant, he could adapt to the changing realities and always looked to see when and where he needed to make adjustments.

In 2004 he changed the defensive scheme and then the offensive scheme in 2005. The changes led to more success, but we did *not* change what we valued. Joe Paterno stood firm to the core bedrock values of what he believed in. Those foundations of success are what carried us over the hump.

In the most trying time in his professional life, with the wolves at the door, he held firm to the beliefs of what Penn State football should be. There was no compromise in a world that constantly demanded a panicked response to every crisis.

The death of his brother was a tough moment for him. George had health problems, and Joe blamed himself for being slow to react and help him. As we stood alongside my uncle George's bed and watched him slowly slip from this mortal existence on a beautiful summer afternoon, I could see the enormous shroud of guilt that was cloaking my father's heart.

I remember walking with Mary out of the hospital. We were behind my parents and halfway down the main hallway. I saw my mother take my father's hand in hers and put her head on his shoulder as they walked. It was a touching moment.

I did my best to try and get my father to understand what he could not grasp. I had read *A River Runs Through It* by Norman Maclean. The story is a true family story, a tale of a two brothers and their divergent paths in life but bound together by a common love of the written word and fly fishing.

There is a moment when Maclean recalls the last sermon he heard his father deliver in the church where he was a pastor. He asks what we are called to do and he says we are to "understand that we can love completely without complete understanding."

I don't know if that message ever got through to my father as it related to his brother. But I do know that over 17 years working alongside my father through good days and bad days, I was angry with him, I was happy with him, and I am sure that he felt the same way about me.

Months after he was gone, I found a letter I'd written to him in October 1991 when I was coaching at the University of Virginia. In that letter I'd expressed what drew me to coaching. I do know that even back in 1991 I did have an understanding of the little things that kept him in coaching.

> Sometimes I wonder if coaching can ever be as fun or as pure as it probably was when you started Dad.
>
> However, I take great solace when I go out on the field and work with some freshmen scout team player that's hustling through the individual drills I put him through because he wants to get better.
>
> And when he does get better it all seems worthwhile again.
>
> Good Luck next week. Love, Jay

Maybe I never gained complete understanding of Joe Paterno. Maybe I did, but I do know that I grew to love my boss and my father completely. That is all that matters.

Chapter 10

Molder of Men

What I came to realize most vividly in the days after Joe Paterno was fired and ultimately died was how, as a coach, my father became a father to so many others. Men and women expressed that to me in the last few months of his life and after his death.

O.J. McDuffie, an NFL star for eight years, came to Penn State as a freshman in 1988 from Warrensville Heights, Ohio. He and my father had their moments, but both had tremendous respect for the other, a respect that grew to love. He pulled me aside at the viewing, pointed to the casket covered in white roses and said, "That man there was a father to me."

I realized that my father was so much more. Yes, he was a patriarch for his own children but also for the scores of student-athletes and others he inspired at Penn State and beyond through his living example.

The Italian name Paterno means "fatherly" and it is a most fitting name for Joe. His coaching style evolved over the years from a demanding taskmaster driving his troops Patton-like into the game to a more fatherly approach. But even in the early days when he was his toughest, there was a genuine love for the student-athletes in his program.

Some of the former players thought he got softer in his old age. It is the same argument kids make about their parents when they perceive looser rules for a younger sibling. Joe was simply adapting to new demographic realities of society around him that, whether he wanted them or not, were creeping into his program.

In his later years, one of the changes from the 1960s and 1970s related to the family dynamics. In earlier years the team was predominantly white and mostly from two-parent homes. Tom Donchez was an exception, coming to Penn State from a single-mother household in the 1970s. My father always had tremendous respect for what his mother had done to get him through high school and to Penn State. Tom has told me many times that he gained a father in Joe Paterno.

By the 1980s and 1990s, the teams were highly integrated and reflected American society with a larger number of young men from single-parent or divorced homes.

More importantly than integrating for integration's sake was the success of the black student-athletes. Through the end of Joe Paterno's career, his graduation rates for black student-athletes were miles ahead of the national average and were on par or even outpacing the rates for his white players.

Penn State's football program was ahead of the curve when it came to racial integration, but Joe always wanted to push it further. In January of 1983 after winning a national championship, he addressed the Penn State board of trustees and urged them to increase diversity. The rate of the football team's diversity was roughly 10 times that of Penn State's student body.

Kenny Jackson was a star member of that national championship team and would become much more than a player to Joe Paterno. Until the end of Joe's life, he became more like a loyal son. Kenny never forgot how Joe Paterno responded when he called his coach for help. In early 1984 Kenny's mother was having heart problems and needed an operation. The cost of the surgery was prohibitive. Kenny had finished his career a few weeks earlier as a two-time All-American wide receiver and was considered a first round lock in the NFL draft a few months later.

Joe called the Cleveland Clinic and explained that Kenny would soon sign a multi-million dollar contract after the draft and would then be able to pay for the surgery. Joe helped get the surgery done, and Kenny's mother lived for nearly three decades after the surgery.

After a tough 1992 season, my father received a fax from Kenny. He offered to come back and coach and in a subsequent phone conversation told his old coach to: "Pay me whatever you can. This isn't about the money."

Joe Paterno remembered Kenny's strong leadership. As a player Kenny and some teammates approached another teammate who had a drug problem.

If the teammate didn't stop, Kenny threatened to go to Joe. Ultimately the team leaders sat down with Joe and told him what they'd done. Joe confronted the young man, who then got help.

Not many college students have the strength to step outside the friendship role with people in their peer group. Joe never forgot that commitment. Kenny became a valuable coach and also helped tune Joe in to evolving social realities.

In 1992 Ki-Jana Carter, a talented freshman running back from Westerville, Ohio, was just starting his Penn State career. His combination of size, speed, and power were rare, a combination perhaps unsurpassed by any running back in Penn State history. Joe saw greatness and resorted to his usual motivational tactics with him. "Hey, Ki-Jana, don't be the last one on the practice field. Go ahead, keep your weight up," he said. "You'll make a great fullback."

Ki-Jana sulked. One of Joe's many strengths was in knowing what he didn't know, and he knew he wasn't reaching Ki-Jana. Kenny told Joe privately that he thought he knew what was bothering the future star.

Ki-Jana was raised by his mother who worked hard at the beauty shop she owned. Ki-Jana was usually the man about the house while his mother worked late. He was used to doing what he wanted, when he wanted. For the first time in Ki-Jana's life, he had a man yelling at him and would have to adjust.

Joe got the point and handled him differently from then on. The relationship between Joe and Ki-Jana grew. A few weeks later, Ki-Jana had some pain in his knee. Team orthopedist Dr. Wayne Sebastianelli came to Joe to talk about it. "Joe," Wayne asked, "what kind of future do you think he has?"

"He can be a great one."

"Then we better redshirt him and clean his knee up for his own good."

There was no hesitation in the coach's mind. Although he could have helped Penn State right away, the decision was made for the student-athlete's welfare. Four years later after a Rose Bowl win and a 12–0 season, Ki-Jana was in Joe's hotel suite with throngs of other well-wishers.

Despite Ki-Jana having one more year of eligibility to play at Penn State, Joe pulled Ki-Jana aside and told him it was time to go. That April he was the first pick in the entire NFL draft and a month later finished his degree from Penn State's Smeal College of Business.

None of that may have ever happened had my father not adjusted.

From then on he'd constantly prod his coaches to learn how to reach each student-athlete. He'd ask: "How can we scratch their bark?"

Brandon Short came to Penn State from a rough housing project where he was raised by his grandmother. Joe Paterno recognized leadership and intelligence in Brandon and wanted to cultivate that. They forged a strong relationship. Brandon has told me many times: "Your father is my father. If it weren't for him, I'd be dead or in jail."

He reminded me of that from halfway around the world on a phone call from his investment office in Dubai. This man, now a brother to me, reminded me how my father's life lessons had helped him rise from the streets of McKeesport to Penn State, to the NFL, to get his MBA at Columbia and on to a career in finance.

Anthony "Spice" Adams came to Penn State from Detroit. His father went to prison when Anthony was just four years old. His mother, Connie, ran Anthony's life so that he could succeed.

She told me how carefully she'd chosen the men she allowed to be role models for her son. Through the recruiting process, she came to believe that Joe Paterno was the man to continue her son's growth. In our visit to Detroit, she told that to us as we stood in their church.

Joe Paterno had doubted how good Anthony was, but after the visit, he was sold on the person we were recruiting. We visited his high school, gym, and church and saw the team of men Connie had put around her son to guide him toward us. "Jay, I don't know how great a player he will be," Joe said. "But his mother is such a beautiful person and the people she has put around her son are impressive. He will be something special because of her."

Anthony was one of those who constantly talked to Joe. My father soon came to understand their relationship was very important to Anthony. Without his own father in his life, he craved that relationship with Joe. Here was a 19-year-old black kid from Detroit relating to a 73-year-old Italian guy from Brooklyn, and the old guy was relating back.

Anthony would even come up and pat him on Joe's butt after a game or a practice. "Coach, that was a great practice," he'd say. "Coach, you did a good job in the game today."

After the end of the 2002 season, Anthony was drafted in the second round.

These were far from Joe Paterno's only success stories. There were the stories of players, switching their position on the team for the good of their careers even if they—themselves—could not see it at the time.

Two of my teammates went through the same story. Andre Collins was a talented safety from Cinnaminson, New Jersey. His mother and father had 19 children, all whom went on to graduate college. Andre was the first of five Collins brothers to play football and graduate from Penn State.

When my father recruited Andre, he went to the house, and all 19 children were lined up and greeted him. Years later Joe would maintain it was one of the most impressive things he'd ever seen in all his years of recruiting.

Andre had gotten offers of a car and money to go to another school and had made up his mind to go there. The ace in the hole was that being under 18 he could not sign without a parent's signature, and Frances Collins knew she wanted her son at Penn State.

A couple of years into his career, Joe informed them that Andre would be moving from safety to linebacker, a move that didn't exactly thrill Andre. Joe explained that Andre had a future beyond college as a linebacker.

Andre earned his place in a long line of All-American linebackers at Penn State. After college Andre went on to play 10 years in the NFL, including winning a Super Bowl championship with the Washington Redskins.

The same year Andre arrived, highly touted lineman Dave Szott also joined the team. Dave's heart was set on playing defense. After a couple of years, Joe called him in and told him he was moving to offense. Dave wanted to leave.

Joe got a phone call from Dave's father, who asked about the move to offense. Joe told his father what he had told Dave. His skill set as a defensive lineman may not get him to the next level, but as an offensive lineman, he could play a long time in the NFL. Dave's father told him to stay.

After he graduated from Penn State, Dave would go on to play 14 years in the NFL.

About a decade and a half later, the story repeated itself with Levi Brown from Granby High School in Norfolk, Virginia. He was convinced he was a great defensive lineman until halfway through his career, when Joe Paterno called him in and told him he was moving to offense. "Levi, as a defensive lineman you may not play after college," he said. "As an offensive tackle, you'll be a top 10 pick."

Levi wasn't interested in hearing the truth at that age. He was determined to leave. His father called Joe and really yelled at him, calling Joe a liar. During recruiting Levi had been told he would be a defensive lineman.

Joe conceded that when we recruited him we believed Levi would play defense, but we now knew Levi's future as a football player would be on offense. After the 2006 season when Levi was an All-Big Ten offensive tackle, a Penn State graduate, and getting ready to be a first-round pick, Levi's father stopped by the house to thank Joe personally. "You were right, Coach," he said.

"No," Joe said, "*your son proved me right.*"

Joe never forgot the gratitude and the trust they had put in him. That April, Levi went to the Arizona Cardinals as the fifth overall pick in the entire NFL draft and signed a contract in excess of $50 million.

But the initial reactions of all three of those young men neither surprised nor disappointed their coach. They were hardly the only stories like that; they are just three of many. Joe never forgot that all the young men who walked in the door harbored lofty aspirations. He understood his responsibility to put them in a position to reach their full potential.

There were failures that haunted him. Two of my teammates had issues with alcohol and never quite lived up to their potential at Penn State on or off the field. As the years passed, they broke the hold of the substance abuse in their lives. Seeing them as grown men who'd defeated their lives' demons gave Joe resolution, but still the nagging question lingered. *What if?* He'd ask himself if he had missed signs, if he could've done more to prevent it.

Joe knew that he was running a team of people, a diverse collection of individuals each bringing a unique past with them. That idea of "scratch their bark" became a staple for him. It was his challenge for each young man.

There are other stories, most not involving football.

One young man was distraught with news from home and came to Bill Kenney, the coach who recruited him. This student-athlete's preschool-aged niece had died, and the family lacked the resources to bury her. Her body would be buried in an unmarked grave.

Bill came to Joe privately and explained the situation. "Bill," Joe said, "talk to John Bove and see what I am allowed to do within NCAA rules."

John Bove was Penn State's compliance coordinator, a stickler for the rules and as good as anyone in the country. After checking with the NCAA,

John informed Joe what he could do. My mother executed the payment exactly as instructed to be in compliance with NCAA rules, so that this student-athlete and his family would find some peace in the midst of such a horrible time.

One thing that his student-athletes could count on was that Joe Paterno would stand with them when times were tough. At the end of one season, a player was accused of a crime on campus.

The office of judicial affairs told him he could appeal and risk being expelled permanently or take a plea and be suspended for one semester. The office did not allow lawyers into the hearings, so he had no legal advice before he chose what looked like the least bad of two bad options.

He was promised that it would be the end of it.

Shortly after the season ended, he was charged by the county district attorney based on his apparent "confession" at his campus hearing. He had been denied legal representation and due process.

There was no undoing his one semester suspension. So he went home to take classes and stay eligible to return for the rest of his college career. After my father died, he shared with me how much my father had kept in touch with him. "He called or wrote me every week to encourage me," he said. "I will never forget that. He was on me every time to stay focused and keep getting my education, even while I was fighting the charges. That meant more to me than you know."

He stayed on his classes, won his case in court, and came back to play three more seasons. His life was helped by Joe Paterno's father-like loyalty to him in his time of greatest trouble.

But Joe's loyalty to his student-athletes did not end when they were done playing. After a few years in the NFL, the once promising career of a former Penn State quarterback was coming to a premature conclusion.

Ernie Accorsi, the general manager of the New York Giants, saw something in Kerry Collins but wanted a second opinion. Ernie had worked at Penn State years earlier and carried a lifelong respect for the place and for Joe Paterno.

He called Joe and asked what he thought about Kerry. Joe gave him his word that Kerry would be a real asset for the Giants. Joe and team owner Wellington Mara were longtime friends, so he trusted Joe's recommendation.

In late winter of 1999, the Giants announced the signing of Kerry Collins to a four-year deal worth roughly $14 million, a big sum for a quarterback viewed as a risk. In the stories about the acquisition, Accorsi mentioned his conversation with my father, which carried a lot of weight and eased the pressure on the controversial signing.

In his second season with the Giants, Kerry led the team to the Super Bowl. As Kerry lit up the Minnesota Vikings in an NFC Championship Game rout, I mentioned to my father how he'd been right about Kerry going to the Giants. "Hey, Kerry made me look good," he said. "It wasn't that I was right."

My father made sure he was on the field in Tampa during warm-ups for that Super Bowl. Kerry and Joe shook hands, and years later Kerry mentioned what that meant to him.

It was a familiar story. When Joe Paterno picked up the phone to go to bat for someone, people listened, and the men he helped were always grateful.

Lance Hamilton came to Penn State as the second of three Hamilton brothers to play at Penn State. Lance was a phenomenal student and after a shot at the NFL he applied to law schools. He had decided to go to Boston University because they had offered a better aid package than Yale.

Joe wanted Lance at Yale and told him he would call up there to see if he could help. The dean of the law school did not know Joe, but he took the call. He pulled Lance's file and called Joe back. After looking at Lance's file and listening to Joe rave about a great student, a football player, and an activist for many causes, he told Joe he would take care of Lance.

Yale brought Lance up and offered him a better financial aid package. Lance made Yale Law Review and proved Joe Paterno right.

But his reach stretched beyond his own sport. There were so many other student-athletes who admired and respected Joe Paterno. His ideals set a course for the entire athletic department. Other coaches like women's volleyball coach Russ Rose, men's basketball coach Bruce Parkhill, and field hockey coach Char Morett expressed their admiration and genuine love for my father not only after he had died but for many years prior to that.

For a couple of years, my father served as both the head football coach and athletic director at Penn State. During that time he attended all kinds of athletic contests at Penn State. He realized all the coaches and student-athletes' commitment to their sports was no less intense than his football team's.

Even when football raked in tens of millions of dollars in profit, he spent the money for football frugally. He'd remind us of other dedicated student-athletes, men and women counting on the money we made to support their sports. "Don't be pigs. We're not alone here," Joe said. "If we don't have to spend it, don't spend it. Every team here wants to win just as badly as we do. Make sure there's enough for everyone."

His awareness and unselfish attitude were not lost of his fellow coaches, and the other student-athletes at Penn State. He didn't need a "One Team" slogan to remind him he was all in for all sports at Penn State.

In 1990 Penn State's men's basketball team fell just short of the NCAA Tournament, losing in the Atlantic 10 conference final against Rutgers. After the game Joe walked into the locker room and asked Coach Parkhill if it would be okay for him to address Parkhill's team.

Joe acknowledged the pain they felt was real. But he told them they would rise up, assuring them they would be back to win the conference championship. Sure enough, the next spring Penn State walked off the court at Rec Hall with a championship win over George Washington and a berth in the NCAA Tournament. Mike Morse, who'd been in that sad locker room and walked off the court with the team, saw Joe, and they both knew what the other was thinking.

Joe winked and smiled at him.

In 1993 Morett's Penn State field hockey team was ranked No. 1 in the country and hosted No. 3 Ohio State. She invited my father to the game. He stayed, watched, and stuck around afterward to congratulate the team.

A few weeks after he died, I received a letter and picture from that post-game celebration from 1993 field hockey team member and family friend Sharon Herlocher. Sharon shared with my family how much my father meant to her and to so many other student-athletes at Penn State. In a letter to my family she wrote: "Your Dad, Granddad, father-in-law and all that he stood for helped every Penn Stater grow, including me. As you all know, his presence lifted everyone around him."

That picture and note are among the most meaningful things I got in the aftermath of this all. The realization that your father's life reached so many people at this school and across this nation is an empowering thing.

But Joe Paterno's reach extended beyond this country. He coached players born in Canada and across the Atlantic from Europe and Africa. There were players born in Jamaica, Italy, Great Britain, Sierra Leone, Ghana, Tonga, Samoa, Zimbabwe, Nigeria, and Liberia.

In the recruiting class that showed up on campus in the fall of 2000, there were two young men from the state of Washington. John Bronson went on to play in the NFL, but Ryan Scott had the interesting family history.

Ryan's father, Raymond, was born the son of a tribal chief in Sierra Leone. Enjoying a sunny disposition, Raymond spoke with a joyful sing-song accent. Ryan's parents saw Penn State as a place where their son could compete on the field and more importantly in the classroom. But Penn State became more than that. On his frequent trips to see his son, Raymond connected with people in the College of Agriculture to improve productivity in Sierra Leone.

Back in Sierra Leone, Ryan's grandfather read about this man, Joe Paterno. What he learned moved him to name Joe an honorary chief in his tribe—complete with garments made from cotton and dyed navy blue from indigo grown on the tribe's land. It was one of the most treasured gifts my father ever received.

One of the hallmarks of Joe Paterno's professional life was his relentless pursuit of excellence and personal integrity, not just for himself but for the student-athletes on his team, the coaches on his staff, and everyone working for him.

NCAA rules were to be followed. Academic integrity had to be maintained not just because of the damage it could do to his program, but for the black eye it would give the entire university. It also applied to off-field behavior and to the rule of law.

In his younger years, there was certainly a tremendous fear of Joe Paterno's wrath and in failing to live up to his standards. But times were much, much different. Campus-wide enforcement of the law was more relaxed as it related to not only football players but for all students. The university was a different place then. Students could have keg parties in the dorms. There was no open container law. Most of the time fights were stopped, and the offending parties were sent home.

In the 1940s Penn State was awash in World War II veterans hardened by years of combat and helped along by the G.I. Bill. After returning to Penn State, my first neighbor was World War II veteran Tom Runyan, who told me great stories of fraternity pranks, kegs *in* Beaver Field, and police who simply instructed them to return things they'd stolen (including a nativity scene from in front of the Post Office). That attitude of live and let live on less serious matters lasted into the late 1980s.

Was it a better time? I don't know. I do know that a lot of those guys were good guys who had a few too many, and no one got seriously hurt. It didn't make them criminals.

Make no mistake, the lax enforcement of transgressions by the university was by no means mirrored by Joe Paterno. Every player dreaded the call from his secretary/staff assistant Cheryl Norman, asking you to come see Joe. The loneliest moments of a player's Penn State career were the quiet minutes in a chair alone outside Joe's office, moments often spent trying to figure out what exactly they had been caught doing and readying their response.

Joe Paterno was always trying to distinguish between the con men and good kids who stumbled. The challenge of a head football coach at the major college level was to evaluate each student-athlete.

It was an idea best summed up by a university staff member I met. Bill Huston, one of the directors of Penn State's judicial affairs, once told me he tried to gauge what he was dealing with every time a student came before him. "Jay," he said, "there is a difference between a bad kid and a good kid that makes a mistake. That is the challenge in my job and in your job."

It reflected back to what Joe Paterno talked about all the time: con men are bad kids. Some may be able to be saved, but it takes a lot more effort. But there comes a time when eventually you may have to cut them loose. The good kids who make mistakes must be shown how they have erred and atone for those errors.

On our team he could handle a couple of con men, but it required a balance he was always evaluating. As it related to gauging the team morale, he sought out "fringe" kids, the guys with strong leadership ability who were not angels. He wanted honest feedback. Often in a coach-player relationship or in an administration-student relationship, the adult seeks out the good egg who will then tell them exactly what the adult wants to hear. "Most of the guys I coach," Joe Paterno said, "I have to spend a little time with, but there is a handful of guys that I end up spending a lot of time with. They are the ones who need the most help. They also can help me the most. If I reach them, I'll get to the whole team."

It is something that everyone in education could learn from. We like to surround ourselves with the best kids, who make us feel wonderful about all we've done.

> Anybody can love something that is beautiful or smart or agile. You will never know love until you can love something that isn't beautiful, isn't bright, isn't glamorous. It takes a special person to love something unattractive, someone unknown. That is the test of love.
>
> Can you accept someone for his inabilities—you might have a guy playing next to you who maybe isn't perfect, but you've got to love him, and maybe that love would enable you to help him.
>
> We don't want to be picking on each other, but rather what can I do to make it easier for my teammate.
>
> Crucial to a team's success.
>
> *Note: found in Joe Paterno's file*

The ones who need the most help challenge us to reflect and re-evaluate our approach. Joe Paterno thrived on being challenged to rethink his approach. It was in boosting those with the farthest to go that Joe Paterno felt he'd done his best work.

Joe used to quote Teddy Roosevelt to the coaching staff after a player had run afoul of his rules. "Youth is a disease," he said. "But it can be cured."

He believed his job was more than coaching them on the field. His cure was to take them from childhood to responsible adulthood. His great strength was the recognition that all men may be created equal, but he also realized that: "When they get to us, some are more equal than others."

There were young men who arrived ready to face anything and everything. John Urschel arrived in January 2009 with a high school academic resume that was the envy of any student on campus. Others arrived much less prepared academically or emotionally or lacking maturity. Joe fought harder to bring them along.

Stephen Pitts finished his college career in 1995 on a straight and narrow academic path by reading Rudyard Kipling's poem "If" at the football senior banquet.

Joe Paterno could see a great number of young men for whom they really were and not how they behaved. One thing I can tell you is how joyful Joe Paterno got when the seemingly "lost sheep" graduated and went on to successful lives.

When he'd talk about a man like quarterback John Shaffer, he was proud. John came from a great Cincinnati family and won all but one of the games he started in his entire career. John was an Academic All-American and has gone on to Goldman Sachs on Wall Street.

But talking about the harder cases made him glow. Ivory Geathers came to Penn State from John's Island, South Carolina. My mother helped tutor him in English, and after a few too many late papers and too many "Yes, Ma'ams," my mom blew up. "I don't want to hear, 'Yes Ma'am.' I want to see you bring the rough draft done on time."

He got the message and earned a Penn State degree as well as a graduate degree.

Men like Anthony Adams, Tamba Hali, and Troy Drayton played in the NFL but, as promised, returned to finish their degrees. Troy came back after an NFL career that lasted over a decade. After commencement he dropped in at Joe's house to show his old coach his new diploma.

There were other challenges and big redemption projects. Joe Paterno often told his coaches and his team: "It's not what happens to you that matters. It is how you *react* to what happens to you."

That philosophy became evident in the story of two 1992 teammates, Bobby Engram and Rickie Sayles. Rickie was a fifth-year senior, and Bobby was a sophomore from South Carolina who had lost his father right after coming to Penn State a year earlier.

One night just before the season started, they got into trouble with the police. When the dust settled the next day, Joe met with them individually, and to their credit, they owned up to what they had done. When Joe told Bobby that he'd been influenced to do something wrong by an older teammate, Bobby stopped him. Bobby told Joe that he—and he alone—was responsible for his own actions.

Joe never forgot that mature display of honesty and strength from a

19-year-old. That prompted Joe to do all he could to keep him in school while serving a one-year suspension. Bobby sat out a year and then played and graduated. During his NFL career that spanned over a decade, Bobby started a foundation for sickle-cell research.

As for Rickie, he also owned up to his mistake and got a one-year suspension. Because he was a senior, it wiped out his college career. He graduated to his life after football. Rickie began a 4-H group for inner-city kids within a group called Penn Civilians. The project has grown to include mentoring and tutoring of children who need help academically.

There were others.

Ahmad Collins was a talented player who couldn't seem to stay on track. Joe called his mother and stepfather and asked to meet with them about Ahmad's future. He told them that he'd have to sit Ahmad out until he got his academic house in order.

After the meeting Ahmad's mother asked to speak to Joe privately. Joe thought for sure she was going to give him hell. Instead she thanked him for trying to guide her son the right way. Then she made a point that Joe Paterno kept in his mind for the rest of his life as a coach. "Coach," she said, "it must be tough to be a father to so many children." At the end of Ahmad's career, we were sitting in our staff meeting and getting an update on academics. Donnie Ferrell, our academic advisor, was giving updates on everyone on the team and saved some good news for Joe. "And Joe," said Donnie with a big smile on his face, "Ahmad Collins is graduating next week."

Joe's smile was bigger than after any game we'd ever won.

There were players who got girlfriends pregnant. Joe Paterno was a realist. While he believed that marriage was the ideal situation for raising children, he also knew that it did occur outside of marriage and often by mistake.

In those moments he did not judge. He urged our staff to do everything within NCAA and university rules to get the right housing and right grants, so that the child would be cared for and the student-athlete could finish his career in the classroom and on the field.

The young fathers who had children in college yet graduated while taking care of their responsibilities made him proud. Others battled addiction or alcoholism, surviving rehab to return to the team and live drug-free sober lives. They, too, made Joe Paterno immensely proud.

But Joe put rules and punishments in place, hoping not to catch people but to help steer them clear of trouble. He'd say, "If there is no threat of going over a cliff, then young people will take all kinds of risks. If there is a cliff at the end of the field, they will put up a fence in their mind or they will not play so close to that edge."

That was why he wanted to aggressively drug test his players. After a year when we did not play as well, some of the kids came to talk to him and informed him there were some kids messing around with drugs. He told our medical staff to boost the number of tests. Every week a good percentage of our team would be tested without exception.

Deterrence was his first goal, not detection. The threat of detection had to be a very real possibility to meet his real goal of drug testing. "I don't test you because I want to say, 'I gotcha,'" he explained. "I test so that you have a crutch. When you are at a party, and someone says, 'Try this,' you have an excuse. You can say to that person, 'Coach could test me tomorrow, and I don't want to get caught.'"

It was a mostly successful philosophy.

In college I had friends who weren't on the team, and some of them smoked weed; some did more dangerous things. Every once in a while, they'd ask if I wanted a try. There was even a time when a very attractive blonde girl offered the chance to take that risk. "Do you want to go get high?" she asked.

It was that crutch that Joe had given me that I used to avoid the temptation and peer pressure. "I can't," I said. "We get drug tested, and I could get hit any time."

"Okay, I can respect that," she said.

That got me clear that night and every night. My friends, who weren't on the team, knew about the drug tests. They didn't put me in those situations out of respect for that. The fear of the testing is probably the main reason I never smoked weed or did any other illegal drugs in college or at any time in my life. Other teammates and players will tell you similar stories.

But there were players who did stumble, and Joe tried to lead them by reaching out and not condemning. He reasoned that if he kicked a young man off the team after a first drug test result that he would fail that young man by simply turning him loose. "The easy thing is to simply eliminate or get rid of a young man when they get in trouble," he said. "It is more difficult to keep them around and try to help them see the right way to do things."

In a society always ready for mob mentality outrage, that isn't always how we see things. Joe Paterno understood the bigger picture that football could be used to change behaviors not for a week or a game but for life.

Punishment was always on the table, though. In Joe's earlier years, punishment was swift and generally very consistent—Old Testament fire and brimstone stuff. But Joe Paterno would be the first to tell you that he grew smarter as he grew older.

As the prosecution of our occasional players' legal issues grew more public, Joe's hands were increasingly tied. In cases involving a trial, Joe was hesitant to act unilaterally, not wanting to essentially proclaim the guilt in the public domain of his player without facts.

He knew administration of a public punishment could negatively impact a young man's ability to get a fair trial. There was no way he wanted the media's demands for him to act swiftly and force his hand.

As he got older, he developed a more measured, reasoned, and fairer response to allegations that came across his desk. Outsiders called it "getting soft."

In 2007 he hit back. In the offseason there was a fight involving members of our team. The media ran with a narrative that late in his career Joe Paterno had sacrificed his ideals and recruited "bad kids," so he could close out his career with more wins.

They cited statistics of charges—not actual convictions. When the actual rate of young men on our team who were actually found guilty was factored against the rate for society and for the campus, we were still well below the rates for both. No one realized the increase in charges was not a reflection of increased activity but rather increased and stricter enforcement in charging all Penn State students.

But that wasn't a good story. It wasn't just here at Penn State. *Sports Illustrated* ran a story in 2011 when they cited what they deemed to be a shocking statistic that 7 percent of all players on top 25 teams had been *charged* with a crime. Not guilty, not convicted, just charged.

The rate of college football players being *charged* was actually lower than the national average for young men of their same age group being *convicted* of crimes. That statistic didn't fit the narrative so it didn't make it into the story.

The 2007 fight started with someone pushing down the girlfriend of one of our players, and our player following the guy back to his apartment. Even after all this time has passed, what happened after that is murky at best. It was even less clear then.

The district attorney decided to grandstand with felony charges and perp walks, making a national show out of a fight that resulted in no serious injuries. Meanwhile, no charges were filed for the underage drinkers at the party or for the host of the party for furnishing alcohol to minors.

It became clear that regardless of the culpability or blame in the fight involving his players, Joe Paterno knew that there were those pursuing this to make their own names. He would not be pulled into assigning guilt to anyone without knowing what really happened.

Amid the media howl, Joe put together a punishment and response that has been forgotten by some of the people who claimed he held his team above the law. Before any trial or any finding of guilt, Joe decided that this was a failure on a team level. Without any evidence pointing to guilty individual members, he assessed a team penalty.

This accomplished two things. First, it would highlight to the team that they were responsible as a group to keep each other *out* of trouble. Second, he would not try and play detective and publicly punish the guys he could only guess were responsible.

That summer the entire team took a couple of Saturdays to build a home for Habitat for Humanity. Then in the fall they got up on Sunday mornings after home games and cleaned the stadium. That job was usually reserved for student-athletes on club teams who used the pay they received to help subsidize their team's expenses.

The football team did the cleaning, and the club teams still got the money for their programs. He wanted his players to understand how fortunate they were to get everything they got as members of the Penn State football team.

It was an effective tool to illustrate his point.

Beaver Stadium the morning after the game is a mess. Nacho cheese, vomit, soft pretzels, cups, and all sorts of soggy garbage litter the stands. Our players waded into that with none of them particularly happy about it. Even the morning after a primetime rout of Notre Dame, they were there cleaning up the stands.

The message was delivered loud and clear. A year later the 2008 team was fundamentally different. The team responded with an 11–1 run that was a field goal on the game's last play at Iowa away from playing for the national title.

On the field you had to prove you were good enough. While off the field, he expected a certain code of conduct, a decorum, and way of living your life. He was John Locke, believing in the innate goodness of man. He was the ideal of the American legal system, assuming all men and women were innocent until proven guilty.

But Joe Paterno never forgot that he was human, that he had fallen on his life's journey. The high standards were there for all of us. But he was realistic and he'd remind us that even the best among us would make mistakes.

But the forgiveness was almost always there, never given but able to be earned. Sometimes there was the ultimate price to be paid—removal from the team. One of the men Joe admired the most was Abraham Lincoln. He had read how reluctant the President was to sign the death warrants for deserters in the Union Army.

Lincoln spared the soldier's life far more often than his officers wanted. In Joe Paterno's case in his later years, he spared his student-athletes perhaps more than some in the media would have liked. In the book *Team of Rivals*, Doris Kearns Goodwin wrote that Lincoln once remarked, "Officers only see the force of military discipline," but that some men were "overcome by a physical fear greater than his will."

Lincoln stated, "Let him fight instead of shooting him."

In a similar vein, Joe took the tougher line. He kept the student-athlete fighting, figuring out the path to redemption, pointing them to follow it to the right conclusion.

Through the disappointment his players felt in failing to live up to the standards, there was the trek on redemption's path. On that path Joe Paterno would forgive the trespasses that he knew were mainly the missteps of youth, of growing into maturity under what had become a national microscope.

But most importantly they knew that their coach was watching them, pushing them, and rooting for them to succeed. Despite their failings there was never a loss of love and always a willingness to forgive if they could prove they'd earned redemption.

Chapter 11

It's Gotta Be the Shoes

On Penn State gamedays, Joe Paterno's black shoes were almost as iconic as his dark glasses. The same went for his team's plain uniforms and footwear. Every game the black Nike shoes seemed to sparkle in the autumn sunlight like they'd just been polished.

There was a good reason for that: they had.

As kids my brother Dave and I would alternate polishing my father's dress shoes. My mother wasn't too excited about this because she feared we'd ruin our clothes with shoe polish. But she relented and got us a wooden shoe shine box, where we kept the polish, rags, and brushes.

One spring day my father offered me 50 cents to shine his shoes—enough for two packs of newly arrived baseball cards at the College Heights Exxon. Anxious to get paid and walk to the gas station, I did a shoddy job on his shoes. I wanted to be the first to score the coveted Reggie Jackson card.

Trusting that I'd done the job correctly, my father paid me before he saw the results of my half-hearted labors. Upon my return I was lectured about taking pride in everything that I did. In my haste I failed to actually *earn* the money I'd received.

There is karma in the world: Reggie Jackson was *not* in that pack.

As I sat in the basement laundry room all alone, it was a sad solitary moment. I sat with my guilt while hearing the sound of a metal zipper clanging as it tumbled in the dryer. I re-polished the shoes to meet his standard.

Standards mattered.

Every time he went to make a speech or to meet a recruit's family, he'd do everything he could to make a great first impression. "Jay," he said, "if you don't shine them right, they won't look right."

"So what?" I asked.

"Look, people will judge you. If your shoes are sloppy, it is a sign that you don't care about every detail. If you care enough that even your shoes are polished, they'll see it."

Eight years later I'd learn even more about the shoes. In my freshman year on Penn State's team, we were approaching the season opener. After Thursday's practice we were all told to bring our shoes up to the equipment room.

I asked equipment manager Tim Shope, a gruff but highly lovable cowboy, why he needed my shoes. "Just get 'em up 'er," he barked.

Assistant equipment manager Brad "Spider" Caldwell pulled me aside to tell me about the shoes. "Jay, we polish them up every Thursday before the game," Spider said.

Looking around the equipment room, I saw the student managers spread out with black shoe polish working on piles of cleats. The smell of polish in the air highlighted the intensity of their work. "Why?" I asked.

"Tradition," Spider replied.

Tradition.

As a student of the game of football, I just loved that word. It evoked memories of Penn State Heisman Trophy winner John Cappelletti banging through the line of scrimmage and into the end zone when I was five years old. That was the year I got hooked on tradition.

Tradition can't be manufactured instantly. Tradition is excellence over time, a gift and a challenge.

In 1986 Penn State's black shoes were tradition but also a rarity among the vast majority of teams wearing white shoes. Our conservative adherence to the black shoes of our ancestors' days was widely ridiculed. It was seen as a sign of Joe Paterno's failure, or worse yet, refusal to keep up with the latest fads.

They may have been right. Joe loved to swim against the tide. The plain uniforms and black shoes were part of that. Even in his last season when teams had five or six different uniforms each season, he took the jerseys back to the 1970s by removing the contrasting color trim. It was simplest and most beautiful uniform in football.

Like all great traditions, there's a story behind the shoes and uniform.

In high school my father's coach took him to a World Series game between the St. Louis Cardinals and the New York Yankees. The Cardinals came out with scuffed shoes and sloppy uniforms. The Yankees emerged in crisp uniforms and something else, which my father's coach pointed out to him. "Look at the Yankees' shoes," the coach said.

There was a smile in my father's eyes 50 years later as he described the Yankees' black shoes shining in the sun. They were immaculately polished. "Jay," my father said, "my coach wanted me to see the Yankees' professionalism while the Cardinals looked like bums."

"Who won that World Series?" I asked.

"Who do you think? The Yankees, and that image was set."

"You weren't a Yankees fan, though."

"I was a Dodger fan. I hated the Yankees, but I respected their tradition."

Tradition.

I love that word. Yankee tradition reminded me of my youth, listening on the radio after bedtime to Mr. October ripping another World Series home run.

Respect for tradition was something that was part of our upbringing in the Paterno household.

But the tradition went beyond the cleats. The Yankees ideal reached beyond shoes. The Yankees have no names on their jerseys. They require their players to shave, keep their hair cut, and don't allow earrings on the field. Anyone familiar with Joe Paterno's Penn State teams recalls those traditions.

The shoes were just one sign; the jerseys were another. But ultimately the whole package represented what Joe Paterno wanted for Penn State's student-athletes.

He sold this idea; Penn State is not for everyone. In recruiting he wanted student-athletes to come to Penn State for the right reasons. Being part of Penn State's football team was a privilege, requiring everyone to give something up for the group.

Isn't that how everything worthwhile in life works? That was his life lesson.

When Joe recruited someone to Penn State, he wanted them to be flattered. He wanted them to know we think they are special enough to pursue success in the classroom and on the field. The way we recruited, it played into that. When his coaches went on the road to visit prospects' homes or schools, Penn State coaches always wore ties. That was Joe's rule to show respect to the student-athletes and their families in recruiting.

While other coaches from other schools wore sweats or golf shirts, we were there in our coats and ties. Other coaches would razz us about it. But we loved being unique and explaining to the prospects and parents why we were in ties on the road and in our office.

We wanted to be different and we asked our players to be different.

It wasn't without issues over time. In the late 1960s, Franco Harris had a mustache when he arrived at Penn State. The staff complained that team rules forbade facial hair and that Joe should do something about it. "Did anyone tell him the rules when we recruited him?" Joe asked.

When it became apparent that no one had informed Franco, Joe allowed Franco to have his mustache because no one had told him.

In the early 2000s, the haircut rule became an issue with some of the black players on the team who wanted braids or dreads. Joe called a team meeting to explain that *everyone* on the team regardless of race had to cut their hair.

But he went further.

He pointed out that Stanley O'Neal, the CEO of Merrill Lynch and a black man, was running one of Wall Street's most prestigious firms. He talked about Ken Chenault, the CEO of American Express, only the third African American CEO of a Fortune 500 Company.

He wanted the student-athletes to consider if O'Neal and Chenault would be CEOs if they had braids. Then he pointed out President George W. Bush's hair. He asked if they believed he would be President of the United States if he had a long ponytail.

Then he compared the CEO's higher compensation with that of an NFL player and noted the lifelong earning potential of a business executive versus the four- or eight-year NFL career.

He understood the unfairness of people judging others by haircuts or by looks, but it was how the real world worked. Joe Paterno wanted his student-athletes to have an understanding of the reality that awaited them, a world that judged everything.

Before the 2005 season, Joe decided to get tougher on all the rules about personal appearance. In a staff meeting we talked about the rule, and the biggest offender was Tamba Hali, an outstanding defensive end. Joe asked if Tamba had been told when he was recruited that he would have to cut his hair. As with Franco Harris 40 years earlier, it turned out Tamba was never told.

In the team meeting, Joe told everyone to cut their hair. Everyone, he explained, except Hali because no one had ever warned him before he came to Penn State. Joe assumed everyone else had been told but did ask anyone else, who'd not been told the rules before they got to Penn State, to raise their hands. Not one hand went up.

At the very next team meeting when the team filed in, it seemed all the haircuts were in order. To Joe's pleasant surprise, about three rows from him sat Tamba Hali with a wide grin on his face and his head shaved. To the day he died, Joe would have gone to war for Tamba Hali because of that show of respect to Penn State's tradition.

A tradition was born in the 1940s to a wide-eyed high school kid from Brooklyn watching the greatest baseball teams in the world battle for a championship. Sixty years later he reminded this Red Sox fan that free agents signed with Boston because they offered the biggest contract without having to make any personal sacrifices to play there.

To be a Yankee, a part of the greatest organization in baseball, is not a right. It is a privilege. It requires the best players in the world to give something up to play for them.

That is all Joe wanted from his student-athletes, an outward sign of shared adherence to a standard. The sign showed each other and those outside the program that being at Penn State was special. That common sacrifice would make it tougher for them to let each other down.

It all started with polished shoes in baseball's Fall Classic and gave birth to a fall classic Penn State football tradition.

What made Joe Paterno's Penn State tradition so special?

It's gotta be the shoes, but it is so much more.

Chapter 12

The Walks Home

There is a moment after playing or coaching a big-time football college game when it is almost eerily silent. The crowd may be roaring, but your mind is still. The preparation for that game is done. All is gone to history; in a moment the realization your work resulted in either success or failure.

The outcome will be forever tallied in either the win or the loss column. A score is written down. The details of the game will be in memories that fade as the minds of those who witnessed what you have done pass from the Earth.

Coaching a big-time football game is a drug, an adrenaline rush flowing through your senses, creating a high. Particularly in the high-profile, tightly fought games you find a focus that zeroes you in on the ebb and flow, the give and take of a great contest.

Once the game is done, a coach has no need for that adrenaline and needs to get it out of his system. You find yourself agitated and edgy. Joe Paterno was that way. My mother made a suggestion to him in the early years of his coaching career. "Why don't you just walk home to clear your mind?" she said.

A tradition was born. We lived just four blocks from campus in a home purchased in August of 1969. It was where Joe would live the rest of his life. The proximity to campus fed him the youthful vibe of a town where 40,000-plus residents were always between the ages of 17 and 22.

It also allowed him to walk to work and to walk home from the stadium after games. The early days were different. There were no cell phone cameras or social media to post pictures on. Joe Paterno walked through fields turned into parking lots of fans enjoying their postgame tailgating feasts. The fans would yell and wave: "Good job, Joe." "Better luck next week, Joe."

It was as though they were grilling in their own backyards and their neighbor, Joe, walked by. It was comfortable, familiar. It was family.

On those late afternoons of the Central Pennsylvania autumn, the mountains cradled the valley in colors vibrant in the fading sunset. As Joe Paterno turned down his street, arching branches of fall colored leaves bathed in sunlight gave the appearance of a gilded vaulted cathedral ceiling.

In 1988 as a member of the team, I started to make those walks home with him after the games.

It was quiet, a time with my father apart from everyone else in the world. As one of five kids, it wasn't easy to get that time one on one with either parent. In football season that time with my father was limited, if it was even available.

Sometimes we barely spoke at all. We would cross Park Avenue leaving campus and walk down a private lane that ran parallel to our neighborhood. The lane led to an old stone home named Lisnaward. Before we got to the house, we would hop over a low fence, cross a yard into our neighborhood, and walk the last two blocks home.

As we neared the end of two seasons of walking home together, the Notre Dame game in 1989 would be my last home game on the team and likely my last walk home with him. The moment was not lost on him.

The game concluded in the evening, and we started our walk after dark. The streetlights lit our way through campus, but the lane was completely dark. We both knew the way instinctively.

He admitted how much he'd enjoyed having me along on his walks. He told me that he had high hopes for my life after college. He told me I should feel no pressure to follow his football career in my own life. "You're interested in politics, you can write, you'd be good on television," he said. "If you want to coach, you can be very good at that, too. But do what you want to do, don't do something because you think I expect you to do something."

"Well, whatever I do, you won't have me to walk home with you again. I hope you can make it without me." I laughed.

Under the streetlight on McKee Street, I could see him smile, too. "I think I'll be able to find my way home," he said, laughing.

In 1995 I returned back to Penn State after a few seasons coaching elsewhere. In June I reminded him that he could have company on the walks home.

"Yeah, it's been a while, hasn't it?" he said, smiling. "You may be surprised that I found my way home without you."

The 1995 season opener game ended with a last-second game-winning field goal and a win over Texas Tech. The walk home routine had changed slightly. Now Tom Venturino drove my father two blocks and dropped him off to avoid the people waiting for him right outside the stadium. The vehicle was a gray pickup truck, so I jumped in the truck bed and rode along.

After two blocks we hopped out on campus. We still walked past some tailgaters and fans, through North Halls, down Holmes Street before finally walking down a gravel alley and onto McKee Street. That was the first of many, many walks we made home after games. There were times when the walks contained great lessons, words he shared that I will never forget.

After a game in the fall of 1998, we were walking home, talking about one of our players whose career hadn't lived up to what we thought it should be. My father stuck with him, and that player was improving as a player and as a student. "You know, Jay," he said, "we have an obligation to him."

"How so?" I asked.

"You know, Jay, once you have kids you'll realize that your happiness is defined by your least happy child. You are only as happy as your least happy child. Every young man we recruit to Penn State was raised by his parents, or maybe just his mother or father, or a grandparent, or someone. They put a lot of time and effort into that child and then they hand them off to us. We have a tremendous responsibility to them because that child's well-being and happiness are in our hands."

"I get what you're saying about the kids we recruit," I said.

"That's the point I wanted to make. Being in a position to determine people's futures or destinies is not something to be taken lightly. It is an awesome responsibility whether you are a coach, or in business, or a parent. The decisions we make about our student-athletes impact their lives. That is why I stick with some of these guys."

He made his point, but in a short walk home, he'd actually made a few points. The one that has stayed with me the most was his point on parenting. When I became a father, I discovered he was right about a parent's happiness.

November 23, 2011

Joe,

This is the time to remember all the young men you have inspired over the decades at Penn State and not just on the gridiron.

I will never forget being at your home after a game and meeting a former player with his young son on his shoulder. He tapped the table and said, "Joe had Sue teach me to read at this table."

He explained that he arrived at Penn State without the ability to read well enough to be scholastically eligible.

Then he said, "Now I'm a lawyer."

Tune out the naysayers piling on you with schadenfreude delight until a flag is thrown or a whistle blown. Those who know you will always believe in you.

You're in my prayers.

Don

The best parts of the walks home were often on campus. As the gray truck would stop at the corner, we'd get out and try to blend in. Inevitably, fans would recognize that Joe Paterno was walking behind them or in front of them. I would listen and I could hear what they'd say: "Hey isn't that?" "Oh my God that's JoePa." "Mom, look that's Joe Paterno."

As we walked by tailgates, sometimes fans approached with a beer or a sandwich or invited us to join them. Kids from tailgates would run across parking lots to ask for him to sign something for them. Many people would ask for Joe to get in a picture. He sincerely hated to tell anyone no.

One thing I did learn is that you never knew who you were going to run into. Fans from other teams were excited to bump into Joe Paterno. Mostly they were just surprised to find that the head coach of a major college football program walked home from games. No police escort home—just a man walking home with his son.

Over the years we were stopped by students, who stopped us, from Asia, Europe, and all over the United States. Two students, who stuck out for me, bumped into us near North Halls. They stopped him to say hello. They were black students and spoke with an accent that clearly indicated they were not from here. That piqued my father's curiosity, so he asked them where they were from.

They explained they were among the Lost Boys who'd escaped a bitter civil war in Sudan. My father was interested in learning more, so he asked them to walk with us. We learned because of their ethnicity within Sudan they had been forced to walk out of their country into refugee camps across the border in Kenya.

When they reached their dorm, they shook my father's hand and thanked him for talking with them. As my father and I continued the walk home he looked at me. "Do you know how lucky we are?" He said. "Do we all realize how lucky we are in this country? Those young men and their families were forced from their homes and had to flee with no idea where they were going or what their future would be."

We didn't talk much about the game the rest of the walk.

On two occasions we did have company. In October of 2001, we defeated Ohio State in a great comeback win. That was his 324th career win, eclipsing the NCAA Division I-A record held by legendary Alabama coach Paul "Bear" Bryant. After the win my 21-month-old son Joseph V. Paterno III came with us.

Joey rode the two blocks from the stadium, and then I carried him on my shoulders, so we would not be slowed down by his little legs. He wore a little brown leather bomber jacket to keep the cold out, and my father got such a kick out of him being with us. "You know, Joey, you don't have any idea what's going on here," Joe Paterno said. "That's good. There's a day you'll wish you could be so oblivious."

"Yeah, Dad," I said, "all he knows is he got to ride in a truck and then walk home with his father and grandfather. That's a big day for him."

Nine years later he would be along with us in late 2010 when my father won his 400th game, a number never before reached in major college football. This time, as a young man a few months from his 11th birthday, he was aware of the moment. By then my father had become his hero.

But all the rides and walks were not idyllic. During the tough 2003 and 2004 seasons, there were a lot of negative comments. During that stretch we won six home games and lost seven, the worst two-year stretch of home games under Joe Paterno.

One older guy sat on a folding chair across the street from the stadium. After each loss he'd yell, "Give it up, Joe." He sat there on his can and yelled about Joe being too old. I laughed because he was no spring chicken himself.

The other comments had to do with the losses and many people expressing that they wanted to see both of us gone. It wasn't easy to hear. True to human nature, they'd yell when we passed in the truck, but no one said anything negative when we got out and started walking.

The man in the truck is somehow less human.

When we were on foot, the people who approached us were supportive and wished us well for the next week's game. Only a couple of times did anyone make a sarcastic comment to our faces. One man made a comment that really upset me, but my father gave me good advice. "Let him go," he said, "if that makes him feel better, so be it. The worst thing you can do is engage someone like that. Remember what I've always told you; don't get into a pissing contest with a skunk."

It was good advice, but as the losses mounted, more and more skunks surfaced.

At the end of the 2004 season, we finished with a big win against Michigan State. What neither he nor I talked about on the way home was if this would be his last game and our last walk home. We just talked about the future and how the win could help us get a couple of big-time recruits. He sensed that one or two important guys could complete the team, giving the program momentum in recruiting and going into the offseason.

In 2005 we started off the season with five wins and no losses headed into a home night game against Ohio State. In one of the most thrilling games ever played, we won 17–10 in an epic defensive battle that re-established us as a national power.

After the game it was complete pandemonium in the stadium as police fought to keep students off the field. Outside the stadium students waited for Joe to come out of the locker room. The grey truck was gone, and now we got into a small Jeep Liberty. The police cleared a way for us to get into the vehicle.

It was reminiscent of a moment from the early morning of January 1983. Penn State had won a national championship about 26 hours before. The trip home had brought us to the football office complex. The lot was filled with students, and they stood atop flat roofs of the buildings adjacent to the lot. It was after midnight as the buses pulled in.

In trying to find my mother, I got separated from my family. I was 14 years old, stuck in a massive crowd, and nervous about getting home. I knew my father was in the football office so I waited there to go home with him. He and the team captains were speaking by bullhorn out a window to the students outside, thanking them and hoping they would disperse. Some of them did.

After trying to wait them out, he realized they weren't going anywhere. We could still hear them outside. He decided we'd go out a back door and try to sneak behind the crowd facing the football office to get to my father's car. Quietly we went outside and were sneaking across the lot. It was straight out of a cartoon like Scooby-Doo and Shaggy trying to sneak past the Mummy or the Phantom. We were about halfway across the back of the lot when I heard it: "Hey, there he is."

Neither my father nor I had to guess who "he" was, nor did we have to guess what the students were going to do next. My dad simply said: "We better run."

We could hear the footsteps, yells, and panting breath of a throng of students chasing us as we dashed to the car. It was the fastest I'd ever run at that point in my life. It was like a scene from a movie as we got in the car and shut the doors just in time. The students swarmed the car and pounded on it yelling, "We're No. 1" or "Joooooooeeeeee" as they shook the car.

To my surprise my friend and neighbor, Mike Hammond, was right at my window. He cheated, knowing what kind of car my dad drove. My dad immediately recognized Mike. "Ask Mike if he needs a ride home," my dad instructed me.

I cracked the window and yelled, "You need a ride?"

Mike laughed as he yelled above the crazy noise. "No way," he said. "If you open the door, they'll be a bunch of people in there."

Nervously my father backed the car up. The students slowly parted but kept pounding on the car and yelling. Many of them walked alongside the car out of the lot until we turned and headed home.

Now nearly 23 years later, my father and I were in another vehicle after a huge win for the program. The students were pounding the side of the Jeep and yelling, "Joe-Pa, Joe-Pa."

The biggest change in the two decades was the presence of constantly flashing cell phone or digital cameras. Venturino was cautiously trying to get through. His inner-New Yorker driver was going crazy, having to drive this slowly. "Hey, Tom," Joe said, "just take your time and be careful. Let's not get anybody hurt."

Students were on the sides and behind the car. Some were jumping in front and turning to snap cell phone pictures. They were walking up to Joe's window and snapping pictures. The flashes were blinding.

"Does everyone have a camera these days?" Joe asked.

"Pretty much," Venturino said.

"Lucky me," Joe said, laughing.

It was a surreal scene. For the game all the students had worn white as part of a White Out. Driving through them was like moving through clouds with constant flashes of lightning from their cameras. I can still picture the faces, college guys yelling, "Yeaaah" and sticking up their index finer. College girls yelling, "We love you, Joe." Others were just startled to see this Jeep pulling up behind them carrying Joe Paterno and in their surprise, hastily scrambling to get out their cameras.

I reminded him of what the victorious Roman generals were always told as they entered Rome to the cheering crowds: "Fame is fleeting."

"Yes it is," my father answered.

Alongside us one student was walking with his hand on the side of the car, yelling to clear a path for Joe. The crowd started to thin out, and as we picked up speed, that student jogged along. Joe was impressed. I put my window down and asked if he was on the track team.

As he jogged he was panting but said, "I'm not on the track team. I'm just so happy."

"Yeah me, too," I said.

Finally we made a turn toward home because Venturino wanted to make sure that we got home safely. But earlier in the trip, I'd learned something valuable.

Earlier as we passed the spot where that man sat yelling, "Give it up, Joe" for two years I said something about a guy who yelled at us.

"Yeah," Joe chuckled, "I wonder where he is tonight."

It was then that I knew he'd heard what I heard the last two years. It was then that I knew he was human like I was. The criticism, while not mortally wounding, did sting. Most people in the world do have bad days at work and good days at work. They just don't have people sitting in chairs, yelling at them as they go home. But neither do they have thousands of students cheering them on their way home after a great day at work.

With the bad comes some good; with the good comes some bad. You're only as happy as your least happy child. Don't get into a pissing contest with a skunk. Meeting the Lost Boys of Sudan, carrying my son, Joey. They were all with me that night.

They were all with me the last time I'd make that walk a little over six years later, when my last walk home from a game would be without him.

Chapter 13

Make an Impact,
Do Unto Others

The Golden Rule of "Do unto others as you would have them do to you" was something my father would say only occasionally, but when you look at the grand sweep of his life, it was a consistent foundation of almost everything he did.

When my father called home in the early 1950s to tell his father he wouldn't be going to law school, his father wasn't initially thrilled. He supported his son's decision but with one condition. He told him to be more than just a coach. He wanted him to "make an impact" on the place. Before that decade ended, his father died of a heart attack. But that challenge never faded from my father's memory.

My father never bombarded us with examples of great things he'd done in his life, but he did tell us stories about certain things that meant a lot to him. He believed in honor. One night after dinner, he told me a story from his time in Korea with the Army right after World War II.

My father was walking by a depot of Army supplies. Some barefoot Korean people—poor from the ravages of war—were bringing what little they had and buying shoes from some U.S. soldiers.

When they had walked about a block farther down, another soldier would stop them and demand to know where they'd gotten U.S. Army-issued shoes and accuse them of stealing. When they tried to explain, he'd take the shoes back and hand them to another soldier, where the scam would be run again. "These were the people we were supposed to be trying to help," my father said. "I couldn't do anything about it. When I brought it up, I was told to keep my mouth shut."

It bothered him that he was powerless to stop the injustice. But he told me that there were other times when he reacted rashly, resorting to violence only when it was justified. "You shouldn't get into fights to try and prove how tough you are, but there are some things worth fighting for," he said.

"Yeah, like when?" I asked.

He pulled another story from his time serving in Korea. He happened upon a soldier trying to force himself on a Korean girl. It was evident to my dad that she needed help. "What did you do, Dad?" I asked.

"I fought him, so the girl could get away."

"Did you win the fight?"

"That's not really important, but yeah, I got the better of him."

There was no smile of satisfaction. That soldier's actions appalled him.

There was also a lesson in human dignity that remained from his time in the Army. While still in Korea, my father was among men asked to participate in a running race with some of the local people and some of the soldiers.

The people of the village presented my father with soap as the prize for winning the race. Realizing the poverty of the people there, he was going to give it back. His commanding officer stopped him. "These are proud people. Soap has a lot of value to them. To give it back would be an insult to them," the officer told him.

My father explained there is pride and human dignity that all men and women have. To have forgone the prize would have been to deny them that pride, that dignity they felt in presenting him the award. He saw the humanity in everyone no matter how exalted or humble their background and he was consistent in that for his entire life.

Just a few weeks after I'd heard that story, I answered the phone at our house on a random Saturday afternoon. One of my father's fraternity brothers was calling to talk to my dad or mom. Neither was home, so I talked to him. Growing up we'd see my Dad's DKE fraternity brothers so we knew them. Some even attained uncle status like "Uncle Kevin" Cash or "Uncle Marty" Gresh. They told us funny stories and read books to us.

The fraternity brother on the phone that Saturday was one I didn't know. But I listened to his stories from my dad's college days. It sounded like he was calling from a bar and may have had a couple of drinks before he picked up the phone to call. It was one of the joys of my father having a listed telephone number.

He said to me, "I've known your father a long, long time. Let me tell you a story about him that you should know. He wouldn't want me to tell you this because your father doesn't like to brag. We were in a diner in Providence down the hill from Brown, getting some dinner. There were a couple of Jewish kids with their dates, getting something to eat. Some punks started to hassle them because they were Jewish. Your father told them to knock it off."

"What were the kids doing?" I asked.

"Times were different then. The Jewish kids were just trying to stay out of trouble so they kept quiet. But the punks kept it up. So your father made us get up, and we beat them up. He defended those kids because at that time they really couldn't defend themselves."

When my dad came home an hour or so later, I followed him into his den. "Dad, did you ever get into a fight at a diner in college?" I asked.

"What?"

He turned and almost glared at me. For a moment I feared I'd brought the wrong subject up, but I continued. "Did you get into a fight at a diner, defending a couple of Jewish kids?"

He hesitated. It was from decades earlier, a story he hadn't thought about in years. I could see a flicker of memory, illuminating a long ago tale. Part of him was wondering where I would have heard about that night. "I talked to one of your fraternity brothers on the phone. He told me the story. The message is by the phone in the kitchen."

I relayed the name of the fraternity brother, and a smile came to my father's face. Then there was a laugh under his breath. "I'll bet he called you from a bar," he said.

"It sounded like it."

"Jay, I wish he wouldn't have told you that. But what is important was that we did the right thing."

"Getting into a fight?"

"Yeah, it wasn't fair what they were doing to those guys and their dates, so we had to stand up for them. A lot of times in life there are people who cannot stand up for themselves. That is when it is most important to take a stand."

It was the right thing to do. Often in life doing the right thing is an easy path to spot but a much tougher road to walk. He agonized the most in those times when the right way wasn't as obvious. Most of the time, he got it right. Even if his vision was flawed, his intent was always the best.

The force of his will was his belief that we are all in this together. Those who could not stand by themselves were our collective responsibility. He told us so many times: "This team is only as strong as our weakest player, only as fast as our slowest athlete, only as smart as the player who knows the least."

That wasn't just a lesson for his coaches and players. It was a lesson that he believed applied to our country and to the world. My parents gave of their time and money to dent the world's problems one act at a time.

They engaged in causes from preventing disease and hunger, to encouraging religion and education, to the Special Olympics. Philanthropy was not just opening a checkbook or wallet; it was opening a heart, a soul, and reaching a mind to share some peace with those in pain. They would also prod others to join them in their causes.

That concept of make an impact through the maxim of "Do unto others" became a ripple from each pebble they dropped in the lake of human injustice. From the networks of people that their example touched, they created a tsunami of good reaching people half a world away.

Some of the names are familiar to Penn State fans—some not as much. Michael Robinson started a foundation to reach back to his high school and community in Richmond, Virginia. Years earlier I had given Michael the book *Days of Grace*, written by Arthur Ashe. "Do you know why I gave you that book?" I asked him.

"Because he's black, and I'm black?" he asked back.

"No, I gave you that book because he is from Richmond, because he was a great champion, and because he was bigger than sports. He used sports to change other people's lives. You have that same gift so use it."

Just a few months after my father died, I went to Richmond to see Michael put on a free camp for the children of Richmond. He used football as the hook to talk to them about school, about social media, and the pressures they faced in the streets where they lived.

Make an impact.

There is former Penn State linebacker Deryck Toles. He learned the value of education from his grandmother, who raised him. She worked at the county board of elections and pushed him to go where he'd get an education.

Early in the recruiting process, she decided Deryck would go to Penn State. It was a place where her grandson would be challenged and inspired. From Warren Harding High School in Ohio, a hotbed of Buckeye greats, Deryck made his own path to Penn State.

But what he did later was even bigger.

He founded an after-school educational program in his home community called Inspiring Minds. They fill the dangerous after-school void, idle hours that can lead to trouble when kids are alone in homes where the adults work. Inspiring Minds pushes kids to reach for higher education, helping them with college visits and helping them navigate the financial forms to get them to their goal.

Make an impact.

O.J. McDuffie left Penn State with a degree, as a first-round draft pick, and spent his entire NFL career as a member of the Miami Dolphins. Beyond playing football he got himself involved in the community by starting the Catch 81 Foundation. His foundation raised money for children's charitable causes throughout South Florida. Causes ranged from abused or neglected foster children to early education, to Boys and Girls Clubs, to single-parent ministries.

From Joe Paterno, O.J. learned the ideals of leaving a mark on society beyond catches and touchdowns.

Make an impact.

Former Penn State player Bryan Scott brought his love of arts and incredible musical talent to school kids through Pick Your Passion Foundation for the Arts. That foundation allows kids to take trips to music and art venues to inspire them to reach for their full potential in what they love and in their school work.

Make an impact.

Before he even left Penn State, wide receiver Scott Shirley started to make a difference. His father was diagnosed with kidney cancer. His family learned that kidney cancer, along with many other rare diseases, suffered from a lack of understanding brought on by a lack of investment in research.

He and teammate Damone Jones began a Lift For Life event at Penn State. By 2013 the event had raised over $1 million. But Scott took it even further. He started a national foundation, Uplifting Athletes, which challenges college football players across the country to give back.

Today Uplifting Athletes chapters are on over a dozen campuses including Penn State, Notre Dame, Nebraska, Ohio State, Illinois, Boston College, North Carolina State, and Northwestern. Each chapter highlights a rare disease and raises money for that disease. In December of 2012, the chapter at the University of Nebraska helped raise $300,000 for pediatric brain cancer research.

The ripple that began with two student-athletes on the Penn State campus has spread across the country.

Make an impact.

Larena Rolli worked as an intern in the Penn State football office. Even with a career and two children, she took a message of philanthropy with her in the days immediately after Joe Paterno's firing.

She teamed with other Penn Staters to form a goal of raising $500,000 for RAINN, a sexual abuse victims group. Appearing on CNN the morning after the Nebraska game in 2012, she said, "Penn Staters learned philanthropy from Joe Paterno. That's what he taught us."

In the first days after his career was ended, Joe Paterno's lessons still reached and inspired others to pick up the cause. They reached their goal.

Make an impact.

My teammate, Bill Spoor, and his wife, Elke, started a ripple in the water. In a remote corner of sub-Saharan Africa, they sponsored one child through her education and matriculation to college. They then expanded support to two dozen children. The project has grown into "Happy Valley Uganda," a name that recalls Bill's time at Penn State. They aim to get that community of young people educated and then have them return home, showing others the way toward a brighter future. Each success sets off another ripple.

In my father's eulogy, I mentioned Bill and what he was doing. He called me afterward and thanked me for using his life as an example of what so many of us learned from my father. "It was well deserved," I told him.

Bill was running with an idea that would change the lives of people so far removed from his own life and he was doing it because he knew what mattered.

Make an impact was international.

Even after his death, Joe Paterno's vision lives on. On the day of his passing, people were asked to make donations in his name to the Pennsylvania Special Olympics or to Penn State's Dance Marathon, which raised money to battle pediatric cancer. In the next few weeks, nearly $1 million was donated in his name to those and other charities.

Most years my parents were out of town for the Penn State Dance Marathon. But after he'd died, I was reminded of one of the few occasions when he'd gotten back in time.

They were vacationing on the island of Hawaii in February of 2009 and were awakened to a tsunami warning. They left the island and got home a day early. In a surprise Dance Marathon appearance, my father brought the 700 dancers and 16,000 people in the building to their feet. Tears and loud applause ensued.

He spoke during family hour, an emotional time when the families of children battling pediatric cancer speak to the weary dancers, who had been awake for 42 straight hours. Some families had a child who'd won the battle, some had lost their child, and others had a child still battling. He listened to the stories the families shared and realized the impact being made by Penn State students.

He stepped up on stage with no idea what he was going to say, but he hit the perfect note. "There are very few times in my life when I'm speechless," he said, "but I am right now. I wish the whole world could see and feel what's in this room right now. I've been 58 years at Penn State. I've never been more proud than right now. I've never been more proud than to walk into this arena and see what you folks have done. When those families came up, I have a tough time keeping my composure. God bless every single one of you. I hope that you will never forget what you can achieve later on in life, what you've achieved here for yourselves, as well as the people you've helped, and how proud you've made everybody who's ever been connected with Penn State."

As he finished he took his glasses off and wiped the tears away. It was only about two minutes, but it was the last time he was at the Dance Marathon.

Five years later I believe the tsunami warning that chased him home wasn't a coincidence. The ripple of "make an impact" carried him on a wave to deliver a moment those in attendance would never forget.

Three years later I would stand on that stage speaking to THON 2012 about the same time on Sunday that he'd spoken three years earlier. My mind went to him on that stage—how proud he'd have been to see the students announce a total of $10.7 million that afternoon. Two years later in 2014 they would raise over $13 million.

Make an impact...

As it haunted my father from his father, now in the void left by my father's passing, I hear him: "Make an impact, do something, don't feel sorry for yourself. Get up, do something, get hustling, make your move, but always make an impact on the world around you, always do unto others."

It lives on.

Chapter 14

Hallowed Be Thy Name

Whether it was holding my father's hand as a child at bedtime prayers or in the locker room after a football game, I can hear his voice unwavering as he began his favorite prayer: "Our father, who art in Heaven, *Hallowed be thy name.*"

Hallowed be thy name.

When we sing the Penn State alma mater, there is a verse that sings, "May no act of ours bring shame, to one heart that loves thy name. May our lives but swell thy fame, Dear Old State, Dear Old State."

Joe Paterno spent his entire adult life serving Penn State, a labor of love to make it a better place. He gave his time to raise funds for the library and the honors college and for students to study the classics. He did everything he could to raise Penn State's profile as one of the world's great research universities.

In my father's childhood in 1930s America, having an Italian last name was not a positive thing. If you became successful, it was assumed you had been in the mafia or you were a criminal or were cutting corners to get ahead.

My father knew the value of a name, the value of the name his father had given him.

He also knew the value of Penn State's name.

Joe taught our players that the honor of being a Penn State player came with responsibilities. They stood as caretakers of a proud tradition of excellence they had to defend and preserve for all who would follow. "Just putting on that uniform doesn't complete your journey," he said. "Tradition is a gift but more importantly a challenge to sustain and to add to through your own actions as you go through your time at Penn State and in the lives you will lead. You have a responsibility as a member of this team. You represent yourself, your family, your team, and Penn State. People will judge you, your family, your team, and this school based on what you do."

When we traveled to bowl games, often the manager of the hotel would comment to Joe about the polite behavior of our players. Flight attendants would comment on the class our players displayed compared to other teams they'd flown. It was the little things—wearing a coat and tie when the team traveled or professional demeanor with the media and in public.

Those were his lessons. "People will see you who may know nothing at all about Penn State," he said. "They will form an impression of our team and our school based on their interaction with you."

It was a theme I would hear over and over again in my career coaching with him. In team meetings he would talk about what the name Penn State meant. "The value of a Penn State degree is only worth what Penn State's name and reputation are worth right now," he said. "It fluctuates, and any mistakes we make can negatively impact that name."

Joe explained to us that the value of a college degree is like a stock. The value rises and falls with the public perception of that school's reputation at any given moment. It is an ever-evolving value.

Excellence in a college football program can enhance the reputation of a school. Each week major college football teams get a three-hour infomercial where they present their university to the public. Conversely an athletics scandal can do tremendous damage to a school's reputation.

Penn State benefitted from the academic and athletic excellence of the student-athletes on the football field each week. The brand of simple uniforms and clean-cut players who excelled in the classroom and on the field gave Penn State's overall image a boost every time we represented on television.

The epic 2005 win against Ohio State and the 2005 season presaged a large jump in applications to Penn State. The return to glory on the field put Penn State on televisions, newspapers, and computer screens around the country with positively glowing articles.

Notre Dame football transformed a small Indiana Catholic college into a university that is a household name. Gonzaga was a relatively unknown Catholic school in Spokane, Washington, until it burst onto the national college basketball scene. The same can be said for the profile of schools like Butler (basketball) or Boise State (football).

What set Penn State apart was Joe Paterno's involvement in the academic philanthropy of the university and his engagement in a vision of a great university. In January 1983 he spoke to Penn State's board of trustees and challenged them to engage in big capital fund-raising campaigns to build Penn State's meager endowment. He chaired campaigns and flew to ask donors for money.

In January 1983 Penn State's endowment stood at $17 million or roughly $39.2 million in 2012 dollars. At the time of Joe Paterno's death in 2012, that endowment had topped $2 billion, a growth of over 510 percent.

Penn State became a school transformed with amazing academic and athletic facilities and a faculty improved and energized by new endowments and top quality students. Joe Paterno could realize the vision and sense that Penn State stood as a university envied around the country with a great campus, tremendous faculty, and an alumni base that always walked proudly. For decades professors, administrators, coaches, and student-athletes had done the right things. Most everything associated with Penn State was revered for our unflinching standard of "Success With Honor."

Much of that changed after the events of November 2011. Where Penn State had once been a name that inspired respect, it became a national punch line. In a November 2011 *Saturday Night Live* skit, the devil is so outraged by what happened at Penn State that he quits. He says, "Evil isn't what it to used to be." A full year later in November 2012, I sat at a New York City fund-raising event for Malaria No More. After emcee Seth Meyers made a remark about Penn State, everyone roared. I wished that our trustees could've been there to hear what I was hearing. Regardless of motive or intent, the actions of the university's board in reaction to this story only added fuel to a raging wildfire.

If they had taken the time to pursue the truth, they could have separated the university from the actions of a long-retired employee, facing charges that overwhelmingly took place away from our campus. The story would have followed a narrative that was much closer to the truth.

In the aftermath of this story breaking, Joe Paterno reiterated he wanted to help defend Penn State, to get the correct history written about this episode. The blame was in the actions of one man, and those actions should not indict an entire university community. The response of the board invited that indictment to stick to Penn State.

Their willingness to pay for the flawed Freeh Report, accept NCAA sanctions, and then write checks to move forward only made Penn State completely guilty in the eyes of the public. It is the classic corporate model in any major scandal.

The formula: admit an error, hire someone with a big former title to write a fictional account blaming three or four people no longer with the company, and then pay off victims of the error. It usually works with corporations. They issue the report, fire some people, and their stock takes a hit before rebounding. If the stock doesn't come back up, the stockholders can sell their stake.

The problem with that formula for Penn State alumni is that they cannot sell their Penn State stock. It is their education, it is their history, and it is a university they love. The people paying attention to this story understand that this isn't Merck or British Petroleum or some other corporation.

Penn Staters realize that our university is not responsible for the actions of one man, but by following the corporate model, the school's board forced our entire university to be considered guilty and responsible by the public at large.

Donald J. Trump @realDonaldTrump 11/17/13 6:40 PM

The wimps that run Penn State should be forced to resign (and be sued) for the pathetic settlement they made and destruction of great legacy

From Twitter

That has damaged the name of Penn State for decades. If you don't believe me, ask anyone over the age of 45 what they think about when you say the name Kent State. That was over four decades ago.

This story will stick to Penn State for a long time. It should never have happened the way it did, but it will provide a case study in faulty crisis management studied in universities around the world.

What was most damaging was the assertion that this happened because there was some faulty deference to a flawed "culture of football" that allowed the offender to do this because we were protecting our football program.

Joe Paterno sat players out who missed classes. He deferred to doctors when they told him injured players could not play. He was never found to have committed any major NCAA violations and in fact never even had a hearing before the organization. He aggressively drug tested his players before it was something that was done by many other schools.

The assertion of a "football culture" flies in the face of decades of truth to the contrary.

It damaged the names of Penn State and Joe Paterno after decades when those names meant a gold standard. Now we're relegated to reviews by outsiders like *former* Senator George Mitchell, who reports that we are "moving toward compliance." Penn State athletics is relegated to officers overseeing the "moral conduct" of an athletic department that had few if any issues in compliance.

But that's the reality of where our university stands right now. The name built by the efforts of so many people has been damaged. When this story hit, those on the board of trustees entrusted with the hallowed name of our school stained it by taking the shortest way through, not the right way through. Their acts brought shame to so many hearts that love the name Penn State.

They allowed the truth to be sacrificed on the altar of expediency and in that they lost decades of work to build the respect of the world for Penn State.

Chapter 15

Give Us This Day...

There was rarely a day that Joe Paterno did not end being a little farther down the path he wanted to travel. He was an early riser, rising early was like getting a head start on everyone else.

His mornings began by boiling his water and stirring in a spoon of Folger's Crystals or Maxwell House, his morning fuel. Adorned in his robe and pajamas, he'd head to his desk, mug in hand, and sit watching films, writing letters, or drawing up game plans.

The house was quiet and dark except for a small lamp on his desk. As a child I could hear the projector running from the kitchen and I'd see my father alone at his desk before the sun came up, always working to stay ahead.

These mornings were important, the quiet pre-dawn time when the phone wouldn't ring, and he was left alone by the world. In these moments he was uninterrupted to build his plans for the next practice, the next day, week, or year. The demands of fame for autographs, appearances, or helping the university's philanthropic efforts did not exist in this stolen time. "Time is your enemy," he would tell his players. "There are things we must get done if we are going to be good enough and we must understand the clock is always running."

The concept of time was evident in the first thing he'd included on our players' printed list of team rules. It was a quote from Malcolm X: "Beware the man who wears no watch. He doesn't respect time."

Time was always the enemy, but it demanded respect.

When you have big plans for student-athletes to excel in the classroom and on the field, time management was always the first lesson. He structured our game week, placing an enormous value on our student-athletes' time. To meet his standards on and off the field, efficiency was paramount. Every practice minute was tightly scripted, and he constantly looked for ways to get more done. He made lots of notes and came back with new ideas: "While we're working on the punt period, is there something we could be doing on the offensive field with the offensive line? Can we get the quarterbacks doing something during that time? I hate to see anyone standing around."

He evaluated everything, challenging us on the value of each drill or practice period. In the back of his mind was a philosophy he had about tired football teams.

He told us a story that Bud Wilkinson, the legendary Oklahoma football coach, once shared with him during a visit to Oklahoma in the 1950s. Bud said, "If just one of my assistants thinks the team looks tired or that we've practiced too much, I listen and we back off."

Bud's lesson stuck with him for decades, and Joe's philosophy built on that concept. "If your team is emotionally down, they can overcome that in a game. But if they are emotionally down and they are tired physically—then you're dead," Joe would say.

Throughout his career he guarded the student-athletes' time and energy jealously. In a big exam week, he would adjust practice and the game plan back, so we didn't need to practice as long. "We're not going to do as much," he'd tell us, "but we will be great at what we do."

In his mind there was no sense spending even one minute more on anything redundant or wasteful. Our weight room was a great example. Players worked out in smaller groups with individual appointments so that they would get maximum efficiency with strength coach John Thomas. The efficiency in the weight room allowed for more time on studies or for them to have a social life. Joe wanted them to keep the priorities in order: academics, athletics, and a social life.

The social life was something he wanted them to experience. He wanted players involved in other campus activities, to meet other people. In the 1960s All-American Mike Reid missed spring practice to play the lead in a campus musical production. During the 2008 presidential campaign, players were involved in registering voters and getting students out to vote.

It was something he wanted for them, a chance to engage other students and to enjoy college. Only through efficient time management could they get the ultimate college football experience.

He was that way with everyone with whom he came into contact. Joe managed his time well, so well that he was able to commit time to raise millions of dollars for Penn State academics while also being involved with corporate and philanthropic boards.

What surprised others on the boards he served was his commitment to being a valuable contributor. He brought notes to the university library board meetings. In capital campaign meetings for Penn State, he brought articles on others' schools endowments or a prominent alum that they should be "hitting up for money."

My friend Ara Kervandjian had my father serve on a board for a small company he had helped start. Many of the other people on the board were businessmen with more experience on corporate boards. Some of them hadn't read the materials before they arrived. "Your dad always read his stuff and he would show up with articles about other companies in the industry," he said. "He would pull out an article with notes on them and ask how national developments would impact us. He wanted to know if we could benefit from anything else someone was doing. He was very challenging. I loved it."

He was keenly aware that time marched forward, and every day was a gift, and every game was a gift. He would tell his team how much they should cherish every game: "You only get to play so many games in your life. Don't waste them."

Then he would challenge them, saying, "Look, there is a difference between being injured and being hurt. If you're injured, the doctors and trainers will keep you out. If you are hurt, you can play. After a couple of weeks, everyone is hurting. Hey, I'm old. Every morning I get up, something new hurts. But we only have a limited number of games we get to play, so if you're not injured, get yourself ready to enjoy these games."

Before the Illinois game in 2010, he made his way to talk to the players as they stretched on the field. He approached a linebacker who'd had some bumps and bruises. I was walking behind him and heard the exchange. "So," Joe asked, "can you go?"

The player shook his head. "I'm only about 90 percent, so I don't think I can go," the player said.

He walked away in disbelief and mentioned it to me after we'd lost the game. "Jay," he said, "90 percent? I'd give anything to be 90 percent and play. Maybe I'm not getting through to these guys."

Joe understood players had aspirations beyond college and had people advising them not to play hurt. It was better not to appear on film at anything less than 100 percent for the pro scouts. He addressed it in a team meeting. "I know some of you have people telling you not to play hurt so you won't have bad films for pro scouts," he said. "If you don't play at all, they won't have anything to look at. They don't draft potential without seeing something on film. If you don't play, you're labeled as injury-prone. Use every day to prove something."

The giant leaps in NFL salaries attracted family and friends—all with advice. Many advised them not to trust the coaches. The game had become a reflection of society with big money creeping in to corrupt and pervert the goal of college athletics. Coaches and coaching salaries in many cases were leading the way.

One scene that replayed itself at least two or three times a year was the sudden appearance of an article highlighting the higher salaries being paid to assistant or head football coaches at other schools. The message from the Penn State assistant coach who provided the numbers was always the same: Penn State coaches were making less than coaches at other schools.

Joe Paterno would laugh and tell us, "None of you are starving. If you think I care, I don't. We're doing fine."

In 1994 he called Rip Scherer, my boss at James Madison University. They were discussing the first college coach's salary of $1 million a year to be made public. Joe worried for two reasons. A barrier had been broken, placing more expectations on coaches, increasing the pressure to win at all costs.

His second worry was big money in college coaching would attract people who did not belong in college football. Money was never his reason to coach. He wasn't greedy, but he was realistic. "Look, I don't mean to preach," he said. "It's not like I took a vow of poverty, but I never set out to coach to make a lot of money either."

After nearly 46 years as Penn State's head coach, his annual salary of just over $1 million ranked him ninth in the 12-team Big Ten. By comparison, coaches who had never won national or conference titles were making $2 million or $3 million a year. There were offensive and defensive coordinators making more than Joe Paterno at that point.

He honestly did not care.

He would say, "How much do I *need*?"

That didn't just apply to his salary. He ran a fiscally frugal football program. If we didn't need to spend money, we didn't. He constantly reminded us that we supported nearly 30 other sports at Penn State all with coaches who needed resources to compete nationally.

In 2011 *Forbes* magazine listed our program as the nation's second most profitable ($53 million a year) and the third most valuable college football program in the country (valued at $100 million). The large football profit margin allowed Penn State's athletics department to be completely self-supporting.

In fact there was a lot of money that came to the academic side because of athletics. On February 1, 2011, just a few months after Joe Paterno's 400th win, Nike announced a $400,000 gift to Penn State's library in honor of Joe Paterno's commitment to raising money for the library.

Assistant coaches complained that we were driving to see recruits while schools we competed against were taking private jets everywhere. He'd waved us off and argued that we didn't need to take private jets everywhere. We'd do it the hard way and we still succeeded.

While other schools were spending $20 or $30 million on football facilities, Joe oversaw the building of our complex in 1998 at a cost of $14 million. Joe Paterno personally raised a good chunk of the money by meeting with the widow of his good friend and 1928 Penn State alumnus Louis Lasch.

Mildred Lasch spent time at our house with myself and assistant coach Kenny Jackson after a bowl game and ultimately decided her husband would have wanted to donate the money. In the mid-1990s Joe froze the football budget for two years to show other coaches in the athletic department that it could be done.

But Joe Paterno worried where this was all going. He talked about the days when there was a section in Beaver Stadium for local kids to sit for $6. That's where I sat growing up. The pressures were not only to win but also to make a lot of money. He feared we were pricing college football out of the reach of the working families who'd made up the loyal fan base for years.

In the early 1990s at the suggestion of assistant coach Bill Kenney, Joe agreed to make the annual spring football game free. In 1998 we drew a crowd over 70,000, so some people saw a chance to generate revenue for the athletic department. Joe stood his ground and explained his rationale to the coaching staff. "We need to keep this free," he said. "There are young kids and families who never get to see us play in person because they can't afford it. Others scratch to put together money to buy season tickets, and we charge them an arm and a leg. We owe them something. We need to get those families who can't afford it into our stadium to see their team play in person."

The game remained a free event through the rest of Joe Paterno's career.

But Joe's overview of need versus want extended beyond the football program. It was the way he lived his life. He decried materialism for material-ism's sake his whole life. In the early 1970s in his book, *Football My Way*, he wrote about the generation then parenting their children. "I think we have to understand, when you talk about youth today and the way they feel, what they're saying to us," he wrote. "They're asking our generation 'What have you done for America and for your fellow man and for what other reason besides making money?' We have tried to buy them off. We've given them cars and we think that's bought respect. All it has really done is make them feel we think material things will satisfy them. That money can buy every-thing. Well, it can't and the kids have proven that by their actions lately."

When Wall Street came crashing down in 2008, he was still amazed by behavior that ran counter to what he believed. As the nation staggered to get a footing to recover, he re-taught the same lessons he'd written about in the 1970s.

It wasn't hollow. In 2001 when he became the all-time winningest coach in college football, a local publisher put together a commemorative maga-zine. Because it was officially licensed, Joe Paterno received a portion of the proceeds. He gave his cut, over $20,000, to charity. When Wheaties put him on the front of their cereal box, he gave all of the money to Helping Hands Ministry started by longtime friend Stan Hamilton. The charity fed and housed hungry and homeless people in northeastern Pennsylvania.

For most of his career, he drove whatever car the university gave him to use. In 1986 while winning a national championship and being named *Sports Illustrated* Sportsman of The Year, he was driving a university-provided car, a compact Ford Escort. The players would tease him about it. He'd laugh and say, "My father used to say: 'Who needs a Cadillac when a Ford will get you to work just as well?'"

Eventually he decided he wanted to buy his own car so he did not have to adapt to a different university car every year. He did research in *ConsumerReports* and bought a Saab after reading the safety crash test data. After a few years, he bought the smallest BMW car and ultimately bought a Mercedes SUV when he had his hip done and needed a higher seat.

He agonized over buying the Mercedes. "What would my father think?" he asked. "A Mercedes? I don't want people to think I have money."

"Dad," I laughed "I think people are aware that you've made some money. I wouldn't worry about it."

"Yeah, but a Mercedes?"

In the end he got a good deal, and a friend told him that the car was actually assembled in the United States. Then he felt better about it, but it was fun to tease him about the Mercedes in his garage.

There was an even bigger lesson for our staff as the university was forced to contain costs. A few years before he retired, he talked to us in a staff meeting about the upcoming fiscal year. The university was facing a large funding cut from the state. In response university president Graham Spanier announced that there would be a salary freeze at Penn State.

In our staff meeting, Joe mentioned that we would fall under that same policy. As a few grumbles emerged, Joe stopped the conversation. "Look, I was due a raise in my contract and asked if I could take that money and give it to you guys," he said. "That is not allowed, so we are all going to forgo any raises, myself included. *If no one else at the school gets a raise, neither will any of us.* None of you guys are starving, and we all have to do our part."

It was a strong reminder that greed did not run his world. It was an even stronger reminder that we were part of the larger university community and not outside of it. The last takeaway was the unselfish nature of Joe Paterno, his willingness to be just like everyone else at the school.

His lone goal was to use the time given him every day. If at sunrise and sundown he'd used that time wisely and had enough for his daily bread, he was content until rising before the next day's dawn.

Chapter 16

Politics

During my childhood and adolescence, political discussions were always part of our lives. My parents wanted us to be aware of the world around us. Nights when my father was home by 7:00, I'd hear the theme music for what was then the *MacNeil/Lehrer NewsHour* on PBS. Old habits die hard, and I watch that whenever I can; the theme music makes me think of my father.

My father was the son of an FDR Democrat. Angelo Lafayette Paterno worked the polls and wards. But he wasn't afraid to cross party lines and wrote speeches for Republican New York Mayor LaGuardia, a New Deal supporter.

My father registered as a Republican in the 1950s after he moved to Penn State because he was told his vote would only matter in the G.O.P. primaries—then the dominant party in local politics. He never told his father.

My father was a moderate, a George H.W. Bush Republican, a pragmatist who wanted solutions developed through reasoned debate and consensus. He was fiscally conservative and socially liberal. Ideas like culture wars, no-tax pledges, and being anti-anything were not really his cup of tea. He scoffed at the idea of ideological "purity tests."

His entire career was spent on a college campus around young people, keeping him plugged into changing demographic and societal realities. His foundation of values never wavered, but he adapted his methods to the times.

He admired Lincoln's political genius, citing his adherence to bedrock beliefs of right and his ability to alter his course, arriving at the desired outcome. Joe Paterno replicated Lincoln's pragmatism in his own workplace leadership.

In discussions he never came across too sure of himself for two reasons. First, he was smart enough to know he didn't have all the answers. Second, he never wanted someone who disagreed to be intimidated into not stating their true beliefs. He wanted to learn from them.

If I argued in the absolute what was still hypothetical, he had a line he'd use. "Maybe someday I'll have all the answers like you do," he said.

Across decades arguing with friends and family members, he learned from us while we learned from him. But there was always open discussion before reaching consensus. The political world of the 21st century was the polar opposite of that. That irked him.

In his later years, he decried what he called "gotcha" politics—the goal of getting a politician to say something on camera that would be used against them. He argued "gotcha" politics eliminated honest consideration of the important issues of the day. "People are more interested in winning the argument or wanting it to seem that they won," he said. "Doing what is right for the country has become secondary."

It was his vast historical perspective, a perspective studying not just the history of this country but also world history as far back as the ancient Greeks.

I'll never forget our staff meeting the morning after President George W. Bush addressed a joint session of Congress on September 20, 2001. When Joe walked into the meeting, a couple of the coaches commented on what a great speech the President had made the night before. As he sat down, he looked at one of the coaches who had commented. "You think that was great?" Joe asked.

A couple of guys nodded.

"It was very well done. I watched it and I saw people congratulating the President," he said.

Joe then looked around the table. His face was solemn. "The President doesn't have a choice, but did you really hear what we're facing? This is going to be a war that lasts years," he said. "The people in that part of the world do not think in weeks or months or even years. Do you know how many empires have gone into Afghanistan and failed?"

He mentioned Alexander the Great, the British Empire, and the Soviets—his well of historical reference on display. But he also mentioned the Crusades as he finished up his point. "This part of the world has been at war for centuries. We have no concept of that here. This is not going to be like Kuwait when they invited us in. Your kids and maybe even your grandkids may be fighting this war. But I'll probably be long gone before this is all over."

Over a decade later when he died, we were still at war in Afghanistan.

But his stance on war shouldn't have been surprising. Nearly 30 years earlier, he had written a book called *Football My Way* and he addressed student activism and the war in Vietnam: "Kids today on college campuses are anti-war and I think they are 100 percent right. No nation that has ever fought a war did a poorer job of selling the action in Vietnam to the people than the United States. We just tried to slip in to Vietnam without ever admitting what we were doing and, all of a sudden, we were caught with our pants down and with several hundred thousand troops fighting an unpopular war. We were gradually sneaking our way into Vietnam and, suddenly, we looked up and we were embarrassed. And now it's impossible for us to defend our position there.

"Then along came Cambodia, another unpopular war that triggered violence on college campuses. The students were angry and they reacted. I don't condone violence but I understand it. They don't want to fight a war that our country has had trouble justifying. I'd hate to be a 19 or 20-year old kid and have to go to Vietnam. I'd go because of the way I was brought up, because of the discipline that I have, but I'd hate to get my arm shot off for what's going on in Vietnam."

As I see soldiers who lost limbs in Iraq, I cannot help but think of what my father wrote. To his last days, he had so much respect for the men and women fighting for our country. But the casualty counts and the reports of young people killed or wounded always stayed with him. He tried to honor every request he could for phone calls, for cards, for pictures when it involved anything having to do with the military.

Beyond his discussions at home, there was a genuine flirtation with politics for him. After I'd gotten involved politically, I was approached in 2009 about running for office in 2010. As rumors spread I decided to talk to my father before he heard it from someone else. He appreciated the conversation and reiterated he'd support whatever I did with my life.

137

Later that fall we stood on the field before a night game in Beaver Stadium. It was an electric environment with deafening crowd noise even in pregame warm-ups. As I was watching the guys throwing, I felt someone tap me on the shoulder. I turned to see my father smiling at me. "You still thinking about running?" he asked.

"Running?"

"You still thinking about running for office?"

He took his right index finger and pointed up at the student section all clad in white and then gestured all the way around the stadium. "This'd be tough to give up," he said with a twinkle in his eye.

Years before, he'd been approached about running for governor. A popular, principled, and successful coach was a tempting target for a party looking for someone electable. I asked him once if he ever really thought about running. "Jay," he said, "of course I thought about it. I thought maybe I could do some good for people. They wanted me to run for governor, and I considered it."

"Why didn't you run?" I asked.

"Running is the easy part. I thought maybe I could win. So I asked the people from the party. Who would run the transportation department for me? They told me they had a guy. I asked who would oversee education. They told me they had a guy. It went on and on. Pretty soon I realized they weren't interested in me actually being the governor. They wanted a guy they could get elected so they could put their friends into position to run everything."

He saw what they wanted because he was blessed with good political instincts. In the 1980s he was invited to the national governor's conference. There he met the son-in-law of 1930s Penn State football alum Hugh Rodham. Hugh had two children—a son, Hugh, who also played at Penn State, and a daughter, Hillary. Hillary's husband, Bill Clinton, was the governor of Arkansas.

Governor Clinton introduced himself to my father. After the conference his father-in-law wrote to my father to thank him for talking with Bill Clinton. My father wrote back and indicated what an impressive young man the governor seemed to be and that he thought he had a bright future.

The other guy I heard him talk about was Senator John Heinz. He was charismatic, educated, and had name recognition and a lot of ketchup money.

When I was young, we made a family trip to south-central Pennsylvania where my father introduced him at a rally during John Heinz's first senate campaign.

Even my sister, Mary, one not always easily impressed, came home impressed with Senator Heinz after sitting next to him at the 1987 Pennsylvania Society Dinner. The day Senator Heinz's plane crashed and he was killed in April of 1991, I remember how upset my father was. The Senator was in his early 50s, and he thought he certainly could've been President.

He was probably right on John Heinz and he was certainly right about then-Governor Clinton. In 1993 President Clinton came to Scranton for his father-in-law's funeral. In the eulogy the President mentioned that his father-in-law thought that there was one perfect man—Joe Paterno.

My father really had some fun with that. "You see, even the President thinks I'm perfect," my dad joked.

"He isn't married to you," my mother quipped.

Three years later President Clinton invited my parents to a state dinner honoring the President of Italy. In attendance were notable Italian-Americans from Martin Scorsese to Jon Bon Jovi.

In the pre-dinner social, my father found himself seated next to someone who looked familiar. The "young man" introduced himself as Nicolas Cage. (My father re-told the story still thinking his name was Gage.)

My father commented on his name not being Italian. Cage informed him that he was born a Coppola but changed it when he got into the business. Coppola was a name my father was familiar with. "So are you related to Francis Coppola?" my father asked.

"Yes, he's my uncle," Nicolas Cage replied.

"And you're in the business?" My father asked.

"Yes, I'm an actor."

"So how's that going for you?"

Informed that Cage had recently won an Oscar, my dad was impressed but not half as impressed as he (and every other male) was by Sophia Loren's dazzling looks and dangerously low-cut dress. My father was at the table next to the President and Sophia Loren. My father had a straight sight line to the President. "I don't think the President took his eyes off her the whole night. But heck, I can't blame him," he said. "I was as guilty as he was." My father laughed.

A few years later in January of 2006, he attended the Alfalfa Club Dinner in the nation's capital. Former President George H.W. Bush saw him and grabbed him. He congratulated him on an amazing season that netted Joe Paterno his record fifth national Coach of the Year Award. "What a great season you had. How'd you do it?" the former President asked.

"Well, we just needed a couple of guys with some balls who didn't care what people told them they couldn't do," my father replied.

He laughed and said, "That's what I've been telling the President he needs. Hey, you have to tell my son that."

His son happened to be the current President of the United States. George H.W. Bush took my dad into a back room where President George W. Bush was seated with some of his cabinet and his mother, Barbara Bush. After greeting each other, President George H. W. Bush turned to my father. "Coach, tell him what you told me," he said. "Tell him what turned it around for you this year."

My father rarely used the term "balls" and he certainly didn't want to say it in front of the President and the former First Lady. He hesitated. "Well, I can't really say what I said out there," my father said.

Then through the hesitation he heard Barbara Bush speak. "Go ahead, Joe, I've heard it before," said the First Lady, laughing.

My father respected the politics of Washington, D.C. He testified at a congressional hearing on steroids headed by then-Senator Joe Biden. Years later as Vice President, Joe Biden told me how much he respected my father for the courage he showed to talk publicly about the issue.

He'd been to White House state dinners under Presidents Ford, Reagan, Clinton, and George H. W. Bush. He'd also met Presidents Eisenhower, Kennedy, Nixon, George W. Bush, and Obama. The process of our nation's capital deeply interested him.

When Newt Gingrich was Speaker of the House, he called Joe Paterno a couple of times for advice. In an interview with Charlie Rose, he shared the advice: "I've talked to Joe Paterno at Penn State a couple times and said, 'All right, I'm not getting this thing done right. What would you change?' And he gave me very good advice about how he coaches, how he brings along his assistant coaches, how he deals with the players."

"What did he say?" Charlie Rose asked.

"He said, 'First of all you have to be clear in your own mind. You've got to know your game plan. Then you've got to meet with all your assistant coaches, listen to them carefully, and then you've got to really ask yourself as a team are you ready to go out and meet with the rest of the team? Because if the coach and the assistant coaches don't have their act together, they're going to be offering very conflicting signals when they go through practice. And you've got to remember that there's practice. Nobody is good all the time the first time.'"

Maybe Joe Paterno would've done okay as a governor.

He kept up with what was happening in the world. President George H. W. Bush raised taxes to try and balance the budget, which he ultimately left on a surplus trajectory for Bill Clinton. My father instantly recognized a decision putting the President's re-election in jeopardy to do the right thing for the country. "For that he has my respect," he said.

He was disappointed when President Obama and speaker John Boehner couldn't bring their sides to a consensus on the 2011 debt ceiling debate. His hope was that both sides could work together and meet somewhere in the middle.

This was always in his mind; we are one nation and should always work together for the benefit of all. In December of 2009 at a bowl trip, we had our annual coach's dinner around his birthday. At our table were several coaches and our team doctor. We got into an animated discussion. It ranks as one of the best meals I ever shared with my father.

We were talking about the President, and a coach from another table made a comment to me: "Well, did you see what *your* President did?"

Before I could even respond my father replied forcefully. "He is *our* President," he said.

It was reflective of the respect he had for the office of President, regardless of party. About a year later, Senator Mitch McConnell told the Heritage Foundation that, "Our top political priority over the next two years should be to deny President Obama a second term."

My father brought that quote up with me. I reminded my father he and I had met Senator McConnell in then-Vice President George Bush's hotel suite at the 1988 Republican National Convention. "Jay, I'm a Republican, but I am rooting for the President. If he succeeds the country succeeds. Isn't that what we should all want?" he asked.

He then spoke in a low voice, getting me to listen more closely. I leaned across the kitchen table to better hear him. It was a late Saturday evening around 10 or 10:30 after a recruiting party. The recruit's parents had left the house, and my mother was busily loading glasses into the dishwasher. His voice had trailed off, so I knew to keep my mouth shut. He wanted to articulate something very carefully. "Jay, I don't agree with some things he's done," he said. "But having said that, I hope President Obama is successful."

I kept my mouth shut as he continued. "It is bigger than just his success. It's taken us centuries to elect someone that doesn't look like you or me."

"I see what you're saying," I said.

"I see a change. Racism isn't gone. Let's not kid ourselves. For the first time, a young black kid growing up in an inner city school can believe that there is no limit to what they can do in this country. That is important for everyone. It's important that we're open to electing the best man or woman for the job."

His awareness of others' perspectives was incredible. He truly believed all men were created equal, that everyone should have the ability to reach for their goals without obstacles based on race or religion. Unusual for his generation, he became completely accepting of differing sexual orientations. Realizing most times there are no easy answers, he constantly evolved while relying on his beliefs of equality and acceptance learned from his father.

Despite his political interest, there was little doubt he wasn't interested in running. He enjoyed helping others when he could. In the 1980 Pennsylvania G.O.P. primary, he introduced George Bush when he campaigned at Penn State. The two struck up a friendship.

Six years later before winning a second national championship, my father was asked about retirement plans. "I would really like to find somebody and help them become President of the United States," he said.

A couple of days later, that article was mailed to him with a humorous note from Vice President George Bush that said, "Keep me in mind!"

A little over a year later, the Vice President would ask him to do just that. After suffering a disastrous third-place finish in the 1988 Iowa caucus, the Vice President called for help. On a chilly February day, my father campaigned in New Hampshire with the Vice President and Boston Red Sox legend Ted Williams. How I would've loved listening to the stories in that car.

That summer I answered our home phone, and a voice asked for Joe Paterno. When I asked who was calling, I heard something unexpected: "This is the office of the Vice President."

"He's not here right now. Can I take a message?" I asked.

The minute he came home, I was right there with a piece of paper I hadn't let go of in the hour since I'd taken the message. The Vice President was calling to ask him to second his nomination at the Republican National Convention in New Orleans. He'd spent a day during the New Hampshire primary helping the campaign, but this was a surprise.

I could tell that my father was truly humbled.

When the time came to go, I was fortunate to get to go with him.

He sent his speech down, so they could put it on the teleprompter. We flew down and headed right to the Superdome to see where he'd be set up. In the final run through, they'd decided it would be more exciting to have my father give his speech from the floor amid the Pennsylvania delegation.

There was no teleprompter there, so my father would have to read his speech. There was just one hitch; he had sent them his only handwritten copy. So off he went to the hotel so he could re-write his speech mainly from memory.

I went for a walk and by the time I got back he had re-written his speech. We walked to the Superdome for the evening session where we were seated in the front row of the Vice President's section just down from Barbara Bush, Dan and Marilyn Quayle, and in front of senator John Tower, Secretary of State George Shultz, and famed actor Charlton Heston—heady stuff for a 19-year-old kid.

Just before his speech, we were led to the floor and into the Pennsylvania delegation. Senators Heinz and Arlen Specter were there. The delegation surged up as my father gave his speech and nailed it. In his speech he mentioned Walter Payton, Coach Bryant of Alabama, and the Yankee Clipper Joe DiMaggio.

Afterward we were leaving, and he got a little nostalgic talking about his FDR Democrat father. At that moment my father realized that he'd just seconded the nomination for the man who would become the President of the United States, and there was someone he wanted to share it with. He said aloud, and to this day I'm not sure if I was ever meant to hear it, "Boy, if my father could see me now."

After Vice President Bush won and became president-elect Bush, my father was asked to be a member of the electoral college and cast one of Pennsylvania's electoral votes. I'm sure he was once again thinking of his father.

President Bush and my father remained friends over the years and would talk occasionally. In the fall of 1999, we were in our pregame meal before playing at Iowa. The manager of the hotel came in to tell Joe he had a phone call from former President Bush.

The former President was in Iowa stumping for his son ahead of the Iowa caucuses a few months away. My father spoke to President Bush and joked that he might not want Iowa voters to know he'd called him the morning of a game versus the home-state Hawkeyes.

For his 80th birthday, the former President invited my father to skydive with him, which my father politely declined.

Years later in 2008, I had my own turn in presidential politics. One of the highlights was a rally on Penn State's campus. Some of our players were involved as well. Lydell Sargeant worked on registering voters, and Gerald Cadogan was going to sing the national anthem. They met with Senator Obama.

When I talked with Senator Obama, one of the things he said was how impressed he was with the two players he'd met. During our visit we called my dad, and I put the Senator on the phone. They had a good laugh.

Afterward when I talked to my father, I could sense the pride he felt that I had taken a stand and had gotten involved. "Jay," he said "I'm not going to get involved in politics any more. Heck, I'm 81. You're the one with young kids. You're the one that has to do something for what you see in their future. I know my father would be proud of you, but I'm proud of you, too." He smiled.

"Thanks, Dad."

After the primary was over, most of the staff was moving on to the next primary. But before they left, I took them to the house to sit down with my father. They all had spent over a month in town and they just wanted to be able to tell people they'd met him.

As we sat around the kitchen table, my father looked at the young faces—people in their 20s involved in a presidential campaign. There was a pinch of envy in my father's voice. "You know in some ways I'm a little jealous," he said. "You guys are just starting out and you're involved in something like this. But I do wish I'd have gotten involved in something like this when I was young. There's no telling where this will lead you in your lives."

For one of the people at the table, I got to see where it would lead. After working at the Department of Education and at the State Department and for United States Agency for International Development (USAID), Ashley Wiegner decided she wanted to do something different in her life.

In November of 2012, I visited her at North Star Academy in Newark, New Jersey, and saw firsthand where her life had led her. In that inner city school, she was inspiring young children to set all their goals on getting a college education. They all came from families where college was so far over the horizon that they didn't dare dream about it.

It's rigorous, a structured but vibrant environment. The kids wear school uniforms and are inspired by their teachers. They're asked to do tough things, be disciplined, and believe that there is no limit to what they can do. I saw responsive, excited students striving to meet the high expectations that were demanded of them.

This was the ground floor of the future of this country. I am sure that as I sat in classrooms and walked the halls of that little old corner school, my father was watching and smiling. For all the politics going on in Washington, this was where the rubber met the road. This is where you reach the children, as he did at the collegiate level for so many years.

Maybe he knew that for all the elections that could be won and all the partisan squabbling he would've gotten into, where he really could change lives was in a classroom and on the football field.

That was his calling.

Chapter 17

It's How You
Play the Game

"When the one great scorer comes to
write against your name, He marks—
not that you won or lost—but how you
played the game."

—Grantland Rice

Now that the one great scorer has come to write against the name Joe
Paterno, there are plenty of wins he could mark, but far more impressive is the way he played the game. In a profession rife with egos and men
cutting corners, he insisted on fair play and a respect for the sportsmanship
of the game.

In all the years I coached for him, the angriest I ever saw him was in
2005. We had a night game at Illinois with its new coach Ron Zook, a guy
my father liked. Before the first half was over, we had a 49–3 lead. With a
couple of minutes left in the half, we put in our backup quarterback Anthony
Morelli to get him a chance to play.

Normally in these situations, Joe would tell us to run the offense and
give the backup quarterback a chance to move the ball and have some success but make sure it was a run-heavy attack.

Kermit Buggs, our graduate assistant coach, was on the field and was responsible to signal in the plays we called upstairs. We had Kermit ask Joe if he wanted us to "run the offense."

"Yeah," Joe said, "run it."

What he meant was *run the ball* every down. What we thought he meant was *run the offense*. A couple of plays later, we faced third and 6 at the Illinois 24-yard line. We sent in a play-action pass. As soon as Morelli made the fake and set up to pass, I could hear Joe (standing about five yards from Kermit) through Kermit's headsets. "No. I don't want any passes," he yelled.

To make matters worse Morelli completed the pass to the Illinois 1-yard line. One play later we scored to go ahead 56–3. On the sideline there was no calming Joe down because he did not want to run up the score.

Usually in those situations with a big lead, you may throw it occasionally through the third quarter. Most coaches wouldn't be mad if you threw the ball on third and long in the second quarter with your backup quarterback in the game. Joe didn't see it that way.

We headed down to the locker room just before halftime and stood outside the locker room. Michael Robinson, Tony Hunt, and some of the other starters on offense were laughing. The minute Joe saw us he walked to me and pointed a finger. "You know Ron Zook is trying to build a program here," he said, "and you guys are trying to embarrass him. I don't like that."

Here we were winning a game 56–3, and he was irate because we were doing too well. But I did feel I needed to defend myself and our offensive staff. "We asked if you wanted us to run the offense, and you said run it," I said.

"Yeah, run it," he answered.

"That meant run first and pass on third down if we had to."

"No, you know I meant run it. Run the ball!"

"We didn't," I said.

"Run the ball!" he yelled, cutting me off.

At that point I don't know if there was anything I could have done in the world that would have made him any madder. What I didn't know is that the last minute of the first half he was giving Buggs the business on the sideline, and the television cameras were drawn to it.

To make sure he was not misunderstood, he reiterated his point to me. "No more passing," he stated rather emphatically.

He turned and headed into the locker room still fuming. When he left I started to laugh. Kermit was still there and he was laughing, but he did have something he wanted to say. "You better not call any passes," he stated. "He yelled at me for the pass, and I told him that I just signaled in what you called."

"Then what did he say?" Coach Galen Hall asked.

"He said," Kermit said, "'I don't care if they call a pass. You change the play to a run.'"

Joe wanted us to play the game *the right way*, to play and coach with sportsmanship and not to exploit an overmatched opponent. He knew there were days when you had the other guy's number. He also knew there were games where the other guy had your number, and you hoped they would treat you the same way.

His insistence on fair play extended to recruiting. In college football the dirtiest, most cutthroat part of our job was recruiting. There is a fairly extensive, and some would say arbitrary, set of NCAA recruiting rules. Joe Paterno insisted that we follow them—all of them. "I'd rather lose a player recruiting the right way," he said. "If we have to cheat to get him here, he's not the right kind of person for our program."

The right kind of person for Penn State was one who came here to do a couple of things. First, he had to want an education. Second, he had to want to be part of a great team and then third, he may have NFL aspirations. Those were the priorities in that order.

There was also another element: they had to relish the challenge to be part of a tough football program with exacting standards.

> Largest Truths of the game:—Conditioning, Spartanism, defense and violence—as distinct from Brutality.
>
> *Note: found in Joe Paterno's files*

To the day he coached his last game he knew that this was a game of conditioning and violence. He talked to our team about what wins big games. "At some point in the game," he said, "you have to make them say, 'ouch.'"

He loved challenges. In 1982 Penn State became the first team in college football history to win the national championship while playing the nation's toughest schedule, including four games against teams ranked in the top five. There is the adrenaline of a big game fought to the last play that cannot be duplicated in any other civilian job.

The games he loved the most were the ones that were tight deep into the fourth quarter, and either his offense won the game or his defense prevented the other team from winning. He also loved when his offense ran out the clock with a punishing ground attack to take control.

It was the conditioning, Spartanism, defense, and controlled violence that made Penn State unique. The brutality side was for bullies, and it usually was the hallmark of an undisciplined team that would make big mistakes late in games because they lacked poise.

His philosophy was unique in his complete indifference to the statistics that everyone else followed. He didn't care about total yards. He looked at yards per play, he looked at third-down conversions, he looked at Red Zone efficiency, he looked at turnovers, and he looked at time of possession.

In most tight games against good opponents, those were the factors that mattered. "Sure," he once said when I asked if they mattered, "they matter. They indicate control of the game's tempo. They may not matter when you're playing a bad team, a bunch of fish, but when you play someone good, controlling the game matters."

That philosophy was carrying him to the end of his career when his team was 8–1 when he was fired. That was how he coached. If we had an identity and knew who we were as a team, everything else was secondary.

That identity was never reached easily. It was the result of hard work, discussion, and ultimately consensus.

If there was one constant in Joe Paterno's life, it was his need to argue, to have his views challenged by a worthy debater or well-crafted argument. Debate kept his mind sharp and forced him to defend or re-evaluate his position.

There was a saying he used when we argued about football, and it illustrated his coaching strength to "get the chalk last."

When presenting a new play or a new defense, a coach would go to the chalkboard, and then everyone would take shots at it, trying to break it down and show why it wouldn't work. One coach would put up a play, and another would go up and draw up the defense to try and stop it. Then the first coach would go back and show how he'd adjust.

The back and forth would continue and then Joe would go up and settle the discussion. "That's all good," he said, "but I get the chalk last."

It was recognition that both football and life were a series of plays and adjustments. The ultimate goal was to succeed by having the chalk last.

He still referenced chalk even during the last 15 years of his career when we used dry-erase boards. "Get the dry erase marker last" just never had the same ring.

There was no hiding his disdain for the dry-erase boards because when he'd go to the board he always seemed to find the pens that were running out of ink. "I miss the old chalkboards," he said. "When you picked up a piece of chalk you always knew it was going to work."

It was the same with the computer video for game films and PowerPoint presentations. While the technology was booting up, he'd laugh. "If this was on tape, we'd be watching it already," he'd say.

But it still came back to "Get the chalk last." That was how he lived. In coaching it was easier. He'd study what another team was doing, create an adjustment, and then anticipate how that team would adjust to his adjustment and have his next move already planned. "Guys," he'd say to the coaches, "give the other guys some credit. At some point they will recognize what we're doing. When they do that, how will we respond? Think a step or two ahead."

Across decades of football, he understood the chess game as well as anyone. Notre Dame coach Lou Holtz looked across the field at my father for a number of games while he was the head coach at North Carolina State and more famously for seven straight years at Notre Dame. After he finished at Notre Dame, he sent my father a picture of the two of them and signed it. Lou Holtz wrote, "Joe, I think you are the best game day coach I have ever seen."

It was Joe's ability to get the chalk last. Holtz knew it well as Penn State won four of the seven Notre Dame matchups, including big upsets in 1987 and 1990. But my father had great respect for Holtz, too, often citing upsets of Penn State while Holtz was at N.C. State.

In 1990 Holtz learned how well Joe could do when he had the chalk last. In November Penn State traveled to South Bend to take on No. 1 Notre Dame. Late in the game with the score tied 21–21, Penn State had the ball and faced a fourth down. Joe decided to punt rather than go for it.

There were a lot of people griping that he was playing for the tie (before college adopted overtime). Joe remained calm, knowing the pressure was on Notre Dame, which needed to win to stay in the hunt for the national championship.

Sure enough, a few plays later Notre Dame's quarterback threw an interception to Penn State safety Darren Perry, setting up Penn State's game-winning field goal as time expired. Joe knew the big picture facing his opponent.

It came into play so many times. In 1995 at Iowa, he called for us to throw a quick hitch out to wide receiver Bobby Engram. He caught it and was immediately blasted by Iowa's defensive back. Bobby came to the sideline and complained. His wide receiver coach told him to calm down. "Relax," he said, "Joe is setting that guy up."

Sure enough, a few plays later, Bobby was back in and ran a fade route past the defensive back, who was playing up. Bobby caught a big touchdown pass in a tough road win.

In 2002 against Michigan State, the Spartans defense was playing aggressively against the run. Joe came down to coach Fran Ganter. "Tell Jay upstairs to throw one deep," he said. "We have to run past these guys."

I did as I was told, and quarterback Zack Mills threw a beautiful touchdown strike to wide receiver Bryant Johnson. During a timeout before our next possession, he came back down to Ganter and asked for "32 A-Opposite," a short-side run play.

"We can't run that," Fran protested. "The safety is down to the short side, and they'll play it."

"We just hit a deep touchdown pass, the safety will be back. Run the A-Opposite, it'll score," Joe said.

"Okay," Fran said.

We were on our own 20-yard line or so. Before the offense went back on the field, Joe went over to our defensive line coach Larry Johnson, whose son, Larry, was our starting tailback. Coach Johnson was talking to his players, and Joe told him to go watch the next play. "Your son is going to go 80 yards for a touchdown," Joe said.

When we came out of the huddle, the Michigan State safeties were back, and Larry went 78 yards for the touchdown. Smiling, Joe walked down to Coach Johnson and pointed his finger at him and said playfully, "I told you."

After the game as Larry told me the story, there was a tear in his eye. His son had run for nearly 300 yards to become only the ninth running back in NCAA history to run for 2,000 yards in a season.

Joe's anticipation of the opponent's adjustment enabled him to get the chalk last.

We weren't always right. In fact sometimes our rigid belief cost us the ability to see what was coming. In 1999 we beat Ohio State while running for over 200 yards, getting outside on a pitch play. The next week we went to Purdue, and the Boilermakers had a great adjustment to keep us from getting outside, but we hadn't anticipated the adjustment. Only a great defensive stand at the end of the game kept us undefeated.

The inability to anticipate had nearly cost us the game.

The idea of getting the chalk last carried into his life. At the dinner table, he trained us to try and see how someone arguing against our point of view would respond to each of our points. The critical thinking, the anticipation of the next move was a skill that he wanted us all to have.

If there was one thing he despised, it was a hard-headed, unchanging, one-size-fits-all approach to problem solving. He taught me that any endeavor involving human beings was going to be complex and ever-changing and required reasoned individual approaches.

But to him, though there was complexity in human behavior, there was predictability based on the study of history. People respond to pressure in a certain number of ways. People respond to adversity or success in certain ways.

He read history, he read Shakespeare, and the ancient classics. He'd cite examples from Homer, to Lincoln, and even the story of Shackleton the explorer, who survived a near Antarctic disaster to get all his men home safely. That was one of the stories he talked about to us as coaches and to me as a son so many times.

He loved the narrative of overcoming adversity, of stiffening your upper lip in the gale force winds of tough times, and emerging to see the sunrise on a better day when the storms had passed.

Unlike many coaches in love with the game plans they formulate every week, Joe Paterno looked at our game plan and tried to beat it. The objective was to challenge your ideas, find the weakness, putting himself in the opponent's shoes.

Whether in scientific study or a political debate or a football game plan, he knew that we as humans had a tendency to shape our plans or hypotheses with a pre-ordained outcome we hope we'll find. We get sloppy, only looking for the information to back up what we already believe. When we do that we don't thoroughly look for factors that may challenge our thinking or prove us wrong.

There was a Lincoln story Joe used to tell us about a farmer with a lone big oak tree next to his farmhouse on the prairie. The farmer saw a squirrel run up the tree trunk and disappear into a hole. The farmer checked the tree and saw it was just starting to rot inside.

The farmer realized that there was a chance the tree would be okay, but also a chance that it might blow over and destroy his house. It provided the only shade on the blazing prairie summer days. But he also didn't want it to fall on his house. He loved the tree and didn't want to cut it down. As he stood on the porch, looking at the tree and facing a decision he said, "I sure wish I'd never seen that squirrel."

Joe Paterno actively looked for those squirrels as best he could. As a leader he challenged us to do the same. If we recruited a player with a parent who had substance abuse problems, he'd tell us to remain vigilant with that player. Once a student-athlete had displayed a lack of interest in school, he was always on the staff to constantly monitor his progress.

His anticipation of changes included the biggest issues of college athletics as well.

After a 1984 Supreme Court decision in *The NCAA v. The Board of Regents of the University of Oklahoma* blew up the NCAA's ownership of television rights for college football games, Joe Paterno was already thinking ahead. He teamed with many others including Chuck Neinas, the Big 8 Conference commissioner from 1971 to 1980, to form the College Football Association. They put together a national television package.

But they also allowed for syndicated regional rights for conferences—and in the case of Penn State, then an independent football power—for their own individual games. When that model started to wane, Joe was an enthusiastic supporter of Penn State's entrance into the Big Ten Conference, announced in 1989. All these years and conference realignment dances later, it's easy to forget that the Penn State bombshell announcement set off that chain of events.

It was the television revenue that was needed to pay for the escalating costs of big-time college athletics that drove realignment. Shortly after Penn State made the move, Arkansas and South Carolina went to the SEC, and Florida State went to the ACC. That forced other football independents led by Miami, Virginia Tech, West Virginia, Syracuse, and Pitt to form the core of the Big East football conference.

The big hole in that league was Penn State. Not coincidentally, it was those schools' rejection of an eastern all-sports conference being brokered by Penn State football coach and athletic director Joe Paterno that led Penn State to the Big Ten.

In his business dealings, he lost in the short term in forming an eastern conference but got the chalk last in joining the more prestigious and lucrative Big Ten conference. Joe Paterno understood the demographics. He advocated for Rutgers in the Big Ten because he saw a state with great football talent and access to large television markets. He wanted the conference to move east, not west.

Be aware of the realities and get the chalk last.

Joe Paterno never shied away from leadership on a national level when it came time to do what was right. He stood at the NCAA convention to advocate for higher academic standards for freshmen when most other coaches wished he would've shut up. His stance earned criticism from other coaches and some leaders at historically black colleges. The new standards were seen as culturally biased because of their use of the SAT or ACT as a standard for eligibility.

What Joe Paterno wanted was to challenge high schools around the country to see the requirements and start to prepare their students for the new standards, which would kick in four years later. That was the aim, and in the decades since passage, graduation rates in big-time college football have risen.

Anticipate the future, get the chalk last.

But where he was strongest was in debate, in discussion. On many, many occasions I saw a coach come into a meeting with what they perceived to be a great idea only to not be able to hold it up in discussion with Joe. If that coach was unable to sell it to him, to persuade him, the idea died. It wasn't Joe's way of being autocratic but rather to test the depth of your idea or concept.

Joe's fundamental belief was that coaching was really three things: organizing, selling, and teaching. Before he adopted team rules or schemes or changed practice routines, it had to be sold to him. Credibility was vital to student-athletes buying in to whatever you wanted them to do, so he knew that the sell had to be convincing.

He reminded us that the best student-athletes could smell a fraud. When we stepped into a meeting, he wanted coaches to be the experts, the most informed people in that room. If you couldn't convince him or anticipate his counterpoints, then either you hadn't thought it through thoroughly or you didn't believe in it. Before you presented your idea, you'd better be ready.

The idea of getting the chalk last also drove a tectonic shift in college football recruiting. Joe decided he was going to offer players early and then ask them to make a decision. It started with the class of players who would arrive on Penn State's campus in 1994.

It was a completely new approach, and the first year, a couple of kids jumped on it. It skyrocketed my first year as recruiting coordinator at Penn State after big-name guys committed early. In my second year as recruiting coordinator, LaVar Arrington, the top-ranked prospect in the country, committed to us before he even finished his junior year of high school.

We were racing ahead of everyone else in the country by evaluating and targeting the best players in our recruiting base and getting them to commit. It was Joe's recognition that some schools weren't as aware of certain players as we were, so we took advantage of our head start.

As everyone else started offering players earlier, Joe started to shift his focus. There were certain players that we offered early, but he made sure we had scholarships in reserve. Every year in late November and December, coaches got fired or switched jobs. Often recruits that had committed to those schools reopened their recruiting. With scholarships still available, we picked up some players that way.

We also were able to find some players who emerged as seniors that other people missed. In 2011 we signed wide receiver Allen Robinson, a late bloomer and future All-American that we were able to get because of Joe's plan to have a couple of scholarships in reserve.

Joe got the chalk last and changed the game of recruiting. Then he adjusted when everyone else caught on. Throughout his life he wanted to win, but he wanted to win the right way. It mattered to him how you played the game, and to win you had to find a way to get the chalk last.

Chapter 18

The Zen of Joe Paterno

Hall of Fame NBA coach Phil Jackson was best known as the Zen master with his philosophies of "Be in the moment" and "Surrender the me for the we." Most people would not expect to see the term Zen and Joe Paterno on the same line, but there was something Zen-like in his approach to coaching.

Joe Paterno espoused the philosophies of being in the moment and the "We over the me" concept across decades of coaching success. But there were other philosophies that he taught as well.

For his entire career when you stepped on the practice fields, you saw in the distance the silhouette of Mount Nittany and the ridgeline running behind it. If you looked down as you crossed onto the field there on the green grass, you noticed a blue line.

The Blue Line.

He would say, "once you cross that Blue Line—you're all mine. When you cross that Blue Line, the only thing that matters is football. You can't do anything about your girlfriend, your family, or your schoolwork. All you can do is focus on getting better while you're here."

The Blue Line separated the present from the past and from anything beyond the moment at hand. The philosophy of the Blue Line was to be carried into other areas of our lives. "When you walk into a classroom, imagine a Blue Line," he said. "All you can do anything about is your classwork. When you are with your family, all you can do is focus on your family. You should have Blue Lines all over your life."

With the academic demands of our student-athletes, focus was important. On our printed practice schedules, there was a box with the names of every player with a class conflict so that we would all know who had to leave early or would arrive late.

When I became a father, he gave me even more advice. "Jay," he said, "this job is hard enough on your family. Don't do what I did. When it is time to go home, go home. But most importantly *when you are home...be home.* Be there mentally. Don't just be physically present. Pay attention to your kids."

That stuck with me: "When you're home—be home".

He taught them—we and us—so many lessons.

Phil Jackson's "Surrender the me for the we" was a Penn State concept for years. In recruiting Joe used to say that he was looking for "we and us" people.

The nameless uniforms, the lack of promotion of individual players, the team-first mentality was the embodiment of his philosophy. Some days we'd throw the ball to win; other days we'd run it. "When we give up individual preferences for the good of the group, then we have a team," he'd say.

In his heart, in the core of his being, he was a man who was put on this Earth to teach.

There are so many lessons.

"You either get better or you get worse. You never stay the same."

That was his daily challenge; get better. If you don't get better today, you got worse and someone else is catching up to you.

"The will to win is important, but the will to prepare is vital."

This was always on his mind. The whole key to getting better every day was to prepare. He'd also say, "It's one thing to itch for something. It's another thing to scratch for it."

"You're never as good as you think you were when you win and you're never as bad as you think you were when you lose."

This one was *always* true. Every time we won, we'd study the video and see all the mistakes we'd gotten away with that should've cost us the game. After every loss we'd find two or three plays that we missed that would've won the game.

"All big games come down to three or four plays. You don't know when they are coming so you must prepare and be intense on every play."

We lost a game because we had an extra point blocked when a player made a small mistake. Iowa picked up the blocked kick and ran it back for two points. Those points would have made the difference between us winning in regulation instead of losing in overtime. A seemingly routine extra point made a huge impact on the game. You never know when those plays are coming. Big games are often decided by a play or two that may have happened in the first half of a game, and only when the game is over do we see the significance of that one play.

"Take care of the little things, and the big things will take care of themselves."

The very reason for success was your foundation. In one note he wrote to himself he reiterated this idea another way: "Perfection comes with simplicity; repetition, confidence, and passion."

You cannot build a grand house without strong foundations to support the structure. Those were the little things that he constantly stressed, the right first step, aiming point, the right angle to defend your gap, taking the right release on a route to avoid the safety help.

Every practice he made notes on the smallest details. In practice he'd jump in and correct the technique or he'd make a note of it and bring it up at the next staff meeting to make sure it was corrected.

He was a constant note taker. At practice, in meetings, on planes, at home, on the road, it didn't matter. Always he had a piece of yellow graph paper and a pencil with him.

As a coach once you saw him make a note while watching the players you coached, you knew the next staff meeting would result in questions about something he'd seen. Sure enough, he'd start off the next meeting going through practice notes and writing notes about your response.

These notes accumulated over the course of a month, a football season, and his life. They were the journal of the little things that led to big successes.

"Publicity is like poison. It'll only hurt you if you swallow it."

I've never been around a coach who cared less about what was written about him—both negatively and positively. He told me a funny story about my mother. One morning early in his career after he'd read a glowing story about himself he was looking at himself in the mirror. "Honey," he yelled to my mother, "do you know how many great coaches there are in this country?"

"One less than *you* think," she yelled back.

It was a funny lesson, one he took to heart. Positive publicity has a tendency to make one complacent. Complacency leads to sloppiness and a lack of focus on the details.

In 2008 that may have cost us a shot at a national championship. We ran through October 9–0 after a three-week stretch at Wisconsin, vs. Michigan, and at Ohio State. We had a week off and were three games away from playing in the national championship game.

All our team heard was how we had an easy run left. As we got closer to the game at Iowa, Joe sensed that we were a little loose. He warned us to be focused and ready to play a motivated, well-prepared Iowa team. His fears were realized when Iowa drove late in the game and kicked the game-winning field goal.

Conversely, negative press can penetrate your psyche, eroding your confidence. Today, friends and family consume all kinds of publicity and tend to share it with guys on the team. Even when I was coaching, I'd tell people that I didn't want to hear what someone said or wrote. If you're not careful, you lose confidence—or worse yet you overreact to what you think others want you to do.

In 2001 we went to Illinois, and our starting quarterback Zack Mills got hurt. The backup, Matt Senneca, had an off night, and we lost the game. We couldn't get anything done throwing the football.

The criticism of Matt was brutal. On Monday rather than watch the tape of the Illinois game and beat him up, I put in a tape from a game earlier in the year when he'd played very well against Northwestern. "Matt," I told him, "the guy who played at Northwestern is the same guy who is going to show up next Saturday. What happened at Illinois was all mental. I know you can throw completions and run this team. The Northwestern tape proves it."

He got the message and threw for 278 yards, ran for 47 more, and led us to the win against Indiana. He was a completely different guy because he refused to swallow the publicity. As he walked off the field, it was one of the proudest moments of my coaching career. But it was a lesson I learned from the best ever.

"It's not what happens to you in life that matters. It's how you react to what happens to you that matters."

160

Joe Paterno was a solution-based guy. You couldn't get him to bemoan any negative circumstances in his life, nor did he ever spend time basking in success. Years of experience always taught him that the moment one event happened—either positive or negative—there would be a consequence, a reaction.

That space in time was what mattered in life. After a loss he looked for the players who upped their effort level and went back to win the next game. After a win he looked to see if anyone was easing up in their efforts.

From many disasters arose great triumphs because of how a team reacted. In 1982 Penn State had beaten No. 2 Nebraska in Week Four. The next game the Nittany Lions went to Alabama and were beaten 42–21 on a blocked punt and interception return that blew the game open.

It wasn't the loss but rather how that team reacted to the loss that he remembered. Team leaders vowed to win the rest of their games. By the last two weeks of the season, Penn State had risen back in the polls. After wins at No. 13 Notre Dame and at home against No. 5 Pitt, Penn State gained the No. 2 ranking and a chance to play No. 1 Georgia for the national title.

From the disaster at Alabama, the team reacted with renewed commitment and won a national championship.

It is how you react.

"While you're falling, think about how you're going to get up on the way down."

When you play good teams, you will not get the better of the man across from you every play. When he gets the better of you, you learn from it and figure how you're going to get him the next play.

In the 1986 Notre Dame game, the Irish were driving to win the game and upset Penn State. Defensive linemen Bob White had been rushing the quarterback using an outside move the whole game, and the Notre Dame lineman was onto it.

At a key moment with Notre Dame within striking distance of the game-winning touchdown, it was time to think about how to get up. In the dark late Indiana afternoon, the home Notre Dame crowd was anticipating another major upset under the watchful eyes of the storied ghosts of a proud program.

White decided he would take the inside move. As the play unfolded, Notre Dame's lineman took the outside, and Bob rushed inside, sacked Notre Dame quarterback Steve Beuerlein, and changed the course of the game.

Bob found a way to get up, and Penn State won the game and went on to win a national championship.

Never stop learning.

The flipside of Joe Paterno, the teacher, was Joe Paterno, the eternal student. His note-taking extended to his reading, where he did his most of his studying. He never cracked a book to read without a notepad nearby.

The list of books he'd championed in his later years usually ran to historical themes and themes of overcoming great adversity. He studied *Team of Rivals* about Lincoln's cabinet. We talked about the books *John Adams*, *1776*, and *Undaunted Courage*, the saga of Lewis and Clark. Joe loved the triumph over disaster story, the epic classics he'd studied and loved in his youth—Virgil's *Aeneid*, *The Iliad*, and *The Odyssey*. He studied the book *When Pride Still Mattered* about Vince Lombardi.

But his literary tastes were not limited to old books or classic tales. Before the turnaround season of 2005, he gave copies of Malcolm Gladwell's book *Blink* to every member of his staff. It was a challenge to look at ourselves and evaluate our assumptions.

Always he made notes, and the notes live on even after his death, many of them taped to his desk blotter. From Lincoln: "Let us have faith that right makes might and in that faith let us to the end do our duty as we understand it."

"I have endured a great deal of ridicule without much malice and have received a great deal of kindness not quite free from ridicule. I am used to it."

From explorer Ernest Shackleton: "I think nothing of the world and the press. They cheer you one minute and howl you down the next. It is what is one's self and what one makes of one's life that matters."

Benjamin Franklin's motto for his library: "To pour forth benefits for the common good is divine."

Ultimately, Joe Paterno led a divine life that poured forth lessons for the common good.

Chapter 19

My Story

Child sexual abuse is a troubling and difficult topic. It happens in homes in every neighborhood, town, city, and state in America. Most of our minds cannot grasp it. In the initial aftermath of allegations, due process becomes a casualty of immediate moral certainty, driving passions in a society demanding swift justice. There's little opportunity to discuss what happened and why.

And it is difficult for those who are victimized to come forward.

In the summer of 1981, I made the 10-minute walk across campus to downtown State College. After I bought a new Journey album, I took a bus to a friend's house in the Park Forest neighborhood.

By late afternoon it was time to take the bus back and walk home from the on-campus stop. I sat by myself with the album under one arm. I just sat looking out the window. I guess I didn't even notice the guy until he pointed at the album under my arm. "Is that any good?" he asked.

"I just got it today," I answered.

The conversation started with a discussion of the album. He mentioned he was visiting, so he asked questions about town or where to eat.

All these years later, I realize his approach was to get me talking about myself, start to size me up. After a few more stops, other people got off the bus. Near campus he told me we were hopping off the bus at the same stop. "I am here for a conference and I am staying at The Nittany Lion Inn," he said.

When we got out, he asked me for directions to the hotel, and I pointed him in the right direction. Then he got to the point of his approaching me. "Why don't you come back there with me?" he asked.

"What for?" I asked.

"Look, I am here for a conference. I have a girlfriend at home and when I am away I do not like to cheat on her."

"What's that got to do with me?" I asked.

My 12-year-old-mind didn't see his angle.

"Well I don't like to sleep with other women. But if you come back to the hotel, we could have oral sex."

"What?" I asked.

"Just come back to the hotel, and we'll have a good time."

"Um," I stammered, "that's really not my thing."

This had taken me by complete surprise. I was uncomfortable and looked around for other people. It was still daylight. Some people were around but too far to hear our conversation but close enough to see if he grabbed me trying to flee.

He didn't give up. "Are you sure?" He asked. "We'll have a really good time."

"I need to go home now. My parents have dinner waiting for me," I said.

I was sick to my stomach and wanted to get home right away.

"It's really okay," he said. "It is okay. There's nothing wrong with it, and as I said, I just don't want to sleep with another woman."

"I'm pretty sure your girlfriend wouldn't be okay with this. I'm going home."

I headed toward my home as quickly as possible.

Confused, I blamed *myself* for his proposition. Now at age 45, I know that is a common reaction. How could this happen in my town? The entire existence of my life I'd believed in this safe, sheltered cocoon of Happy Valley.

His offer made *me* feel guilty. The truth, which isn't always easy for a child to see, was that I'd done nothing wrong. I'd gotten on a bus and politely answered a stranger's questions and then walked away when he did something inappropriate.

But when I walked into my house, I told no one in my family about what had happened to me.

I feared that I'd be judged. The feelings I was grappling with were all directed internally. Did I somehow invite that? What was wrong with me that some man would ask me to do that?

All these years later, I look back and recall how I felt because of something I didn't do, something I avoided. Then I try to imagine a young man who was sexually abused by someone they knew and trusted. There is no way I can imagine what they must be feeling, but my experience has shown me part of what the internal reaction must be like.

What has been wrought by all that happened had a lasting impact on the victims and so many people in this community. It became a worldwide story and for my father it began a tumultuous run through the last weeks of his life.

It all unraveled in the course of seven fateful days in November, and no one who lived through it, around it, or near it will ever be the same.

Chapter 20

Runaway Train
Coming

Friday, November 4, 2011

There are sounds that take on a special quality at night, the hooting of an owl, the barking of a dog, the squeal of a tire, the whistling of the wind, or the snapping of a tree branch under the weight of ice or snow.

On my return from a recruiting trip, I stopped to get gas. At the Circle K in Rootstown, Ohio, just off an I-76 ramp, I filled up and got a receipt at 9:11 PM. As I stood outside filling the tank, I heard a distant train whistle, probably a freight line rumbling across this flat expanse of eastern Ohio.

I paused in the cold night and listened. It was bitter, but there was no wind—just the sounds of trucks on the interstate and the train whistle. I'd heard that whistle before, always a warning that a train was coming and to clear the tracks.

A runaway train was coming toward my life, a train loaded with enough hazardous material to wreak havoc in the lives of my family, town, university, and our team.

We certainly couldn't have seen it coming from where our day started. Our team was headed into a free weekend with the Big Ten's best record. Wanting to give his players a weekend to go home, Joe Paterno had us on the field at 6:30 AM. There was excitement in the air about the three remaining games that would determine the fate of our season. Our team had great confidence.

Under the lights before dawn, we saw the sun peek over the ridge of Mount Nittany. That weekend most players traveled home. Coaches traveled to recruit prospective student-athletes.

A few hours later while driving west on I-80 to Ohio for recruiting, I got a call from my brother Scott.

"Well, it is about to break," Scott said.

"What is about to break?" I asked.

"Jerry."

Silence.

Since being questioned by state police investigators, I knew that name would reference one man—Jerry Sandusky. I'd known him most of my life. He worked for my father as a defensive coordinator for many years.

When I returned to coach at Penn State, I worked on the same staff with him for five seasons. He and I did not always see eye to eye professionally, but I respected what he'd done as a coach and for The Second Mile, an organization he started to help young people across Pennsylvania.

A grand jury investigation into alleged child sex abuse offenses against Jerry had become public after a report in *The* (Harrisburg) *Patriot-News* in March, but the report didn't create much of a media stir.

Scott called and told me there were reports that the attorney general was ready to charge the defendant. "How bad is it?" I asked.

"It is not good."

"No kidding. What about Dad?"

"Dad is not under any investigation."

My first hope was that this would not result in any problems for my father. He lived a moral life for almost 85 years. The investigation proved there was no attempted cover-up to assign to Joe Paterno.

That put my worries to rest as I kept on with my day. I stopped at Howland High School and then at Cleveland Heights to watch a practice before making it to Akron to watch a state playoff game.

As I watched the warm-ups and game, my mind wandered off to what was happening back home. I became cognizant of my Penn State jacket and what people would see in that name in the future.

On the drive home, I called and talked with friends, old friends who were Penn Staters. A little after 11:00, I talked with my friend Paul Levine.

Paul, an attorney before becoming a writer of mystery novels, had great legal perspective. Not many people can rival his intense love of Penn State. By the time I pulled into my driveway at 12:30 AM, it became apparent that this story would be a problem for Penn State.

The collision was coming, the unstoppable force barreling down on people who were neither prepared nor ready to make decisions to divert the train or get out of the way. Behind that lead locomotive was a wave, an invasion of media the likes of which our world had never seen, that would steamroll all we'd known for decades.

I still couldn't quite see far enough to know what threat loomed just beyond the horizon.

Chapter 21

Storm Clouds

Saturday, November 5, 2011–Sunday, November 6, 2011

It was after midnight when I pulled into the driveway. After exiting the car, I stood outside, inhaling the chilly air while gazing at the starry sky. I made my way up to my room for the last good night of sleep I would have for weeks.

In the morning I hoped to enjoy a rare fall Saturday with my kids, a plan that ended early.

My phone buzzed, and I saw the name "Scott Paterno." By the time I hung up, I learned that the grand jury presentment had been placed on the attorney general's website "in error." Error or not, it was captured and reposted by multiple media outlets.

Presentments are one-sided documents lacking cross-examination and presentation of evidence contrary to the state's case. Its aim is only one thing—to get an indictment. The attorney general presented the case in the most sensationalized terminology to create momentum for a trial.

The presentment mentioned a graduate assistant coach had witnessed Sandusky in the shower with a boy in 2002, using the words "anal rape," even though the witness never had. The next sentence stated that the assistant had told Joe Paterno what he saw, implying Joe was told about an "anal rape."

It was the leadoff for the case, a bold inaccuracy for the world to read and believe. Before long Penn State fans had figured out the graduate assistant coach was Mike McQueary.

Around 10:30 Scott called me telling me Monday would likely bring perjury charges against Penn State athletic director Tim Curley and university vice president Gary Schultz. That news swept across the country. "Jay, Mom's in Philly for Special Olympics meetings. You've got to go check on Dad," he said.

I put down the phone and headed over. In the den I asked how he was doing with the news about Tim Curley. Tim's indictment hit close to home. Tim had grown up in State College, been a member of Penn State's football team, a graduate assistant coach, and the recruiting coordinator. Ultimately, he got into athletic administration, rising to become athletic director in 1993.

After a few minutes, I was comfortable that he'd be okay and headed home. When the Michigan-Iowa game came on at noon, I was seated in my den. Shortly after noon my phone buzzed again and the name Pete Thamel, *The New York Times* college football writer, came up.

Our conversation was about the presentment. I told him I had not gotten to read it yet as I had been traveling all day before. He expressed his disgust at the serious issues in that document. "Jay," he said, "this is going to be a front page story for us tomorrow."

Ominous clouds were gathering on the horizon.

I called Guido D'Elia, who was in charge of communications and brand management for football. "Pete Thamel just called. This is Page One tomorrow," I said.

I gave him Thamel's cell number. When Guido called back, his voice betrayed concern. "Jay, this is not good," he said.

"Not good?"

"Yeah, his attitude with me was this: I can't believe you're actually trying to spin this."

"Guido, Joe didn't know."

"They don't care."

"So what?" I said. "The truth is that the first time Joe was *ever* made aware of anything he went to his superiors, and that was all he could do."

"They don't care."

That exchange was telling. The media didn't care about what actually happened. The forces of Salem had been unleashed and wouldn't rest until someone had ascended the gallows to hang.

By halftime of the Michigan-Iowa game, it was the lead story on ESPN, and I had more media calls. I now grasped this story would go beyond being a sports story.

My father and I talked again later that day. I wanted to be sure he was still okay and be sure he would have some dinner. When my mom was out of town, he had a couple of go-to dinners. One was calling for pizza, the other was a yellow jar of Mancini roasted peppers or fried peppers he'd heat up in a saucepan and eat with some sharp provolone. He assured me he was okay.

All day I hoped my oldest son, Joey, wasn't paying attention when the football announcers on TV talked about the emerging story. My son was born after Sandusky's career was over, but he had met him and knew he'd coached at Penn State.

Sandusky's adopted son, Matt, coached his daughter's soccer team, and my daughter was on that team. My daughter had been at Sandusky's house for her friend's birthday party just a few months earlier, and I feared how she'd react when she saw this.

After the Michigan-Iowa halftime, Joey wandered into my office, but I was on the phone. My son walked into my office and sat on a big chair in the corner. To the left of him, the blinds were open to the street.

He was confused. Sitting in an oversized chair, he looked even younger and smaller. He asked me what was going on. By then the reports were also talking about Tim Curley, a man Joey knew well.

It was a short conversation. I probably failed as a father, but I just wasn't ready to have that conversation. Although I was 43, I struggled to grasp this. Maybe that's why I ducked the question. He just looked too young to hear what had to be said. "Dad, what is going on? What is happening with Mr. Curley?" he asked.

There was genuine concern in his voice. "What's going to happen to Granddad?" he asked.

"Look, Joe," I snapped. "I don't know what is happening. I just don't know what to tell you. I don't think Mr. Curley did anything wrong."

"Why are they gonna arrest him?"

"Joe, sometimes they get it wrong."

"What did Mr. Sandusky do?"

"Joe, I can't talk about that now."

I regret how I handled it with terse answers—avoiding meaningful responses that may have fostered understanding. His confusion, unresolved by his father, remained obvious on his face. That afternoon I just wasn't up to the task.

After watching our next opponent Nebraska lose to Northwestern, I was fried. The story was creeping into all areas of my mind. The plans to cook out and watch the Alabama-LSU game together fell through. The constant updates and the running text on the bottom of the screen were things I didn't want to have to see with him.

By the time the game was over, I started to drift off to sleep, hoping, just praying that I would wake and find that a nightmare was over. It was just beginning.

Sunday morning after 7:30 Mass, I returned to my house with *The New York Times* and the story right there. Their prominent coverage was likely an accelerant in the fire that had started.

By the time we gathered at the football offices Sunday afternoon, we were all trying to keep our heads focused on the Nebraska game six days away. The meeting we had with Joe Paterno that day was brief. We recapped what we had seen from Nebraska in the game they'd played the day before.

Then we all studied the latest video on our opponent like we did every Sunday. In the meeting rooms as we watched tape, there was banter about other games that Saturday. Throughout the building there was concern about the charges against Sandusky and the charges facing Curley. No matter how much we tried not to talk about it, we did talk about it. It was human nature.

Our phones were ringing from friends, family, coaches at other schools, and reporters poking to see if they could get anyone to talk on the record. We tried to ignore it as best as we could.

Most of us figured that Tim and Gary would be on leave once the charges were announced. Some of us even suspected they would charge president Graham Spanier with something. That would create momentous change at Penn State, a place where stability has been the bedrock of long-term excellence.

As day turned to night and the work day drew to a late close none of us—and I mean none of us—were in any way prepared for what was to come. It was just not something anyone could even remotely comprehend.

I drove home that night, having no inkling the clouds were gathering.

Chapter 22

The Storm Hits

Monday, November 7, 2011–Tuesday, November 8, 2011
Monday morning as I walked into the football offices there were no cameras yet, but I knew they'd show up. I went into Tom Venturino's office and asked if we planned to lock the door to keep camera crews out of the building.

He looked at me like I was crazy.

Sure enough, later that morning a camera crew was in the building looking to get shots of the locker room where the alleged assaults had occurred. We went on lockdown.

Late that morning a full athletic department meeting was called for noon. In the meeting president Graham Spanier tried to still the waters, but there was no way to calm the emotions. As interim athletic director Mark Sherburne ran the meeting along with Dr. Spanier, everyone in that room knew it was bad—just not as bad as I knew it was.

Athletic director Tim Curley was highly respected by our coaches and student-athletes. The charges against him were incomprehensible to everyone.

After the meeting, track coach Beth Alford-Sullivan gave me a big hug. Other coaches offered encouragement, but I felt a sense of guilt that Sandusky, who had been a part of our football program, was possibly responsible for bringing all this to pass.

Ninety miles away the state attorney general Linda Kelly held a press conference, announcing charges against Tim Curley and Gary Schultz. Many of the questions involved Joe Paterno. Linda credited Joe for his cooperation. It was clear he was not the target of any investigation. That should have ended it, but another comment stole the show.

The state police commissioner stated that he felt Joe Paterno had failed his "moral obligation" to protect children. It wasn't his call to make that judgment. Whether it was intentional or not, I don't know.

No matter the intent, the "moral obligation" concept became the headline.

Back in our offices, we were unaware of the speed with which the story was accelerating. We continued preparing for the game we had to play against Nebraska in five days.

Tuesday morning the focus turned to Joe and his usual Tuesday game week press conference. Joe had decided to issue a statement at the press conference and face this head on.

Since the story had broken, the university had issued one statement and then fallen completely silent. What we did not know was that the trustees had pulled President Spanier from leadership.

Guido D'Elia and I talked about the press conference and, while we were nervous, I felt that Joe would address the issue and get the truth out there in the media. Maybe that is what the board of trustees feared the most. Late Tuesday morning the trustees cancelled Joe's press conference. At the stadium the media was lined up, awaiting the press conference. Sports information director Jeff Nelson announced that it had been cancelled, fueling speculation that rocketed out of control.

I got a call, relaying a rumor that Graham Spanier had called off the press conference and was going to fire Joe to save himself. I drove to my father's house, where Scott, Guido, my sister Mary, and my mother had become besieged by dozens of reporters who'd left the stadium and gathered across the street from the house. You can see media mob scenes on television, but it can't prepare you for being in the middle of it. I waded through reporters entering the house amid the din of shouted questions.

Inside the house no one had any idea what was going on with the administration. We reached out.

Mary got Penn State trustee Ed Hintz on the phone, and he claimed not to really know anything. In a cryptic exchange, Ed indicated he'd talk with

Mary at the football game Saturday to which Mary responded, "Ed, I'm not going to be at the game if my father is not still coaching."

Ed said nothing, avoiding the topic.

I took an unlisted cell phone I had and placed a call to Dave Joyner, another trustee I knew well. Dave had played at Penn State. "Dave, it's Jay Paterno," he said.

"Hi, Jay," his voice betrayed a bit of surprise.

"Dave, what's going on?"

"I don't know."

"Dave, I know you can't talk, but let me share what we're hearing. We're hearing that Graham pulled the press conference and is going to fire Joe Paterno."

"Jay, I haven't heard that."

"Whether it is true or not, Joe wants to discuss this. But absent that I want to give you an opinion. Take it for what it is worth."

"Okay."

"Look, there is only one guy in all this that can stand on the national stage and defend Penn State and carry us through this. It's Joe. The best move would be for you guys to state that Joe reported the crime, hasn't been charged, and will remain the coach. That will shut this off. There's also a belief that Graham may be charged. What that means is that you'll be trying to hire a football coach with an interim AD and an interim president. Let Joe stay on and help that process. I know you guys think you can have your pick of any college head coach you want. Most of them will not step into this mess."

"I hear you."

"Dave, one last thing—just talk with Joe. He can help Penn State no matter what happens. Just talk to him."

Months later when trying to defend their actions, the trustees falsely stated that neither Joe nor anyone from our family ever reached out to the board.

As we headed to practice, everyone going into and out of the building was being hassled by media. Joe faced a gauntlet at the house and also at the football office. Media members were surrounding the practice fields to get photos and video.

After practice on Tuesday, Joe had given the okay to hire outside help. Guido knew that as the university remained silent, the storm was, unlike a hurricane, *gaining* strength after it had made landfall here.

After practice Ben Bouma, Guido, and I sat with names and numbers of crisis management experts. Joe had grown impatient with the way the administration was handling the situation and agreed to hire someone to help defend the university.

Mary had finally convinced Joe to hire someone. Joe agreed to use in excess of $100,000 of *his own money* to pay for help for Penn State; there wasn't time to wait for the university to figure out what to do.

At 7:00 PM we started to discuss options. Mary had the name of Dan McGinn as someone who could help us handle crisis management. He was recommended by a number of people we knew.

After research we decided that Dan McGinn was the first pick. He was based in D.C., and had been part of the firm brought in to clean up the situation left at Duke after the lacrosse mess there a few years earlier.

Guido called him, and Dan answered.

"Dan McGinn, this is Guido D'Elia calling from Penn State. I suppose you know why we're calling."

"Yes," Dan said.

"We are interested in getting you to help us."

"First, I have one question. Who will I be representing?"

"Well, Coach Paterno and Penn State."

Dan wanted to know which one would take precedence because he was pretty sure the interests of both parties wouldn't remain aligned—a statement born of experience.

When we hung up with Dan, we were not sure he was taking the case until he called back giving his explanation doing so. "Look, I am only taking this case because of what I know about Joe Paterno and his reputation," Dan said.

It was a long night of calls and arrangements between Guido, Ben, Scott, and Mary. Through media contacts we tried to stamp out the inaccurate stories, but it was blowing out of control.

By midnight we'd done all we could do, and I drove Ben to his hotel in downtown State College. As we drove down Beaver Avenue, the students were on the streets blocking the road. Nothing had happened yet, but there was still time.

I went to bed, feeling we had taken positive steps. But Dan's prediction of divergent interests would come true in less than a day.

On Thursday the university finally came to realize they needed crisis management help. They called McGinn. If they'd only talked to Joe, we could've all worked together.

Lincoln Principles

Refrain from reading attacks upon yourself so you won't be provoked.

Don't be terrified by an excited populace and hindered from speaking your honest sentiments.

It's not entirely safe to allow a misrepresentation to go uncontradicted.

Remember that the *truth* is generally the best vindication against slander.

Do the very best you know how—the very best you can—and keep doing so until the end.

If you yield to even one false charge, you may open yourself up to other unjust attacks.

If both factions or neither shall harass you, you will probably be about right. Beware of being assailed by one and praised by the other.

The probability that you may fall in the struggle ought not to deter you from the support of a cause you believe to be just.

Note: found in Joe Paterno's files

Chapter 23

Retirement

Wednesday, November 9, 2011
Wednesday morning I drove to work, thinking of Saturday's game plan. Running a parallel track in my mind was a timetable. A plane was taking off from Washington Dulles Airport to bring crisis management consultant Dan McGinn and his colleague Mike Clements to town.

My hope was that Joe would survive the next few weeks and coach one more year. As the prominent national figure at our school, I believed he could lead our university out of this mess. But the university administration's silence was making things much worse. They failed to get the heinous narrative away from the school and onto the real perpetrator.

I hoped Dan could circle the wagons, but his perspective on the divergent paths of the school and my father would be right on target. He knew different parties had different interests, potentially putting the administration and my father at odds.

While I was getting ready for practice, Dan was in discussion with Joe at the house. Dan and Mike sat at the kitchen table working with my brother Scott and my father to plot the next steps. Across the street every major news organization waited for anything to come from our house.

Joe told Dan what he had told me a day earlier—that it might be time to retire. They decided that the best course would be to issue a retirement statement that expressed remorse, concern for the victims, and offered the school a way to move forward.

There was an exhaustive conversation about the wording. It had to be exactly right. The major sticking point and one that would be re-read and misunderstood was: "With the benefit of hindsight, I wish I had done more."

Everyone in the room knew that the phrase "I wish I had done more" would be taken by itself and excerpted without the lead-in phrase. It would take on a much different meaning and be seen as an admission of guilt.

If anyone had been aware of other such alleged incidents, who would not have tried to do more?

In the end, Joe was insistent on that phrase staying in—an honest statement of his principles.

JOE PATERNO'S FULL STATEMENT:

State College, PA., November 9, 2011

I am absolutely devastated by the developments in this case. I grieve for the children and their families, and I pray for their comfort and relief.

I have come to work every day for the last 61 years with one clear goal in mind: To serve the best interests of this university and the young men who have been entrusted to my care. I have the same goal today.

That's why I have decided to announce my retirement effective at the end of this season. At this moment the Board of Trustees should not spend a single minute discussing my status. They have far more important matters to address. I want to make this as easy for them as I possibly can. This is a tragedy. It is one of the great sorrows of my life. With the benefit of hindsight, I wish I had done more.

My goals now are to keep my commitments to my players and staff and finish the season with dignity and determination. And then I will spend the rest of my life doing everything I can to help this University.

At 9:30 Guido D'Elia called me. He was still at the house with everyone else. "Jay," he said, "it's Guido."

"What's up?" I asked.

"I just wanted give you a heads up. Joe is going to announce his retirement at the end of the season."

Silence.

I felt sad for my father, but in my heart I knew it was probably the right call.

"You okay?" Guido asked.

"Yeah," I lied.

A couple of tears rolled down my cheeks, but I held it together. Sixty-one years now cut down to two months.

"Look Jay, there is just no way out of this. No way. It is what Joe wants, and Dan doesn't see any other way."

"I got it," I said.

"Hey, I just wanted to call you first. Joe is going to have a staff meeting and tell you guys together. The statement will go out at the same time."

"Okay."

"Pull it together and go in the meeting like you don't know."

Ending the call felt like closing the book on a huge chapter of my life, and I would've given everything to turn it back. After a few moments, I got myself together. I heard the office page system call us to a staff meeting.

"Coaches, please report to the meeting room," the voice summoned us.

Down the hall I heard Joe. "Let's go guys," he said.

His voice remained consistent, the same call he made every day, betraying nothing of what he was about to say to us.

When I walked into the meeting, there was tension brought on mostly by the events now engulfing us. Among the coaches I alone knew what was coming. My insides were churning. Always a true professional, Joe began the meeting going over the notes from the previous day's practice. "Jay," he said, "did I see a reverse throwback to the quarterback? You guys aren't practicing something you're not going to use, are you?"

"No," I answered, "there's a lot of man coverage, so it may be a good red zone call."

"Well make sure you get it right. I like it, and we may need it. But don't practice something you're not going to use."

"Oh, we'll use it."

Then he asked a couple of questions about the defense before he decided to go over that afternoon's practice.

How can he be so cool and professional? I asked myself. *He's about to tell us he is retiring after six decades and all he can do is talk about this week's game.*

After we discussed what we would do on the practice field that afternoon, Joe hesitated. "Look guys, I have something else I have to talk about. Right now a release is going out that I am going to retire at the end of the year."

More silence.

"This thing has gotten out of hand, and I had planned to retire at the end of the year anyway. The guys think that it would get my future out of the discussion and allow us to turn the focus to the victims and what is best for the school."

The room went quiet. Some shed tears. I stayed as stoic as possible— fortunate to have already known what was coming.

We discussed the best way for the team to find out, deciding to call a team meeting, even though we knew that most of the players would already know. Joe wanted to face them and tell them himself.

My next worry was for my children, mostly my three oldest. After the meeting I rushed to call Kelley and have her bring the kids to the office so I could tell them myself. "Kelley," I said.

"Yeah, what's up?"

"Joe is retiring."

"What?"

"Joe is announcing now that he is retiring at the end of the year."

"Are you okay?" She asked.

"Yeah, I'm not happy, but I'm okay. I'm just going to enjoy these last two months and soak it all in."

"Okay."

"I need you to bring the three oldest kids in. I want them to hear it from me. Keep the radio off in the car."

"When do you want me to come in?"

"As soon as you can. We have a team meeting at 11, so if you get here now, I can tell them before I go into that."

The weight of what had already happened finally hit me all at once, and I sat down in my office chair. I looked to my left out across the practice fields and beyond to Mount Nittany and down the valley. It was sunny and mild—much too mild for early November. I'd been coming to these fields all my life, and with the announcement today, it became a real possibility that my days on those fields would end.

My attention turned to my children. My son Joey, one of my 11-year-old twins, was the one I was most worried about. With this sudden change, I was concerned the impact would be too great for his 11-year-old mind to comprehend.

After a few minutes of finishing my team practice preparation, I went downstairs to meet my kids at the front door. They knew something was wrong. Their faces started to go from happy to blank. I could see fear in my daughter Lizzie's usually happy eyes. There was no easy way for me to do it, so I got them to my office, closed the door, and got right to the point. "Guys, Granddad is announcing that he is retiring at the end of the year," I said.

Their tears began right away.

"What does that mean?" nine-year-old Lizzie asked.

"It means that when the season is over he won't be coaching anymore," I said.

Then Joey sat up and with tears in his eyes he spoke. "Dad, that is not fair," he said.

"Joey, look. Here's the thing. Granddad is almost 85 years old. He's had a long career. It is time. He'll be happier," I said.

"It's still not fair," he said.

Caroline was quiet, but she started writing something.

"Guys, it may or may not be fair. What we have to do is enjoy the next two months so we remember all the things Granddad and your father do. It will be the last two months he and I coach together. Now you'll get to spend more time with him like we did at the beach last summer," I said.

Lizzie and Joey were still upset, but they liked the idea of getting to spend more time with my dad. Normally a talker, Caroline was very quiet. Joey was the most emotional. "Joey, here's the deal," I said. "You can come to practice every day. I want you to come over after school and watch practice, so you get to see your grandfather and your father working together. When you're 50 years old, I want you to remember how we worked together."

This idea perked him up a little. Like my father I had always tried to keep my kids away from practice, but it was time to eliminate that barrier for a few weeks.

I excused myself to go down to the team meeting, leaving Kelley with the three kids in my office. By now Joe had met with all the other staff in the building to thank them for all their help. As we went into the team meeting room, it was as quiet as I can ever remember it being. The players knew why they were there.

Joe walked in with a green sweater on and stood at the podium. How many years of team meetings had he led? How many times had he stood in front of his teams and given them a lesson that would make them better as students, athletes as a team, and as people?

The room was dead silent.

Behind him on the wall was a giant Penn State logo. That image, that logo had been a mark of excellence. But in the past few days, all the work put in over decades to make that mark a sign of pride had been under assault. But Joe stood there proud of the men in the room and still proud of all he and we had stood for.

Joe started by telling them that he was retiring. "I wanted to announce it today, so we could put it behind us, so the school can move forward, so the focus can now shift to the victims," he said.

Joe talked about the challenge ahead for them. He reminded us that our team was 8–1 with Nebraska coming in, and we led the Big Ten. "Look," he said, "we've lost one game to Alabama. There is still a lot of football left to play, and a lot can happen for you, so I want you to focus on that. All the stuff that has happened this week wasn't your fault. I feel badly that you've had to put up with all of this."

Then he transitioned to his time at Penn State. He started to talk about all the years he'd been here and all the people who had sat in his team meetings over the years. "You know there are a lot of guys that have played here before you. They've always played hard and always played the way we want Penn State to play. They made sacrifices to make this place something special. Most of you will be here next year after I am done. But what I want you to know: you share something with all the guys who played here before you. No matter what happens we will always—all of us—we will always be teammates."

His voice started to break. Even from my last row seat in the back left of the team auditorium and through his thick glasses, I could see his emotion. But his posture was unbowed. He stood proudly with his head up. What I remember most was the quiet, the absolute silence.

His resolve stiffened and after reaching to wipe a tear away he set his gaze to the young men before him—young men he had always valued as his own, sons for him to care for, teach, and to guide.

In that moment he saw decades of young men he'd led and coached, as if they were all there in that room with him. He spoke to *all* of them. "We will always be Penn State football players and teammates—always until the day we die," he said as his voice was cracking again. "And *no one*, no one can take that away."

He turned to his left and walked slowly out of the meeting room as the team rose to their feet and gave him a standing ovation. Each step he took to cover the 15 feet or so out the door was slow and deliberate. His gait was what it had always been—just slower as though he was imprinting each step of that path into his memory forever.

As I looked at the standing players, many were crying.

Most of the players dispersed and went back to their classes. Some gathered in the locker room, still in shock, still saddened.

I made my way upstairs to my wife and kids. Coaching is a journey, and when you become a coach, you commit your family to that journey whether they want to be on that ride with you or not. Slowly I opened the door to my office back up and found my family still upset. My wife sat head held high, but the emotions of the moment were getting to her.

My daughter Caroline handed me a piece of paper. "Daddy," she said. "I wrote a poem for you."

It was like a punch in the chest that stops you from being able to move forward or anywhere at all. As I read the words, I couldn't breathe.

> Nov/9/2011
> By: Caroline
> Age: 11
>
> Memories
> Memories last forever,
>   & are

always the same.
The future is different,
　　with all
　sorts of curves.
My memories will last
　　forever
Here with You

"It is beautiful," I said as the tears began to well up in my eyes.

I knew that I had to go by the house to see my parents. There was no doubt that the finality of it would not be easy. I hugged my kids, grabbed my coat, and walked them down to the front of the building.

As the five-minute drive to my parent's house concluded, I reached the crest of the hill to their house where I could see the throng of media still on the neighbor's lawn across the street. When I pulled into the driveway and made the walk up to the front door, I politely deflected their questions. Inside I made my way back to the kitchen table. Seated there were the new advisors. I met them both quickly, not knowing what to make of these men who'd advised my father to announce his retirement.

My first reaction was relief. We clearly needed the help and a professional plan. There were a lot of us around the table but not my father. I excused myself to go see him in his den.

I opened the door slowly, not really sure what I would say. "Dad?"

"Yeah, come on in," he said.

He was seated in his chair behind the door. How many times had I walked into that den to see him there with a pencil and a yellow graph paper tablet in his hand?

"You okay?" I asked.

"Yeah, I'm okay. Look, Jay I told you before that I was most likely going to retire when the season was over anyway. I just didn't want everyone to make a big fuss about it. Are you okay? Kelley and the kids?"

"Yeah, we'll be okay," I lied to shield the heartache I felt watching him go through this. "Joey's taking this pretty hard, so I told him he could come to practice the rest of the year."

"That's great. Now look, take care of your family."

"Dad, it's been a great ride. Let's end this all the right way."

"That's right. We have a job to do for this team, so let's make sure we don't let them down. Now that this is out of the way, we can get ourselves focused back on the game and get the media off this team."

"I hope you're right," I said.

Turning from the den, I walked back to the kitchen, a beehive of activity. Outside I saw port-a-johns had been set up in Sunset Park, which was adjacent to our house. Apparently some journalists had peed in the park, so someone suggested a temporary solution. McKee Street was barricaded.

Dan turned toward the task at hand. This was his first day, but, as we like our quarterbacks to do in a tough game, he kept his poise. "Have we talked to anyone from the board since we released the statement?" Dan asked.

My sister Mary and brother Scott both came up empty. Scott had reached out to the university's legal counsel, but no one from the university had called back.

"Well, until we talk to them we don't know if they've accepted this move yet," Dan said.

"What are they going to do?" I asked.

"They could fire him now," Mary said.

"They can't do that. I think if they didn't make that move last night, they wouldn't create a shitstorm on a Wednesday of game week for the biggest game of the year for us," I said.

"In these situations you never know," Dan said.

In typical fashion my mother saw to it that Dan and Mike, two men she'd never met before, were not going to eat anything other than a home-cooked meal for lunch. She had heated up some of her tomato soup.

Over soup, Dan looked at me and asked me, "How do you see this all ending?"

"I see us winning the next two games. I don't know if we'll *win* at Wisconsin, but I still see us winning the Big Ten, and Joe's career ends in the Rose Bowl."

"Wow," Dan said, "I hope you're right."

"If he gets to retire, it will end that way. I don't know if we'll win the Rose Bowl, but we'll get there," I said. "That in itself would be a win."

Dan didn't know me, and I didn't know him, but we were forced to trust each other. We had no alternative.

This sit-down lunch made me think about bygone days staying at my grandmother's house in Latrobe, Pennsylvania. It didn't matter if we were muddy from playing in the creek behind their house. When it was time for lunch, we all sat down and ate at the table. There was always a great spread: deli meats, soup, great bread, pickles—lots of pickles. I can still see that table, the place settings, and the bird feeders outside her kitchen window alive with activity.

My attention snapped back to the present. Texts from friends or former players were coming in. People I knew from all over were changing plans, booking tickets, and finding a way to get here. No one wanted to miss Joe's last game in Beaver Stadium.

Our conversations and strategy were all a blur. My dad walked back and forth between his den and the kitchen. He popped his head in and smiled as he looked at the table. "I hope they're feeding you guys enough," he said. "Dan, Mike, now don't be shy; eat up." Joe laughed.

He looked at me and summoned me to talk to him. We stood in the room outside his den where he spoke as a father, not as a boss. "Now look, are you okay?" he asked, lowering his head so he could look at me over his glasses.

The look he gave me was a firm smile that demanded I tell him the truth. He'd talked to me like that a thousand times.

"Dad, I'm okay. Look, I knew this day had to come eventually."

"I know but…"

"I'm okay. So let's go get this done the next few weeks."

"Okay, that's what I want to hear." He smiled.

Then he looked down at his watch. The clock was running.

"Are you ready for your meetings? You better get going."

"I got ya."

As I walked out the front door, the throng of media snapped to attention. The camera shutters started snapping, and questions started to get yelled. The questions were about Joe's retirement, about Sandusky, asking if I would make any statement.

At the Lasch building, I headed in, changed into my practice clothes, and went up to my office. I shut my door and found some peace as I sat silently, trying to clear my mind. My mind reverted back to the moment, being professional. It was the way he'd trained us all for decades.

I got up and headed to the meeting room, knowing the team would watch to see how I conducted myself today and the rest of the year. As I walked across the locker room, I could feel a lot of the eyes following me. But strength had come to me from my faith. My quarterbacks meeting was conducted as if nothing unusual had happened.

Afterward Shane McGregor, an outstanding young man, came up to me and shared with me how much my father meant to him and thanked me. My professional demeanor nearly got shattered.

Keeping it together, I went to the equipment room. Joey was waiting there for me. The excitement of being at practice was visible on his face. It was bittersweet, but my 11-year-old mini-me was enjoying the day.

Head equipment manager Brad Caldwell gave Joey a quarterback wristband, so he'd have all the plays. Joey's biggest Christmas morning smile lit up his face as he put it on. It was like Brad had given him the secrets of the universe as he looked at the game plan on the wristband. "Dad," he asked, "can I be a mini-coach, like your assistant?"

"You sure can."

He smiled again, the first smiles in days. Brad gave him a pat on the back and smiled.

"Okay Joey, let's get out to practice. You can't be late," I said.

As we headed out to the field, I stopped. Joey waved at his grandfather, and I told him to stay on the sideline. He would stand with the team doctors and administrators.

As I had done for 17 seasons, I walked across the practice field and looked to Mount Nittany. This day was different. Today there were photographers and reporters trying to sneak through the trees to get videos and pictures of Joe on the field.

But I ignored them, stopping for a moment to put myself into the practice mind-set. My only concern, my singular focus, had to be on this practice for the Nebraska game.

Resuming my walk across the field, I looked back to Mount Nittany. Then it struck me. In my sight on this unseasonably mild November late afternoon were the two most iconic silhouettes this town would ever know. Even with his back to me, there was no mistaking Joe Paterno's silhouette. He stood about 20 or 30 yards away, and past him in the eastern distance was Mount Nittany aglow in the purple light of the late afternoon sunset to my back. Above both Joe and the mountain was a bright, round full moon.

It stopped me right in my tracks. I looked back at my son then back at my father. Three generations of Joseph Vincent Paterno all on one field. Then I absorbed that image of the mountain, the moon, and a man I would fight for with my life—the life he'd given me—if needed.

I reached for my cell phone camera to take the picture. It was one of those perfect pictures, an image that will never leave you. But I stopped. *I'll get that shot tomorrow*, I told myself. *The weather is supposed to be exactly the same, so I can snap it tomorrow.*

Tomorrow.

Chapter 24

The Firing, Tempest, and Et Tu Brute

"I have seen tempests, when the scolding winds have riv'd the knotty oaks, and I have seen Th' ambitious ocean swell and rage and foam, to be exalted with the threatening clouds; But never till to-night, never till now, Did I go through a tempest dropping fire."

—*Casca, Act I Scene III,*
Shakespeare's Julius Caesar

Wednesday, November 9, 2011–Thursday, November 10, 2011 If ever there was a lesson of focusing on practice, this was it. What was going through Joe's head? He seemed completely engaged and unworried moving all over the field taking notes.

We worked through the section of practice where we work on trick plays. We completed Bone Right Over 42 Pitch Reverse Pass, the same throwback pass to the quarterback we'd talked about in the meeting. "Hey, you'd better call that Saturday," he shouted to me in his shrill voice.

"You got it," I said.

Quarterback Matt McGloin looked at me and smiled. "He's right," McGloin said. "You better call that one when I'm in there Saturday." Matt laughed.

All practice our players were locked in despite having to walk past a campus-wide media siege for days. The practice field must have seemed like a place of escape. I know it was for me and I could sense that Joe felt at peace doing what God had put him on this Earth to do.

Every once in a while, I looked over and saw my son shadowing us from the sideline. I could see him smiling in the late afternoon sun, his wristband on his arm. My heart just went out to him. His world had been ripped open, the routine of day-to-day life destroyed by the national soap opera.

How to explain all this to an 11-year-old?

Focus, focus, focus on practice.

As practice moved along, I saw the brilliant sunset. The pink and purple sky was stretched to the west. I inhaled and took it in.

After practice Joe walked the media gauntlet to his car only to drive through throngs of people outside his house when he got home. While university administrators were out of sight, the media knew Joe had to emerge from his house and office to do his job. Video of him headed to practice or into his house became the B-roll video on cable news. Joe Paterno was *the* visual.

Immediately after practice I drove home with Joey. It had been an emotional day. When we returned home, my friend Mike Hughes and his wife were at the house with trays of food from Rotelli, a restaurant in town they owned. They were there to support us. My wife and I have been blessed in State College to have great friends. From the earliest moments of this, our friends' support was unwavering.

I was at peace with Joe's retirement. There was now a finish line, a moment when I would walk off the field with him for the very last time. There was comfort knowing it was coming, so I could hold every moment in my heart to remember.

We ate dinner with the kids and talked about the retirement. The older ones hadn't been to school. We'd pulled them out, knowing there was no way to protect them from things the other middle schoolers might say to them.

With the events of the day having unfolded, I figured it was safe to go play some night tennis with my friends. Sometime in the late spring, we had started playing once a week. The usual attendees were there: my friends Ara, Kerry, Charles, Charles, Spyro, Eddie, and Neil. Another player, Joe Posnanski, was a writer living in town for the fall while working on his book about my father.

The courts are bordered on three sides by large evergreen trees, a peaceful isolated setting. It was a brilliantly clear night, unseasonably warm with a big bright full moon.

When I got to the court, I had a sense of calm. "Do you think that everything's okay?" Posnanski asked me.

"Hey, I can't believe they'd do anything now," I said. "Joe's retiring, and it's Wednesday. To be fair to this team, they certainly shouldn't do anything on Wednesday of a game week."

For the first time in days I was free, running around the court. My mind was clear of the storm, and I floated above the chaos.

Across town the trustees had called an emergency meeting. They took exception to what they perceived to be a football coach telling them how to do their business and rationalized that Joe's statement was an insult to them.

They focused on the wrong words. Their egos and agendas forced them to focus on "At this moment the board of trustees should not spend a single minute discussing my status." The university was facing bigger problems than football, but they missed the point.

Joe correctly asserted that, "they have far more important matters to address." They also ignored the last sentence: "And I will spend the rest of my life doing everything I can to help this university."

On the tennis courts at about 9:55 PM, we decided to call it a night. As we stood gathering our stuff, my friend Kerry Small's cell phone was buzzing. "Somebody get that," Kerry said.

I was closest and I could see on the phone that it was my wife Kelley calling. "It's Kelley," I said. "I'll get it."

Charles picked up his phone at that time and said, "Hey, she called me, too."

"That's not a good sign," I said as I picked up Kerry's phone.

"Hello," I said.

"Jay?" she asked.

"Yeah, what's up?" I asked.

"Why didn't you pick up *your* phone?" she asked "You need to call your sister Mary right away."

"What is going on?" I asked.

"The trustees are meeting, and she thinks they're gonna fire your dad."

I couldn't imagine they would do this. There was no way. He'd already said he wanted to retire.

"I'll call her," I said.

I walked away from the courts calling my sister. No answer.

Then Ara spoke up, "Let's go to the clubhouse and see if we can find out what's going on."

We walked down, and I sat on the green carpeted steps in the entryway. To my left was Posnanski. He was not a journalist now. He was a friend.

At 9:50 I sent a text to trustee Dave Joyner that said, "Dave, I just need a heads up if possible. Is the board going to accept Joe's retirement?"

No response.

I sent a text to my sister. Then my phone rang. It was Mary. "Hello," I said.

"They fired Dad," she said.

"What?" I asked.

"They fired Dad effective immediately. They brought a note to the house. He called them and they fired him," she said.

Too shocked to cry, all I could manage was to say the one word my father never wanted to hear any of us say, a word I had never heard him utter even at his angriest: "Fuck."

Posnanski sat there. Out of the clubhouse bar came a friend, and even now my mind cannot tell you who it was or even recognize the voice. It said, "They're saying on TV that there is a press conference."

The rest of the tennis group came out, and I told them what they already suspected, but were hoping couldn't possibly be true.

Shock.

For Penn Staters and for college football fans this was a moment that no one will ever forget. Instead of my friends, including Posnanski, getting on their phones, they gathered around me. True friends. They all acknowledged what we all knew to be true.

The firing was an act of cowardice designed to cover the asses of the trustees. End of story.

SENT: Wednesday November 09, 2011 10:52 PM
TO: Jay Paterno

Jay,

What a travesty. In response to horrible things, the board
of trustees does a horrible thing. When I was younger,
I envied the guys that got to play for your dad, but it is
YOU who is to be envied. It would be nice to have played
for the greatest coach who ever lived, but how special it
must be to be the son of one of the finest MEN who walked
the earth. He is in our prayers. You and your family are
all in our prayers. Nothing has changed from a week
ago—your dad's greatest reward is still to come. Penn
State may not want JoePa now, but when the time comes,
God will welcome him with open arms.

God bless you all Jay
—Calvin

Now as I reflect, I recall in Arthur Miller's *The Crucible* the critical
moment when they tell the innocent John Proctor that they must post
his phony signed confession on the door of the church for all to see. He
refuses the entreaties of the town elders who know in their hearts he is
innocent. He refuses his wife imploring him to allow the confession to
be posted. "Because it is my name! Because I cannot have another in my
life! Because I lie and sign myself to lies," Proctor said. "How may I live
without my name?"

At that moment the trustees chose to condemn an innocent man. But
in their actions, they also offered up the name of Penn State, an honorable
name earned over decades. In a moment of fear and panic, they destroyed
it. For the damage done to the Penn State name, all the money, all the
investigations, and all the public relations firms they hire cannot repair
what they've done.

As a son of undying loyalty on and off the field, I knew that I was probably at risk. Thanking my friends I got back into my car and drove Posnanski
back to his car. When we arrived at the parking lot, I called a friend who

was in the room when the press conference started, and he relayed to me the play by play.

Posnanski sat in my old GMC Suburban as events that would forever change my life rocketed across campus through my phone. All week Posnanski could sense what many of us could sense—grenades were being tossed, and the university leadership was hiding behind Joe Paterno.

I hung up. I didn't know if they would come for me next. I didn't know if I would coach in three days. A career and life of stability was now one where nothing was certain.

I called my sister back, and she relayed to me that Mom and Dad wanted to be alone the rest of the night. It seemed incomprehensible that my father would never coach another football game again at Penn State.

The students reacted with anger but in a mostly nonviolent way. Announcing the firing at 10:00 PM meant that students were at home, watching and ready to react. In what later was termed a riot, the media focused on one visual, the visual of an isolated group of students overturning a television truck.

It was a statement of blame. While I do not condone it, the isolated act was an understandable reaction to a media invasion that had turned their world upside down. The vast majority of the students were gathering to be there for each other. They wanted to voice their opinions after enduring five days of this invasion. Eventually many made their way to my parents' home.

Finally I made the left turn into my driveway and opened the garage door. As I pulled into my garage, the door into the house opened. Through the open door, Joey's face appeared.

My heart was rent.

Turning off the car, I took a deep breath before getting out and facing what was going to be the worst moment in all of this. Slowly I opened the door and headed over to my son, who had tears running down his cheeks. His idol—my father, his grandfather—had been stripped of his job for sins he never committed.

What hurt me the most was that he had been fired despite *reporting* the alleged crime. When I got to the door, I hugged him. It is a moment I will never forget as a father. "Dad," he sobbed, "Why? Why did they do this to Granddad?"

Every parent dreads the "Why" questions about the world when there are no good answers, no way to justify what happened. With him punished for doing the right thing, how could I explain that to my son?

"Joe, I don't know if you'll understand now," I said.

"Dad, why?" he asked.

"Joe, they had to blame someone. But know this. *Know this.* Your grandfather did the right thing. If he knew that doing what is right would cost him all this, he would do it all over again."

"Why did they fire him?"

I decided to be honest.

"Because there are people in the world who have hearts that are not good. Your grandfather is a good man. For that, some people have envy and hatred in their hearts for him."

Often the truth can be confusing to adults, even more so to a child.

Joey followed me upstairs as I went into my bathroom to brush my teeth. He sat on the edge of the tub. I finished brushing my teeth and turned toward him. It was now well past when he should be asleep. "Joey, you've got to get to bed," I said.

His eyes were still red and puffy. He hesitated, and I knew he wanted to ask something. "Joe, what do you want to ask me?" I asked. "Dad...when this is all over, will we still be Penn State fans?" he asked.

Everything screeched to a halt. The world stopped spinning, and I was completely thrown. It was a question I hadn't even pondered yet. I answered honestly in a way that was as painful a statement as I have ever spoken. "Joey...I don't know," I said. "I just don't know, son."

He left the room to go to bed, and I sat on the edge of the tub. *I just don't know.*

As I made my way to bed, Kelley was awake, saddened by what had happened to my father and unsure of what was to become of her husband. The television was on, and as I changed channels, the images on the screen of every channel were Penn State students marching through downtown.

The tempest dropping fire had been unleashed.

The students wound their way to my parents' home, and my parents appeared at the door in images immediately beamed to satellites and then around the globe. My father was wearing a grey sweatshirt while my mother was in her red robe—a robe she'd probably had for 20 years. Despite the fame that my father had gained as a coach, these two lived simple lives. If ever there was proof of that, here was that moment.

The students cheered—an expression of gratitude for decades of service to Penn State.

Earlier after the retirement announcement, students, alumni, and fans of Penn State had realized that Saturday would be the last home game of Joe's career—one last afternoon together on the storied gridiron he'd helped build. There would be a chance to cheer, tip their hats, and say "Thank you" for all the years, all the memories and all the pride.

The firing took that away. It was all over now and if it can ever be said of someone with such a long career, the end came all too soon.

As my father turned to go back into his house, he turned and spoke the last words he'd ever utter on television after a career in the public spotlight. "We are Penn State," he said.

It wasn't a cheer. It was a reminder that despite all that had happened we still stood for something worth defending.

Across town my wife and I discussed for an hour what might happen. "Kelley, everything is minute to minute and hour to hour. I may get fired tomorrow morning. We just have to hang on and fight through," I said.

Part of me doubted that I could walk onto the practice field Thursday afternoon, knowing that Joe would no longer be there. It was all I could do to not allow my heart to be consumed with hatred.

For years I had stayed up watching big news stories. Tonight I was in that maelstrom; I was in that tempest dropping fire.

I checked my phone, and emails were pouring in. Most were from people I didn't know, but one came from a name I've known since elementary school. Mark Kavanaugh and I have been friends for years. Mark was never one to pour out his emotions, but what he wrote that night will be with me the rest of my life.

> **SENT:** Thursday, November 10, 2011 12:35 AM
> **TO:** Jay Paterno
>
> I don't know where to begin or where to end.....
>
> I love you. I love your family. I love your father. I love my Alma Mater. I love my home town.

An awful man set fire to our village. That's not your Dad's fault...far from it.

Outside of my own immediate family, there has been no greater influence in my life than the example provided by Joe Paterno. But that should be obvious. Because I'm from State College. I'm a Penn Stater.

I'm sorry things have gone this way. I'd do anything to change it. But nothing changes my long-standing opinion of your dad, and I'm confident I speak for the majority of Penn Staters.

I know its mid-season and you're still trying to accomplish goals that are within the team's grasp, but please keep in touch when you can. You're one of my closest friends (in case you didn't know that).

Mark

My tears started immediately. "Are you okay?" Kelley asked me in the dark.

Through my emotions I read to her what Mark had written. Words cannot even begin to express what that email meant to me.

Sometime in the night, I started to hear the wind pick up and raindrops hitting the skylights in our bedroom. A few drops started, and then the pace picked up until it became a heavy downpour. The noise level rose, and I just listened to it.

Julius Caesar was heavy on my mind. Brutus and his men had killed Julius Caesar. The question in my mind was how far they would go—was I next?

Brutus: Do You know them?

Lucius: No, sir; their hats are pluck'd about their ears, And half their faces buried in their cloaks, That by no means I may discover them by any mark of favor.

Brutus: O conspiracy, Sham'st thou to show thy dangerous brow by night, when evils are most free? O, then, by day where wilt though find a cavern dark enough to mask thy monstrous visage?

They announced a unanimous vote. Unanimous. Not one of the trustees voted for my father. Not a one? Then it hit me. *It was about the anonymity in unanimity.* As the men in Shakespeare's play had come to Brutus' home to convince him to join their plot, they covered their faces. The unanimity gave them their cloaks to mask what they had done come the light of day.

But I knew many of them. They'd walked into my parents' home after many football games over the years. Some brought friends and clients to impress with a postgame meal at Paterno's home.

But this night those same people on the board had fired him. My mind recalled deep, long-running connections.

My first thoughts fell on a trustee named Anne Riley. One of my most vivid childhood memories came at just over seven years old. I was in our basement and heard something going on up in the kitchen. I went upstairs and caught sight of my father pulling Anne's father, Ridge Riley, across the floor to perform CPR on him. "Get downstairs," my father yelled.

I did what I was told and after a lot of commotion, Ridge Riley was taken to the hospital, but he had already died in our kitchen. He was visiting my father to continue work on the book *The Road to Number One*, a chronicle of Penn State football history.

How would he have written about this chapter?

In her father's moment of greatest need, my mother and father tried to save his life. In my father's hour of greatest need, where was she?

My mind went down the list of trustee names I could recall.

Paul Suhey.

Paul's family and my own family had a history intertwined over decades. Paul's parents and my father had known each other since my father's first days on campus. But even with that, people who knew Paul had been warning me for years that Paul bragged that he got on the board so he "could get rid of Joe."

I don't put much stock in rumors and I had no way of knowing if that was true, but I thought back to the intertwined family history.

Paul's mother, Ginger, was my godmother. After her husband's death, my father tried to be a help. Paul's younger brother, Matt, will tell you how much he valued my father for his efforts to help him during Matt's college career at Penn State.

But there was more to it. I recalled Paul starting a sports medicine clinic in Jacksonville, Florida, and who did he ask to come down and speak to high school athletic directors and coaches? Joe Paterno.

In this critical moment, where was that family loyalty?

The names kept coming.

Couldn't attorney Jesse Arnelle have seen what he was doing wrong? Couldn't he see the values of Joe Paterno, who recruited him 60 years ago? Couldn't he see that due process, a core American legal value, was being violated here?

Surely he couldn't stay silent as they voted to fire Joe.

My mind went on.

Ed Hintz, a longtime family friend. He and his wife had been in my parents' home so many times I couldn't begin to guess. When Ed and his wife, Helen, had faced some troubles in their own lives, my mother continually reached out to Helen to support her and support their family.

I thought about Mary, reaching out to Ed to see if he would support my father. He had been evasive on the phone. Did he say to my sister that he would go to the wall for my father? No. With his failure to stand up for my father, Ed had succeeded in creating a messy end to a career that had withstood the tests of time.

There were others there who were often at the house after games. In the house they would sing Joe's praises while they drank his wine and dined on food that my mother cooked. But they lacked the ability to stand up for someone they claimed was a friend.

Amid the rain pounding on the roof that night, we still didn't know who was calling the shots. But I knew there were three who figured prominently in this. John Surma announced the firing, the firing of a man who had known his family for over 40 years. John's brother, Vic, had played here in the late 1960s and early 1970s and for years was supportive of Joe. Once Vic's son had walked on and didn't get a scholarship, Vic turned into one of Joe's most outspoken critics. I am sure John Surma heard his brother's complaints and the constant harping about Joe.

Steve Garban came to mind, another member of the board who had played at Penn State and been a lifelong "friend" of Joe Paterno. He was the lone trustee who had shown up at Joe's house in November of 2004 to ask him to step down.

In his administrative career at Penn State, Garban could always count on Joe Paterno to run a football program that was successful on and off the field. But on the fiscal side, which was the part that impacted Garban's job the most, Joe could always be counted on to run a frugal program that did not waste money.

For the decades of service, faithful to the end, what did Joe Paterno get from Steve Garban? Silence.

He sat there as John Surma read the words.

For all the meals Sue cooked to raise millions for the university, what did she get? For all the times Joe stayed put at Penn State, what did he get?

Not so much as a phone call or meeting from Friday through the moment they fired him. After 60 years of university leadership, they didn't even try to get in a room with him to talk about how they could all work together to move forward to do what was best for Penn State.

They sent Fran Ganter with a piece of paper with Surma's name and phone number to call. It was in Fran's handwriting. I knew the truth.

Regardless of how I felt about the vote, I resented the fact that they had so little respect for Joe's perspective. I resented that they didn't even involve him in helping this school navigate the future. Above all I resented the lack of respect for what he had done for this school, the lack of respect for the sacrifices he had made and our family had made in his time away from his home to help build a proud program and promote the university.

The rain kept falling.

Chapter 25

Survivor's Guilt

Thursday, November 10, 2011–Friday, November 11, 2011

The rains stopped. But sleep had eluded me so long I figured it was time to stop chasing it. With the day's first light, all that had been true at the previous day's dawn would be false today.

It was 5:48 AM.

All night no one had contacted me from the university. We got a vague text about a 7:00 AM meeting. I went to the bathroom and started to brush my teeth.

Buzz. I looked down and read the text on my phone at 5:51 AM: "I need to see you when you come in"

It was from interim head coach Tom Bradley. I called my brother Scott who answered immediately. "What's up?" he asked.

"I think I'm getting fired. I just got a text to come see Tom at the office."

He gave me some good advice. After I hung up, I went in to see Kelley. She sat up and looked at me. I sat down on the edge of the bed. "I think I'm getting fired. I just got a text from Tom, telling me he needed to see me as soon as I get in," I said.

"What are you gonna do?"

"Well, I'm going to see how my dad's doing," I said. "That's the most important thing."

It was still dark when I drove to see my father. As I arrived at the house, I knew he'd be awake. He was in his den in his reclining chair probably where he'd been all night. Without a word I walked across the room to his desk chair and sat. The house was still dark except for a lamp on behind him. He looked tired, not crestfallen—just tired.

There was a cup of coffee on the small table next to his chair. For the first time in his life, he didn't need the coffee. If he wanted, he could have just gone back to bed and said, "The hell with all of you. I did all I could and I don't have to answer for anything."

But that was not his way.

"Coach," I said, "I think I am going to get fired."

"What makes you think that?" he asked.

"I got a text to come in right away," I said.

"Well, I don't think they will, but I've been wrong before."

"This is such a mess. I'm not sure what to do."

"Jay, you have an obligation to the guys you coach, to the university, and to try and help Tom Bradley."

I understood that but to help the university that had turned its back on him? That was a lot to ask. We both knew going into work was like walking into a pit of vipers, but he was insistent. "Jay," he said, "you know in your heart what you have to do."

He was right. Part of me wanted to walk out and make a statement ripping everyone and everything. I was in that kind of mood.

I got down to the brunt of it. "Dad," I asked, "what happened?"

"Mike [McQueary] came to me, and it was the first I'd ever heard anything like this. I knew I wasn't the one to handle this, so I did what I was supposed to do. I couldn't go running with things I didn't know were true. I went to Tim and Gary."

"Why them?"

"I didn't see it. I knew Tim and Gary are capable people. Mike had to tell them what he saw. I don't know what he told them, but there was nothing else I could do."

"Dad, I know you did the right thing. I know the truth. What happened isn't fair."

"Jay, you better get back to work," he said.

"I just don't want to go without you."

"This day was going to come sooner or later."

He waved me out. In silence I walked slowly toward uncertainty, leaving behind a past that was almost constant in its certainty.

As I drove away up McKee Street, I saw Penn State field hockey coach Char Morett, a friend and neighbor of my parents. She was walking her dog and, though I tried to drive by without making eye contact, she saw me. Almost immediately she began to cry, so I slowed down to talk.

I hustled to the office for our staff meeting. Afterward I went in and met with Tom Bradley. He asked me to shut the door to his office. "Jay, they want to know if you plan to keep coaching the rest of the year," he said.

At least I wasn't getting fired...yet. "Tom, I owe it to the guys on the staff and on the team to do my job," I said.

"Okay, I'll tell them."

I don't know exactly who "they" were, but I didn't need to know and I didn't particularly care. If they wanted to fire me, they could fire me, but I wasn't going to run.

We had a team meeting that morning, and in it I sensed confusion but also anger. These young men were forced to bear the brunt of the administration's miscalculations. The season they'd worked so hard for, a team on the verge of realizing their goals, had the man who'd led them pulled from them.

The offensive staff went into our meeting and planned out the first plays of the game, putting together a 12-play script. Each week we'd give the script to Joe, who'd either make changes or say that it looked good.

This week we were on our own. We decided to start the game with the fullback dive play that was a favorite of Joe's and then follow it up with the toss crack play he liked and that scored against Ohio State in 2005. It was a subtle way of honoring him, a way that he would understand.

We decided to deliver the script to him at his house. The offensive staff, along with Larry Johnson and Kermit Buggs from the defensive staff, rode over to the house. Upon arriving we walked the media gauntlet. The coaches really had their eyes opened to the chaos outside my parents' home.

The six assistant coaches who went to the door had combined to work for Joe Paterno for over a century. A couple of the graduate assistant coaches came along as well. We were welcomed and seated at the round kitchen table. Joe came out to see us. Behind him the curtains, normally open to let in the sunlight, were drawn to block the view of the media behind the house.

Joe wore a button-down sweater and a dress shirt but no tie, which he normally wore for meetings. We presented the game plan to him, and he gave it a quick look over. "Well, it's really not up to me anymore guys, but I think you have some good stuff here," he said.

There was a quiet acknowledgment of that new reality, but I believe we were all still in a state of shock. When something so solid in your life is ripped away suddenly, there is no time to grasp what has just occurred.

Men I had never seen cry were wiping tears away from their eyes as they thanked Joe Paterno for what he had meant to them and to their lives.

On the walk to the door, I understood I was walking out to keep coaching while my father, my former coach and my boss, was left behind. It was when the pain of survivor's guilt tore my heart.

How could I rightfully carry on when he was not able to finish what he had started? When I got back to my desk at work, I put my head down and just felt the pain.

That afternoon, members of the Football Letterman's Club asked to speak to the team. They take great pride in Penn State football, and it tore them up to see what had happened to Joe Paterno. But they'd learned Joe Paterno's lessons. They wanted to support this team, to help them continue to fight. What Joe Paterno had said to the team on Wednesday had echoed beyond the meeting room walls and reached the men who played in years past.

LETTER FROM THE FORMER PLAYERS TO THE TEAM:

Dear Squad,

The events of this week have been unprecedented and historic at Penn State and more specifically within the football program. Through all of the media scrutiny and turmoil it seems like your game against Nebraska has become an afterthought. In fact, many of you may feel abandoned, hurt, troubled and uncertain of the future. Please know that as members of the Penn State Football Family this is not your burden to shoulder alone as we, the Football Lettermen's Club, stand with you. We stand with you now and forever.

Understand this: You guys will have the opportunity to demonstrate to the world, in a public forum, that Penn

State Football will continue to succeed and flourish in a way that will make us all proud. It is easy for the critics to sit back and say otherwise but it will be hard for them to continue to say it after you take this first step and climb the first rung this Saturday. We, as former players, know that the most important thing at this moment is to remain united and strong in the face of adversity. We also want you to know that you are as much a part of us as we were once in your position and that we care about you.

As Joe has said to us (and you as well) that this is "YOUR TEAM" and that "it is up to you to forge your own destiny."

You rarely hear of us or see us and that is by design as we respect the need for you to find your way through the Penn State Football experience without our interference. But understand: We always have your back and will always be with you currently and for the rest of your lives.

Proudly,
The Penn State Football
Letterman's Club.

After that letter was read to the team, there was an addendum that was sent over to be read. Joe was aware that the lettermen were going to read a letter, and it was sent to him. After he read the heartfelt words, he wanted to add something to the letter.

THE LETTER FROM JOE PATERNO

P.S. Things being different than my last meeting with our team it's great to know that your older teammates care so much about you and Penn State Football tradition. Remember what I said you will always be teammates and you will always be Penn State Football players.

Be Proud- Be your best.

Beat Nebraska.

It breaks my heart that I can't be at the game.

These were the last words that Joe Paterno ever communicated to his team.

After that meeting, practice was a surreal experience. We practiced at our indoor practice facility to keep all the distractions away. Inside there were still distractions.

McQueary had become a focal point of the story, and there was pressure from the administration to prevent him from coaching in the game. The details of those discussions weren't made known to us, but as we practiced he walked the perimeter of the field on his phone. I don't know who he was talking to, nor do I know the substance of the conversation.

Finally, after practice my family and I took dinner over to my parents. As we arrived at the house, I got out of the car and crossed the street to the assembled media. I asked them to respect the privacy of my children. To their credit they honored my request.

When my children got out of the car, it was a shock. A trip to see their grandparents had changed. Throngs of people were across the street with cameras and microphones. My youngest daughter had a confused look on her face that I can still see.

When we got into the house, we talked about the kids' days at school, we talked about family, we talked about everything but what was going on outside the house. My father pulled me aside to see how practice had gone. "Dad," I said, "it is not the same."

"Jay, it was going to have to change sometime."

"I know, but this whole thing is a mess. I'm not sure they're going to let Mike coach on Saturday. For that matter I'm not sure they'll let me."

He looked at me and just shook his head. "I honestly don't know who is running the store," he said.

"No one does. Not only is no one running the store, no one's watching out for it either," I said.

At dinner we did have some lighthearted moments. My seven-year-old son, Zack, had a concern. "Now that Granddad doesn't have a job will they send him back to Italy?" he asked.

From the mouths of babes came a much-needed moment of levity. There wouldn't be many more.

By Friday morning the circus was in full swing. Added to the usual big-game chaos, media hordes were running all over town. There were legitimate security concerns because some people advocated cancelling the game, and protests were being planned.

Everyone in the athletic department received a form to keep by our phones and fill out in the event we received a called-in bomb threat. Atop the sheet it instructed us to: "Be Calm, Be Courteous, Listen Carefully, Do Not Interrupt."

Among the questions we were to ask: What kind of bomb is it? What will make it explode? Did you place the bomb? Why? On the back of the sheet we were to circle all the adjectives of the caller's voice, among them: Calm, Loud, Nasal, Slurred, Deep Breathing.

By late morning I had a meeting with the crew doing the game on television. Each week we met with them to give them information on the team and general insights to make the broadcast more entertaining. Before I went in, Guido D'Elia grabbed me. "There are people in this meeting on the news side of ESPN," he said. "That means they're looking for a quote or news. They'll be listening to see if you have anything they can run on the ticker at the bottom of ESPN."

At that point Penn State had our own category on the ESPN ticker. Alongside NCAA Football, NFL, NBA, and NHL was Penn State all by itself with ticker updates from the latest developments.

As I went into the meeting, the crew was Dave Pasch and Chris Spielman. I was comfortable because I knew them. Spielman had done an earlier game that year. The Friday before that game, Joe recalled his recruiting visit to Spielman's home decades earlier. He described the living room exactly as it was. Chris couldn't believe it.

Despite our familiarity I was careful not to trip any wires that would create a news event.

That morning I was told the school wanted me to coach from the sideline rather than upstairs where I usually was during games. I knew it might be emotional. I talked with a former player who told me to keep my poise on the sideline. "They want you to blow up, so avoid their trap," he warned.

Then he asked about my son, Joey. I assured him that he was okay, but I wanted him to stay home from the game. My friend talked me into allowing him to go to the game, so he could see a new reality for himself. "It will be better for him to accept it now," he said.

The rest of the afternoon followed a fairly normal Friday routine. Unknown to me, though, trouble was brewing across town. My parents had decided to get out of town Saturday, but my father was coughing up blood.

The doctor decided to bring him in for a test before they left town. The problem was that there was no way to move Joe Paterno without the world's assembled media knowing. They put a blanket over him to keep him out of sight. Then they opened the garage and drove away.

No one saw him, and they assumed he was still in the house. As he got out of the neighborhood, he sat up. As they passed Beaver Stadium he wondered aloud something that will stay with my sister and mother forever. "Good old Beaver Stadium...I wonder if I'll ever set foot in there again," he said.

At the hospital he went in a back door and got chest X-rays. No one knew what the problem was, but the trip was on hold.

I knew none of this.

As Friday drew to a close I drove home, making a left turn up a hill into my neighborhood. In the distance I could see the stadium lights. How many Fridays had I driven past that stadium and dreamt about the next day's game? As I drove up the hill, I looked at the stadium, slowed to a stop, and realized that this may the last time I coached in that stadium.

November 10, 2011

Dear Jay,

I cannot imagine your feelings and those of your family as you move through this drama. When I called my Dad last night he was crying. He said the only events in his life that he can recall having that kind of impact on him were the Kennedy assassination and 9/11. My night was completely sleepless, as it was for the members of the silent vast majority who know the real Joe Paterno.

Obviously the board handled this with no class. Just as Joe brought class and prestige to the program, we all knew the school would operate with less class when he was no longer there. This is not cancer and this is not death. With the benefit of some time and perspective all of us will come to terms with what happened. The damage done to Joe will begin to soften and improve among his critics. It is now a process.

There will be positive lessons to be learned from the events of the past week. Frankly, the week has rocked me to my core. I spent much time last night discussing the fact that it is amazing what it takes to remind one of what a cruel and ugly world it can be. There are too many people who love to hate.

The worst of this is seeing your parents hurt...

You do not worry about what you cannot control and you do not worry about those who do not understand what you are all about. Like the greatest teachers, your dad has had a positive impact on countless lives. That impact continues to positively impact our society for generations. What on earth could be better than that!

Your Friend,
Charles

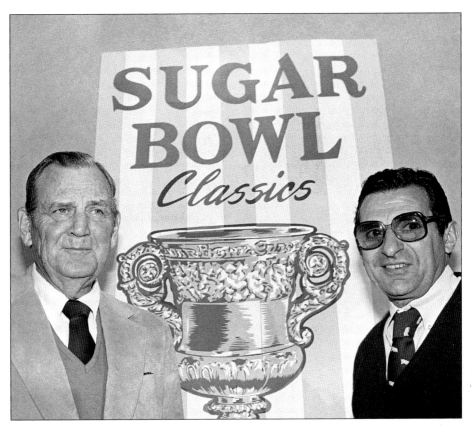

Coaching luminaries, Alabama's Paul "Bear" Bryant and Penn State's Joe Paterno, pose before facing each other in the Sugar Bowl. Bryant called our house to convince Joe to play in the New Orleans-based game. (AP Images)

During the recruiting process, Joe Paterno shrewdly targeted quarterback Kerry Collins, who won Big Ten Offensive Player of the Year honors in 1994, rather than Miami-bound Frank Costa. (AP Images)

A 2006 first-round draft pick, Tamba Hali, who fled civil war in Liberia, is one of the many well-rounded student-athletes to play for Joe Paterno. (AP Images)

Penn State safety Mark Rubin strips quarterback Terrelle Pryor, which was a game-changing play in Penn State's 13–6 win at Ohio State in 2008. (AP Images)

Despite the attacks launched at Joe Paterno, Penn State fans and students remain prideful during the game vs. Nebraska, the first contest the Nittany Lions played without Joe as their coach. (AP Images)

Penn State students express their support for Joe Paterno during Thanksgiving of 2011.

Quarterback Michael Robinson, who had a special relationship with Joe and me, rushes for a first down against Wisconsin. (AP Images)

Michael Robinson listens to the applause after he spoke so eloquently at Joe Paterno's memorial service. The former Penn State star flew 10,000 miles just to be at the service for a seven-hour period. (AP Images)

Two figures close to Joe Paterno, former Penn State quarterback Todd Blackledge (left) and Nike co-founder Phil Knight (right), take the stage at Joe's moving memorial service. (AP Images)

Emotions get the best of Nike co-founder Phil Knight as he vehemently defends Joe Paterno during his impassioned speech at the memorial service. (AP Images)

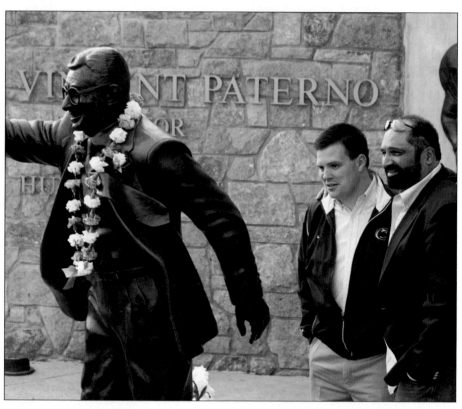

Legendary Penn State running back Franco Harris and I visit the statue of Joe Paterno before the 2012 Blue-White scrimmage. (AP Images)

Chapter 26

World Turned Upside Down

Saturday, November 12, 2011

Saturday—a day that I knew would come eventually had arrived too soon. Everyone knew Joe Paterno was mortal and at some point he'd no longer be Penn State's coach—just not yet and not like this.

Mortality and morality were not in short supply this fall morning.

For the first time since 1949, Penn State football would take the field without Joe Paterno on the staff. Even though he'd told me to keep coaching, I couldn't help but feel some disloyalty in doing so.

It would be vital for me to handle my emotions. That morning I went to my den and wrote a letter to my parents. It was the love and support they'd given me that enabled me to become a decent human being. I wanted to put into writing how I felt—a letter to make up for lost time between my parents and me.

As some tears came, I stopped writing, pausing because I didn't want to ruin the words on the paper, words I'd meant to say for years, words I *owed* them. I *owed* them because I was far from a model child, because they'd always given me a place to come home to and reground my life.

Once my father had sent me an article about perseverance. In the article was a quote from a note Richard Nixon had written to Ted Kennedy after Chappaquiddick. The quote was, "A man's not finished until he quits."

I put that lesson into the letter for my parents and things I should have said a long time ago. Near the end of the letter, I shared a sentiment that in my heart I found to be almost always true: "I know that we haven't always seen eye to eye, but it was usually because I had to grow up to be on your level."

After finishing the letter, I went up to say goodbye to Kelley. "Stay strong," she urged. "I know it's gonna be tough but stay strong."

There were hugs from my five kids on the way out before I started up the car, sat for just a moment, and then drove into the future.

Across town my father woke to find he was coughing up more blood. Although the day before he had slipped away to get a chest X-ray, he'd have to go back.

Dr. Sebastianelli arranged to get Joe into the back of the hospital unnoticed. Every movement in his life would lead to a rumor. With satellite trucks, cameras, and journalists set up across the street, he would be followed. It wasn't easy moving one of the most visible people in the world. As he'd done Friday, Joe got under a blanket in the backseat of the car while the garage door was still closed.

About that same time, I was driving to the hotel where our team stayed Friday night on a road that ran alongside Spring Creek. It is a pretty drive in the fall.

Before pregame church services, I was greeted by Father David Griffin. Our campus priests Father Matthew and Father David are good friends. I could see the sadness as I shook Father David's hand before Mass. I knew he felt much of the same pain I was feeling.

It would be a familiar theme throughout the day.

Normally I'm focused in our pregame Masses. But my mind kept wandering to thoughts of my mother and father. Just days earlier Joe had been planning for this game. Now he was relegated to watching it at home on television.

In my mind I pictured him in his den that afternoon, watching this team play—a team he'd brought to the brink of a Big Ten title and top 10 national ranking, a team he'd taught to sacrifice personal preferences for the team cause.

Just three days earlier, Dan McGinn asked me how I saw all of this ending. Twelve hours after I'd spoken about a Rose Bowl berth, it was all over, and there would be no Hollywood ending.

My attention returned to Father David talking about the seniors on our team, playing for the last time in Beaver Stadium. From Mass we went into a solemn pregame meal.

As I left the hotel to continue my usual pregame routine, the thoughts that this could be the last time I did this were heavy on my mind. Everything was new because Joe Paterno was not there, but I knew every step might be the last I would leave on this path.

By the time I pulled into my parents' driveway, I got my thoughts together so that the assembled media across the street would not see any emotion.

I walked into the kitchen with the letter I had for my parents and yelled for my mother and father. No one answered, which seemed odd given that they were essentially trapped within their own home.

My sister Diana was on the phone talking. On the counter in the kitchen was a note in my mother's handwriting. It said, "Call and tell them we may be late. Joe coughed up blood again, and we went to the hospital."

Talking on the wall phone by the kitchen sink, she knew my eyes had seen the note. I was processing what was written. She hung up the phone quickly and saw a puzzled look on my face. "You weren't supposed to see that," she said. "Well, I did. What's going on?" I asked.

"It's nothing."

I knew she was lying. My father never went to the hospital. "Jay, you weren't supposed to see that. Dad didn't want you to know. He wanted you to focus on the game."

"I'll try," I said

Then I gave her the note for my parents before heading to the door to walk to the game. As I left the house, the media filmed, clicked photos, and yelled questions as I started up my parents' sidewalk as I had so many times before.

On my shoulders I wore my father's coat. It was unique, instantly recognizable to everyone as *his* coat. That was what I wanted. I was angry, wanting to yell in defiance. I resented the people who'd done this to my father, to our university, and to me.

So I wore his coat and I walked with my head held high. I wore no Penn State logos for the first half of the game. In fact a few of the coaches had talked about wearing black armbands or ties in tribute to Joe. Many of us felt Penn State's administration had abandoned us, turning their backs on Joe Paterno and on us.

But I had to manage the defiance I felt. I took my usual path through campus and past some tailgaters. They walked to me, embraced me, yelled to me: "Your father should be here," "We miss your father," "We love Joe."

There was a group that I passed on my way every home game. Each week they wished me luck. This week all of them came to me with sadness in their eyes. Some were crying. Where there had always been good-natured ribbing, now there were hugs, emotional hugs.

When I finally reached the football building, I went to my office. As I looked at my game plan, I heard a knock. It was Tom Bradley. "Jay, you usually walk over to the game from here, right?" he asked.

"Yeah."

"They want you to take the bus. It's about security. They may have protesters and are concerned about your safety."

"Okay."

He asked if I was okay, so I assured him I was fine and he left. A few minutes later coach Bill Kenney came in and closed the door. "Jay, are you okay?" he asked.

"Of course not, but I will be," I said.

"Look, you're on the sideline. Keep your cool, don't get emotional. All eyes will be on you and everything you do this afternoon. You can't break down. *Do not* let them see that."

"I got it. If I have any trouble, I'll find you."

"Do that. Just keep talking and stay in it. They can't wait to see you fail. Like your father would tell you, just keep your poise."

Already I'd gotten the same message in an earlier text from Scott. They knew the weight I was carrying, but they didn't know all of it. My mind kept going back to my father in the hospital.

At 10 AM an email came through from Amy Mann, a member of the athletic department:

SUBJECT: Bomb Threat @ Beaver Stadium

UNIVERSITY PARK, Pa.—Penn State received an anonymous bomb threat Friday night (Nov. 11) for Beaver Stadium. Police and FBI are investigating. Police, who have had the stadium secured since Tuesday, used bomb-sniffing dogs as well as additional personnel to check the

stadium and nothing was found. They searched the area
again this morning, and again found nothing.

Finally it came time to board the bus. We left Joe's seat open—a reminder
by omission.

The ride was emotional with the fans turning out and cheering us on.
There was a burden on the shoulders of every Penn Stater, and it was evident
in their faces. I could sense it.

But the fans could yell and cheer, and it was their primal scream therapy.
In just over a week this Happy Valley, this noble university, had been torn
down by lies, and where we stood proud was bound to each other as never
before by the casting of collective guilt.

No one yet knew the truth, but they knew their players were innocent
and they knew that the coach they loved, the coach they longed to say goodbye to, was taken from them. So they came and they cheered the team and
they raised their voices.

Finally the bus pulled up, and as we exited, I could hear the yells and the
cheers and the support and feel the love. The crowd at the stadium when
the buses arrived was huge.

I walked onto the field for the pregame warm-ups and I saw so many
familiar faces. Guys from the 1970s like Mike Guman, from the 1990s like
Ki-Jana Carter and Brandon Short, and from the 2000s like quarterback
Zack Mills were all part of more than 100 former players on our sideline.
Generations of men whose lives had been molded, changed, or impacted by
Joe Paterno were there to support us and support him. I hugged so many of
them, and the tears were in all of our eyes.

Ki-Jana and Ken Jackson grabbed me and reminded me to be strong
and not let anyone see what I was feeling inside.

At the same time, my wife and oldest son, Joey, were heading into the
stadium to sit in the suites. I didn't want them to go, especially alone, but
our friend Chris Jelic agreed to come up from Pittsburgh and go to the
game with them.

My wife felt it was important for Joey to go. He picked a T-shirt with
my father's face on the front to wear. As they entered the stadium suites,
they found themselves on the elevator with trustees Steve Garban and Paul
Suhey, part of the board that fired Joe.

Kelley stood silent but proudly defiant. She wanted them to see her still-proud son. Later, when Chris told me, I saw my wife's strength as never before.

On the field the game was at hand. When both teams came back to the field, there was a pre-arranged joint team prayer that was to be a moment of silence. A Nebraska coach led the prayer. I resented our administration allowing their coach to lead the prayer—as though no one at our school was fit to lead the prayer. Looking back, I understand why it happened, but my emotions at the time were as I just described.

I also felt that the administration was unfairly overplaying the emotion of the day. They'd talked about this team starting the healing process. This was a football game. A game does temporarily lift our spirits through moments of escape, but it doesn't heal anything.

When the prayer was going on, I thought of my father in the hospital. My mind was wondering what was going on there. At the same time, Penn State was kicking off their first game without Joe Paterno. He was in a hospital a block or two from the stadium, finding out he had a mass in his lungs.

All game the sun bathed the stadium in golden fall light—aural sunshine for a valley that had weathered such a brutal media storm for over a week. Even now the details of the game are hard to remember.

After halftime we got going. We were behind 17–0 but scored a third-quarter touchdown to get back in the game. The fans and the team were roaring back to life.

With nine and a half minutes left to go in the game, the defense got the ball back on a turnover. After making a fourth and 1, we ran two plays that netted two yards. Facing third and 8, quarterback Matt McGloin completed a pass to wide receiver Justin Brown for a first down to set us up at the Nebraska 22-yard line. On the very first play in the red zone, I knew exactly what I was going to call. "I want gimmick 4," I said as I signaled in the play.

On the headsets I heard Galen Hall ask what I had called. "Bone Rt Over 42 Reverse Pitch Pass…it's the throwback," I said. "This one's for the boss."

We broke the huddle and lined up. When the pitch went to the tailback, Nebraska's defense flew to the ball. Then the tailback flipped it to the receiver, Curtis Drake, who ran around the end until he pulled up and threw the ball. McGloin made the catch and nearly scored. We called it just as I had promised my father in his last staff meeting. I hoped he was watching.

The very next play we scored to close the gap to 17–14.

It would be nice if the game story ended with a comeback win, but messy reality often interrupts perfect endings. We fought until we were stopped on a critical fourth down and 1. Even after the defeat, our fans stood and cheered both teams. For a few hours on the field, we'd had an escape from the chaos of the week.

But it would return.

On my way off the field, I was grabbed by ESPN's Tom Rinaldi. Tom asked me some questions, and I held until he asked what I wanted to say to Joe. Then I cried, saying that I wished he'd been here. I thanked Tom and headed off the field.

After the game sports information director Jeff Nelson told me I had media requests, which was not abnormal. But I warned Jeff that this would be chaotic. This would be the media's first crack at a member of the Paterno family since the firing. After interim president Rodney Erickson went in and droned on about the steps they were taking, which no one reported on, interim head coach Tom Bradley went in. After he was done, I went in, and for the next 13 minutes or so, it was a battle to maintain my poise.

A few minutes into the postgame questions, I was asked if Joe had planned to watch the game on television and I visibly hesitated because I realized that he had probably been at the hospital.

I was asked a few times about what he was doing and where my family was during the game. In my dealings with the media, I hadn't lied. I've avoided questions—avoidance but not dishonesty.

That afternoon my head was still spinning. There was no way for me to know what the media knew. Did anyone know he was at the hospital? Would we be able to keep that quiet?

Amid the questions I kept coming back to lessons I'd learned about handling media and press conferences. It was the toughest 10 minutes of media I'd ever faced up to that point in my life. As I stood to go after answering the questions, I had to push my way through the reporters to get out of the room. Thankfully my friend Ben Bouma was there to help get me out.

Outside the media room, my friend Mike Hammond was waiting for us. Mike and Ben had decided to walk home with me. With all the uncertainty, I realized that it wouldn't be a good idea to make that walk alone. On the way home as we walked through the last tailgates of the home season and maybe the last tailgates I'd see as a member of Penn State's staff, I noticed the sadness in the eyes of fans who approached me. This was the first day of Penn State football after Joe Paterno with so much uncertainty ahead.

There wasn't a lot any of us could say to each other. People still had on their blue jerseys. Young boys still threw the football around. For them this game was just a tough loss. For their parents and grandparents it was so much more. It was the closing of a big book, a long saga that they had been a part of for decades.

Sure it would continue, but it would never, ever be the same, and they knew it.

I knew it.

Each step toward the house marked a last walk in my life. By the time we reached the border of my parents' neighborhood on Park Avenue, I noticed neighborhood kids having a bake sale. We stopped to buy brownies and cookies, and the photographers who had been following us snapped pictures.

We walked down Holmes Street, past the house where Mike had grown up two blocks from my childhood home. Now he was here when this part of my life was ending.

As we emerged onto McKee Street, the media snapped to life, yelling questions and taking pictures. What had always been a quiet walk home from the games with my father had ended now with me not even knowing where he was or what was wrong with him.

As I got into the house, Diana informed me that he had not returned yet, but that everything was okay. Nothing could have been further from the truth.

The world had turned upside down.

SENT: Saturday November 12, 2011 5:32 PM
TO: Jay Paterno
SUBJECT: tears for your father

Bottom line, Jay Paterno: The most powerful, the most influential man at Penn State, your father, knew that a boy was raped and he looked the other way. Joe Paterno does not deserve a single tear. Shame on the whole rotten lot of you who place football higher than a life of a child. I hope the class actions suits that are coming your way bring you to your knees and force you to understand that ALL tears should be for those forsaken children, not your lousy, worthless, empty football program

Edwina

Chapter 27

Up Against It

Thursday, January 19, 2012

It had been nearly a week since my father went back into the hospital. As I walked in, I thought about what hospitals mean: happy healings, childbirths, or sad diagnoses or the end of a life. I walked the main hallway with my head down, hoping to avoid being seen by anyone who would tell people that my father was back in the hospital. Privacy was long gone, but there were some small shreds we tried to hold onto and protect.

A week earlier we were all sitting at the kitchen table with a crowd of people. The next day my brother Scott and I had to help Joe get into his bed. After a life of great health and incredible self-reliance, it bothered him to require help, but my parents' upbeat outlook convinced me that everything would be okay.

I stopped into the hospital to see him that weekend and during the next week. He didn't talk much, but he listened and he talked when he had something to say. He laughed and made jokes. His spirits were high as if nothing was wrong except needing some rest. We talked about starting our walks again in a few weeks.

The walks were fleeting moments we had outside the house, but so much had changed with his illness. But we knew he'd make it through. My father and I would walk together again; he always came back from everything.

Thursday morning it started to change. They put a tube in to try and clear his lungs. He was on a ventilator. Thursday evening I drove to see him and stayed about an hour. Though he'd had a setback, he seemed solid and strong. When it was time to go, I was upbeat.

On my way out of the hospital, I bumped into my dad's doctor. Quietly he relayed what was happening with my dad. My upbeat outlook ran into reality. "Jay, your dad is really up against it," he said.

"Up against it?" I asked.

"He's up against it."

When your father is 85 and battling cancer, you know what he is "up against." I still refused to believe the worst; he'd come back. He'd been up against it so many times in his life and every time he fought back. This couldn't be different. There was just no way.

As I drove away, the sky was brilliant. The sun was setting beyond the stadium into a bright yellow on the far horizon, giving way to orange light, darkening blue skies, and a purple light on the clouds. It was an incredible canvas onto which God chose to paint a masterpiece.

It was like the hundreds of sunsets I'd seen on the practice fields at Penn State on crisp autumn nights when the sun's last light would cast a purple aura over Mount Nittany. After many of those glorious sunsets my father would ask me, "Did you catch that sunset?"

On that Thursday night, I hoped my father could see this one from his room.

Chapter 28

The Final Hours

Friday, January 20, 2012–Sunday, January 22, 2012
Friday morning I got a call from Mary that I was needed at the hospital very soon. After hearing the previous evening that my father was "up against it," it was the last message I wanted. At the hospital I learned that my worst fears were real so I decided to stay there until he was out of danger or…

I didn't want to even think that.

My father didn't look like he was fading. He was aware, nodding when you talked to him. He slept a lot, but we talked to him.

Morning stretched into afternoon.

Two days before, a group of Penn State's trustees had met with a reporter from *The New York Times*, asserting Joe Paterno had to be fired because of his moral failings and a failure of leadership. The story had run on Thursday.

That story was out there as I sat next to my father, watching the last sands of his life's hourglass starting to run out. I harbored anger toward the trustees, but being next to my father I remembered his lifelong advice: "Don't get in a pissing contest with a skunk."

I forgot my anger to focus on being there for my father.

Perhaps all children watching an ill parent fighting the last fight of their life come to a place where you want what is easiest for them. Selfishly you hope that they survive, but a moment arrives when you know their survival to a life they never wanted is just selfish on your part.

You hope that if their time is fated, that God allows it to come painlessly and in a dignified manner.

By late Friday afternoon, I had come to the realization.

My kids stopped by with Kelley. I kept a brave face and optimism for them. I suspect my wife saw through me and knew I was lying, but she too wanted to believe.

I talked to my dad when he was awake. I kept quiet when he was sleeping. When I talked he'd nod. The afternoon stretched into evening. Every time I looked at the clock, I thought of "tempus Fugit," the Latin phrase for "time flies" from two years of Latin I'd taken in high school because *he* made me.

Now I was painfully aware of time's unceasing march—my father's life now measured in hours. Outside it was growing dark, and I wondered if that day's sunset was to be my father's last. I did not know if he would make the dawn.

As it grew late, my mother and sisters went home, and I was alone with my father. As he drifted off to sleep, I made notes on my iPad about my father, my life with him, memories from childhood, and coaching with him.

I recalled great wins and tough losses, times when we fought and times when we hugged.

Sitting alone in a hospital room with him, I listened to him breathe and watched the heart rate monitor. I wanted a sign, something to tell me he would be okay, he would pull through.

I drifted to sleep in a chair in the room. Every hour or so, a nurse would come in to check on him, give him a new IV, or adjust his medication. It would jolt me from my sleep, and I would sit there quietly. In 17 years coaching with him, we'd shared some tough days. As Friday turned to Saturday, there was nowhere on Earth I would have rather been.

As the sun began to rise on Saturday, my mother and sisters came back. I needed to go home and clean up. At home I saw my children, and the oldest ones knew something serious was going on. The kids all wanted to go see Granddad. By the time I arrived back at the hospital, my brother Dave had returned.

The minutes of that day seemed to fly by, but the moments will never leave me. We laughed a lot. We cried and told stories, so my father could hear in our voices just how much we loved him.

When my kids came in, I saw scared looks on their faces, and it broke my heart. He squeezed their hands, he listened to them and he tried to impart last lessons to them. He knew the end was near and he wanted them to know how much he loved them.

After some time Kelley took the kids home except for my oldest son, Joey. He didn't want to leave; he felt so much loyalty to my father. The previous two months had forced him to deal with an ever-changing set of life circumstances, and this end was too fast in coming.

The rest of the morning and early afternoon he stayed. Mary and Diana were there, my mother was there, and Dave came in and out. I pulled up Pandora to listen to music. I turned on a Frank Sinatra channel, and his iconic voice filled the room.

Pandora pulled up "Somewhere Over The Rainbow" by Hawaiian singer Israel Kamakawiwo'ole. Even now when I hear that song, it takes me to that time when I held onto hope that my father would survive. A few songs later, my mother was in the room, and Louis Armstrong's classic, "What A Wonderful World" came on. It is one of my mother's favorite songs and the song Diana danced to for her first wedding dance with her husband, Gary.

Tears came to my mother's eyes. I witnessed one of the most beautiful moments of my entire life. In a sterile hospital room full of monitors and the scent of sickness, a light shone on my mother and father. My father's eyes opened wide as my mother pressed her forehead to his, grabbed his hand, and through the tears sang along in a voice strong and clear.

Part of me felt I should leave them there, allow them that moment. But God wanted me there to see true love. After two months of chaos and things crashing down, my mother's commitment to my father never wavered. All of us can only hope that after so many years of marriage that we, too, will have a bond as strong.

In the heat of hell on Earth, my mother walked along with my father to this conclusion and shared a moment like that with him. Best of all my father knew how much they loved each other.

I read Dylan Thomas' classic poem "Do Not Go Gentle into That Good Night." How badly I wanted my father to "Rage, rage against the dying of the light."

There was a moment of pride as I watched my son read Rudyard Kipling's poem "If" to my father, a poem my father had shared with me and now had taken on a whole new meaning in my life. As Joey read it to him, I saw my father fighting the ventilator to mouth the words of the poem from memory along with my son.

After reading the poem, Joey promised he'd do better in school and in sports. Then I saw a tear in my father's eye. Perhaps my father realized how much this boy, just a week or so past his 12th birthday, had been forced to grow up so quickly. There were few delusions that my father would live to see what his grandchildren would become, and those words probably hit to the core of that.

As the tear appeared, I could see my father straining to raise himself. As he did he mouthed the words, "Just do your best" to Joey. He mouthed it twice to make sure he saw what he meant.

Mary said to Joey, "Did you see that, Joey? He said to do your best."

A little later he asked us if he could be alone with my father. Through the window in my father's hospital room, I could see in from the hall. Joey was talking to his grandfather. Someday, maybe when I am lying in a hospital bed he'll tell me what he said. But I will never forget seeing that young man growing up so fast in a last afternoon spent with his dying grandfather.

Throughout the afternoon and evening, all of us—children and grandchildren—had moments alone to tell my father something we wanted him to hear before he died. Through the hospital room window, the scene played out over and over with no one wanting something left unsaid.

Later in the afternoon, Father Matthew and Father David performed a Mass for us. We all assembled in my father's room. We knew this would be the last Mass we shared together, the last of a Catholic tradition that my parents' families had given them.

After Mass I saw Dr. Dranov and tried to get an idea of what we were in for. He told Mary and I that a remote chance existed that he'd pull through, but there was also a chance he would not make it through the evening. He told us we might reach a point of no turning back whereupon the decision would have to be made to let God's will take its course and put him on a morphine drip so the pain would not be too great.

It is a decision that has to be made by families every day all over America.

Across campus some trustees had gotten wind that Joe was not doing well. Having just been in an article questioning Joe's morality, it was not going to be good timing to have publicly attacked a dying man. A trustee who lived in town was trying to find out how bad things were with Joe and he was trying to reach out to us through a mutual friend. I was angry. Dan McGinn and Scott got similar calls.

I called Scott, and he shared my resentment. "I wish they would've called and talked to Joe just once in early November before they fired him," Scott said.

"If they're looking for some deathbed absolution from Dad, they are not going to get it. No way in hell," I said. "I am as mad as you are, but let Wick and Dan call these guys back. Dad is not doing well. Right now you need to be a son, not his lawyer. That's the best thing you can do for him and for yourself."

Before dinner I started to text very close friends of Joe that we would like them to come see Joe before Sunday. They all came. Each and every one dropped what they were doing to be there.

Former players, including Franco Harris, came to see him. He smiled and told me how proud I should be of my father's life. Guido D'Elia came in, Dr. Wayne Sebastianelli, who had patched Joe up a few times, came to see him. Tom Venturino, who'd worked for Joe's brother George before coming to Penn State a quarter of a century earlier, came by.

Everyone who came by got a few moments alone with Joe. He could hear what they said and he nodded as they spoke. He was there in body and mind, but for the first time in his life, he couldn't exert his mind's will over the systems that kept him alive.

Kenny Jackson and I had both coached with him, so we talked football with my father. I kidded him about always having a trick play in his back pocket. "Dad," I said, "if you have any more of those trick plays left or if you have a play call that can turn this around, now would be the time to pull out that sheet of paper."

I took out a pad and diagramed the plays of calls he'd made in big games. There was a touchdown pass to beat Nebraska in 1982, a wide receiver screen to beat Michigan State in 1995, a double reverse that broke open the Fiesta Bowl against Texas, a deep pass to beat Georgia for the 1982 National Championship, the post route to beat Michigan in 1994, the wheel route to beat Ohio State in 2001, and the corner route to beat Northwestern in 2005. He was smiling and following the diagrams. For a few moments, we were back in a staff meeting.

Finally Tim Curley came by. Joe had not seen Tim since all of this had happened, and Joe rose up in his bed, extended his hands to Tim, and started to mouth how sorry he was for what Tim was going through.

Joe had watched Tim Curley grow from college to become one of the most respected athletic directors in the country. Tim helped build a welcoming family atmosphere for student-athletes and coaches, a program that competed at the highest levels in the classroom and in athletic competition. Now he had been forced out, and the atmosphere he had built was being replaced by an atmosphere of fear.

But at that moment, it made Joe happy to see the love all of these men had for him.

Around 9:00 I started to get some texts from people, telling me how sorry they were about my father. A student website reported that Joe had died. That report was picked up by CBS News, who carried it all over the world. People were starting to gather at my father's statue to mourn. Across town friends at a party toasted my father's life.

I had to leave the room and leave my father's side to call Scott and Dan McGinn to see what we should do. It was decided that we should tweet something out. Here I was amid the last hours of my father's life forced to leave his room and cross the hall to go on social media.

Jay Paterno @jaypaterno 1/21/12 9:22 PM

@jaypaterno I appreciate the support & prayers. Joe is continuing to fight.

From Twitter

The post went all over the place, but I knew I was just delaying the inevitable. The end was at hand, but selfishly I wanted him to make it back out of the hospital and give everyone the finger. But even had he made it, he wouldn't have done that.

By late evening it was clear that my mother and sisters needed some sleep, so I told them to go home. I agreed to stay through the night again. I did not want him to be alone if the end would come. My brother-in-law Gary and Dave stayed a while, too. The three of us talked about my father, mostly laughing at funny stories from years long past.

In the middle of the night, my father and I were alone again in his room.

On the television in the room, I had ESPN's Australian Open coverage on. I could hear Chris Fowler's voice calling the action. I'd known Chris Fowler for years, and my father had known him even longer. Chris had lived in State College while his father was a professor at Penn State.

It was a long night. Nurses came in often; they were so kind and sympathetic. Part of me knew that they go through this almost every day with other patients, but they made me feel unique and special and for that I'm eternally grateful.

The night moved slowly. I talked to him when he seemed to be awake. When he slept I would take out my iPad and note memories that were flooding back to me. From childhood, my wedding, moments long forgotten, my father's impending mortality unlocked stories for me to talk about with him one more time. I wanted to hear his voice one more time, but I knew it was lost forever.

Every time a nurse came in, I looked at the time. The night marched on and on. I looked out the window to the parking lot several floors below and in the light I could see it was snowing outside. But light was starting to come, the inevitable last sunrise of my father's life.

The rest of my family started to arrive. I asked Wayne Sebastianelli to sneak in a bottle of Old Granddad. With my mother, my siblings, and Guido assembled, we poured the bourbon and had a toast to my father. Mary gave some to my dad, and he smiled.

This was to be a difficult day for my mother if she was going to have to make any decisions about my father. However, once all of his children were in place he started to slip quietly away.

I could see what was happening. He'd waited until all his children were there and would go before my mother had to make a decision. Even to the end, he went the way he wanted and only when he was ready to go.

Text message sent to my friends on January 22, 2012

10:11 AM "Joe Paterno passed away a few moments ago. As was his way he fought all the way and left on his own terms."

"The courage of life is often a less dramatic spectacle than the courage of a final moment; but it is no less a magnificent mixture of triumph and tragedy." —John F. Kennedy

Chapter 29

A Public Mourning

Sunday, January 22, 2012–Wednesday, January 25, 2012
Outside the window I saw a world covered in a blanket of pure white snow, a blanket that had fallen during the night. The world around us just for that brief moment was clean and whole. We had seen my father die, and nothing could hurt him anymore.

Quietly I edged out to a room across the hall where we met to start discussing what came next. The discussion with Guido D'Elia and my brothers was focused on getting my mother out of the hospital's back door and safely back home before we gave a release to the media.

My father had died less than 15 minutes earlier, and we were across the hall discussing media releases, public memorial services, and viewings. Even in this moment, there was work to do. It was unreal and it robbed me of the reality to accept and mourn.

There was also security to consider. It sounds morbid to say it now, but there was genuine concern that my father's body be moved privately. We certainly did not want any pictures of him to surface. Dignity was a concern. None of us wanted our children to have the specter of pictures of their dead grandfather on the Internet.

I give the people at Mount Nittany Medical Center all the credit in the world. Nothing can prep anyone for this, but they did a great job protecting us.

Once my mother was home, we issued a release confirming the inevitable. We decided on a preliminary plan of a public on-campus viewing all day Tuesday and Wednesday morning followed by a private funeral. Then we would have a public memorial service on Thursday in the basketball arena, the Bryce Jordan Center.

As I got up to leave, Guido grabbed my arm. Joe was like a second father to him and Joe looked at Guido like a member of our family. "Jay," Guido said, "get home, see your kids, and get working on what you're going to say on Thursday. This is really important."

After going to my mother's house, we returned to my house and sat around the dining room table. Kelley came into the room from time to time as we discussed what would happen the next few days.

Months later I found my notes from that meeting. Guido wanted to have a player from all six decades of Joe Paterno's career speak at the memorial service. It was tough to narrow it down. For the 1960s we agreed on Charlie Pittman, for the 1980s it was Todd Blackledge, and for the 2000s it would be Michael Robinson. For the 1970s a few names got tossed until Jimmy Cefalo's name jumped at us. For the 1990s Guido chose Chris Marrone, a player who had *not* played in the NFL. Despite a career-ending injury in college, Chris found Joe remained committed to him through graduation and a successful career that carried him to the Defense Department as an aide to Donald Rumsfeld.

There was one hitch. Michael Robinson was in Hawaii to play in the NFL's Pro Bowl. He agreed to come back, but he needed to find a way back. Phil Knight agreed to give Michael a ride on the Nike jet to the West Coast immediately after the memorial service. Michael would make a 10,000-mile round-trip to be at Penn State for seven hours to honor his coach. He would be in town just seven hours, but his words would echo long after he'd headed back.

At one point I remembered something my father had said to me after going to the Jewish funeral of longtime friend Sid Friedman. "You know, Jay," he laughed, "the Jewish people do it right. You die one day, and the next they mourn, get you in the ground, and off they go. I hope you guys will do the same for me."

Retelling the story to Guido, we both laughed. "Boy, would he be mad at us," Guido said.

After it was decided what the plans would be, the attention turned to what I would say at the nationally televised memorial. It would be scrutinized by people looking for anger and for signals about how we felt about the trustees and administration that had turned on Joe Paterno. I got to work.

The rest of the day people brought food to the house, and relatives were in and out of our home. I asked my mother where their burial plots were, and she revealed that she and my father had never picked them. "Mom, you never picked a plot?" I asked.

"No," she said.

"Mom, Dad was 85 and had lung cancer."

"We just never thought it would happen," she laughed a little.

Optimistic to the very end, my parents really did believe he would beat his lung cancer. We divided up the jobs among the five kids. My brother Dave would get all the logistics done as they related to getting people from place to place. He and my sisters would also help Mom pick the burial plot.

Scott and I would help handle the public part of this with help from Guido, Dan, and Mara Vandlik, who worked for Dan. In my house we worked amid the din of five children and barking of a new dog.

After dark on Sunday evening, a campus vigil was held on the steps of Old Main, the main administrative building on campus. The band played moving renditions of "Amazing Grace" and Penn State's alma mater. Many of the students took candles and marched through the snow to the statue of Joe. The stadium lights were on as they would remain on through Friday morning. The low clouds, the snowfall, and the bright lights cast a calming aural glow. It seemed that the stadium lights were pushing upward into the heavens.

Guido called me. "Jay," he said, "you've got to go up to the statue. The students are there with candles and the snow. It looks like it is a Frank Capra movie. It looks like it is all in black and white."

Kelley and I parked a distance away from the statue and walked up. The light of the candles, the snow, and the silence are things I can never forget. It did look like the moment had been shot in black and white.

It was so hard to grasp that he was really gone.

By Monday it was decided that my sister Mary and I would do the television interviews that had been requested. I would go on the TODAY Show with Matt Lauer. We also decided to go on CBS with Charlie Rose as well as on CNN with Soledad O'Brien.

Monday morning I also got a call from Ashley Wiegner, a friend who'd worked on the Obama campaign with me and was then working for the administration. The call was to serve two purposes. The first was to say how sorry she was for me and for the loss of my father. The second reason for the call was that the White House wanted the best number to reach me, so the President could offer his condolences. The White House called to set up the time, and I indicated that I'd like to get my mom on the phone when they called.

Early Monday afternoon I was seated at the kitchen table when the call came in. My brothers were in the room along with my sister Diana. When I answered my mom was across the room and came to sit down beside me. The staff assistant got me and then announced that she was connecting me to the President. "Hello, Mr. President," I said.

Then the familiar voice of President Obama came across the line and filled the room as my mother and I sat at the table. "Jay, I wanted to call. Both Michelle and I wanted to offer our condolences to you and your family."

"Thank you, Mr. President. My mother is here with me as well," I said.

"Mrs. Paterno, your husband was beloved by so many, and he will be missed. You both worked so hard to build a great institution," the President said.

"Well, we're not finished," my mother said.

"I wouldn't expect anything less. I was honored to have a chance to spend some time with him last year," the President said.

We talked for a few minutes before hanging up, and there was just silence in the room.

As Monday ran into Tuesday, I was still not sleeping very much. So many friends, so many people came by to see us. I woke long before the alarm went off, and we headed to do the *TODAY Show* appearance at 6:10 AM.

The next interview was at 7:40 with CBS, followed by a CNN interview. The interviews were done from the Hillel Prayer Room in the spiritual center. Mary and I did one segment, and as we went to commercial, Charlie Rose said something to the effect of, "When we come back we'll ask members of the Paterno family how they feel about university administration officials attending the memorial."

During the break Mary mumbled to me that we hadn't prepped for that question. I mumbled back to her that no matter who they asked, I would answer the question. There was no doubt that the question was coming. "Jay, there's been a lot made of whether officials from Penn State should attend the memorial for your father, especially given the way his career ended at the university. How do you as a family feel about that?" Charlie's co-host asked.

"To focus on that really takes away from what we're trying to do here in the next couple of days. We're celebrating a 61-year career here at Penn State. We're celebrating 85 years of a life lived at a very, very high level of integrity, morality, of loyalty to Penn State. So obviously we want all Penn Staters to feel welcome."

The next interview was the most challenging of all. CNN's Soledad O'Brien was in a diner, covering the Florida presidential primary. Through my earpiece her voice was being drowned out by diner sounds, glasses clinking, and silverware hitting plates. It was all I could do not to laugh because I could not see her, but my mind pictured the *Saturday Night Live* Cheezborger! skit scene from the 1970s.

The public viewing began later that morning with the current team followed by former players. Many of the current players I hadn't seen in a few weeks, and it was good to see them. After that came the former players, and it was steady stream of familiar faces and so many hugs and tears. It meant so much to my mother—individual moments with men representing lives she and my father had changed.

By the time the last players filed out, it was close to noon. The plan was for our family to greet the team and former players and then leave. Someone mentioned a long line of people who'd waited for hours to come through, so I sent my wife home and decided to stay.

It was the best decision I made that week. I met so many people and heard how much my father meant to them whether they'd met him or not. It had an enormous impact on the eulogy I eventually wrote. As the day went, I realized I was not going to eulogize my father for my pain alone, but I would have to also speak for countless others.

In mid-afternoon I took a quick break to do a sit-down interview with ESPN's Tom Rinaldi followed by an interview with Ivan Maisel. I've known Ivan for a while and I have tremendous respect for him as a college football writer. He and I have spoken many times about the history of the game.

He grew up in a Jewish family in Alabama, reading the Torah and following Coach Bryant. I grew up Catholic in Pennsylvania at the foot of Coach Paterno. But we both loved and respected the traditions of each other's football loyalty as well as our differing religious traditions. Ivan grasped this moment, maybe better than anyone due to his experience watching the state of Alabama mourn Coach Bryant's passing 29 years earlier.

I spent the rest of the afternoon greeting people at the viewing. Scott and Dave were there as well. Finally around 6:30 I decided I should go home for an hour or two to get off my feet. When I arrived home, I met Wright Thompson, another talented ESPN writer. He was here for the week and was searching for a small personal moment amid the week of public mourning. He was with my childhood friend, JB Morris.

I agreed to allow him to tag along when I went back up to the viewing in an hour. Wright followed at a respectful distance as Mary and I finished greeting people.

When the room cleared of all visitors, my mother and several of the grandchildren went up and knelt and prayed. My niece Nicole kissed the casket.

Then I drove over to the statue. I wanted to see all the flowers and tributes that had been left there. Then the moment Wright had been looking for presented itself and he captured it perfectly.

> STATE COLLEGE, Pa. — Jay Paterno parked his minivan on the side of Porter Road, looking at the solemn crowd gathered around the statue of his dad. It was Tuesday night, and a shrine had been forming near Joe's feet for days. Someone left a war medal. There were dozens of flower arrangements, 30-year-old seat cushions and a houndstooth cap. For a moment, he took in the scene: the bronze statue, the flickering tea candles, the bright lights of the football stadium kept lit in memory since Joe Paterno died.

> Visting the Joe Paterno statue gave his son, Jay, solace.

> Jay pulled a hood over his head and slipped in among the crowd. Nobody recognized him. His father didn't seem so far away here. It was comforting. He bent down to read a card: "There's a new angel in heaven." A handmade poster showed Joe walking through gates with carefully drawn wings on his back. The only

sounds came from wind and sniffles, and Jay zipped his
coat against the cold. He stood next to a schoolteacher
from Pittsburgh who worked all day, then drove three
winding hours, bringing her dog, Rufus, for company.
She went to the public visitation and then came here,
to say goodbye. Before driving home in the dark, she
wanted a photograph in front of the statue, so she
turned to the stranger on her right.

"Would you mind getting a picture with the dog?" She
asked, handing over her camera.

"One...two...three," Jay said.

She looked at the lens, and Rufus managed not to
squirm too much. Then, as the candle she lit burned, she
stood still. Maybe she was praying. But something else
was working in her memory. A familiar voice. She looked
again.

"You're not ...," she asked quietly.

Jay Paterno nodded.

The schoolteacher from Pittsburgh collapsed in his
arms.

It turned out that teacher, Carol, had come up after school to go to the
viewing and visit the statue before driving home to be at school the next
morning. I don't know if anyone can ever explain how much it meant to me.
When I got home, I told my family and friends about that moment.

Dear Jay,

Just got home from the Pasquerilla Chapel and decided I
had to write you a note. On my way out when I thanked
you for allowing the public viewing, your reply was "the
honor is all ours." Such a classy statement. It choked
me up. And then I watched your interview with Tom

Rinaldi, one of the best interviews I have ever seen.

A great man is no longer with us, but his legacy will live on forever through the university he helped build, and through his family. I have tremendous admiration for the way Joe, you and your entire family has handled the very difficult situation over the past several months. If I was in your situation, I don't think I could have been so restrained after the awful attacks by the media and others. Your family has continued to show everyone the honor and class that stands behind the Paterno name.

I recall the last time I saw Joe. I was with my wife and two of our kids in Sunset Park throwing a football around. And you and Joe walked by—the two of you just slowly strolled around the perimeter of the park. A touching sight. My youngest son wanted to go over and say "hi" but I told him it was your alone time.

Like so many others, I suppose I looked at Joe as a father figure. I am very grateful for his advice— although I never had but short, casual conversations with him. But I was able to use a lot of his words to guide my actions over the last 30 years. I look forward to learning more of his wisdom when I read the many books that will be written about him in the coming years. Maybe your family will write one someday?

My condolences to you and the entire family. I look forward to the many future celebrations of Joe Paterno's contributions and achievements, and the future strengthening of his legacy.

Thank you again for allowing us to grieve (and celebrate) with you.

> Warm regards.
> Ben

Wednesday morning I went back to greet more people at the viewing that led up to the funeral. The funeral service was beautiful, really beautiful. That it was in the spiritual center that my mother and father had given so much to and on a campus they loved meant even more. They'd met at the library that was across the street. We'd lived five blocks away.

Father Matthew delivered a powerful and funny eulogy about my dad. Mary spoke, delivering her remarks with a touch of humor that my dad would've loved. Dave spoke, and I was so glad for him to have that moment to talk about his relationship with my father. Finally Scott spoke about the round kitchen table we had at the house and the significance of that table.

But the funeral seemed to pass by in an instant. After the funeral we would have a long procession to the graveside service. The hearse was to be followed by the familiar blue bus that took Joe to every home game. His seat, the front right seat, was left open. In the driver's seat was Bill Coral, who drove the bus on game days for years.

On my way to the bus, I ran into a familiar face. It was Dave Richardson. He worked stadium security for years and always found Joe on the crowded postgame field and walked him to the locker room. He had a tear in his eye on this cold, icy day and he hugged me. "Jay," he asked, "I just came here because I wanted to walk your dad out one last time."

I nodded and told him my father would be honored.

As I walked toward the bus, I could not help but think of Dave's silhouette walking alongside with one hand on the hearse as Joe left the mortal playing fields one last time.

What I was perhaps most unprepared for was the thousands of people along the procession route. The people lined the streets for miles; it went on and on. There were so many faces I did not recognize, but so many that I did. As we neared the Bryce Jordan Center and Beaver Stadium, I saw the teams of all the sports lined up along the road in their team sweats.

I remember the signs: "We Love You Joe," "Make an Impact," "WE are because HE was."

The turn down College Avenue slowed us to a crawl. The people were on the street narrowing the two lanes to one. Here on the streets I'd walked my entire life. On the streets my father first came to in 1950, he was saluted for his life lived in this community.

Finally we arrived at the graveside service. On the snowy hillside, I saw close friends standing. I remember the men dressed in dark overcoats standing solemnly as we carried my father to his final resting place. These friends had waited in the cold for an hour to pay their respects.

The grandchildren sat around my mother at the graveside service. The younger children were with her, and they were a comfort to her. I saw my daughter Lizzie's big brown eyes welling with tears. I saw the oldest grandchildren—Brian, Matthew, and Olivia—struck with a sadness that comes from being old enough to know what has been lost.

I saw my mother's brother, Dave, filled with such pain. He knew the man who had been lost and a truth that contradicted the way his brother-in-law had been portrayed the last few months of his life.

The sun was setting up the hill from us, and inside the tent it was getting dark. There was sadness but also rage welling up within me. How could his life end now? I just wanted to be alone with him, just wanted to hear his voice tell me it would all be okay.

When the service was over, I stayed until everyone left. I was all alone with him. I talked to him, I asked for his help. But there were no answers, so I walked alone across a snowy road into the rest of my life.

Chapter 30

Give Them No Tear!

Thursday, January 26, 2012

After Wednesday's funeral I spent time at a reception with family and friends before riding over to the football stadium lounge for another reception. Once there I was greeted by hundreds of players. Stories flowed, bringing smiles, hugs, and laughs.

How he would have loved to have been there. A team reunion is unlike anything except, I would imagine, military reunions. Men share funny stories about disasters narrowly avoided on the field, in the classroom, or on campus.

Because my father was not here, in his place I heard the memories. I was asked to speak to the group, which sparked something in my soul. I told them how much they meant to my father, how much he loved them and to be in the locker room before a big game. I shared his wishes to fight the false narrative tearing down what we'd all done honorably at Penn State.

As I read Rudyard Kipling's poem "If" to them, I saw them nodding along, recognizing life's lessons they'd learned from Joe rooted in that poetry.

At the end I reminded them that we ended every game kneeling as a team, holding hands, and reciting the Lord's Prayer. We all knelt and prayed together as they'd done when they were on the team.

Once home I stayed up late talking with friends. It calmed me as I had a speech to deliver to 12,000 people and a national television audience, one requiring me to keep my emotions in check while telling the world about a man that meant so much to me. And I had to be sure that I didn't touch upon the unresolved scandal that led to his firing, which clouded the last months of his life.

Armed with the strength of my convictions, I had very little fear. I'd read and re-written what I had every day that week. The pressure to deliver was at a whole new level. As the closing speaker, I had to plant the flag of an incomparable life atop the mountains Joe's life had scaled.

Thursday morning I rewrote the beginning with clearer vision. This was done as it had been all week, with friends and kids coming in and out of the house. It was a wonderfully busy chaos. Guido D'Elia had read it and decided to change the event's ending. He was going to show a video after I spoke, but when he saw how I planned to conclude, he moved the video ahead of my eulogy. "It's beautiful, Jay," he said.

Kerry Small, a close friend, had stopped by for another read-through. We tweaked a couple of sentences after reading through it two more times. "You'll do great," he said.

I knew the words were right, but I worried about my ability to deliver it without getting overly emotional. I felt people needed me to speak with clear strength.

In the den Kelley was busy getting tickets for the service to people. The tickets made available to the public were gone in seven minutes. As she always does in crunch time, Kelley came through handling over 200 requests from our friends alone.

After vowing never to fly again, even my 87-year-old father-in-law was compelled to get here. He and his wife overcame bad weather, several delays, and an overnight stay along the way to get here. They arrived from Florida to pay their respects late Tuesday morning.

All Thursday morning the doorbell rang as people arrived in a steady stream to pick up tickets and popped into the living room to see how I was doing.

Finally it was time to go.

At the Bryce Jordan Center I went into a room with the other speakers: Phil Knight, the CEO of Nike; Susan Welch, the dean of Penn State's College of Liberal Arts; Lauren Perroti, a student in the Paterno Fellows Program; and players Kenny Jackson, Charlie Pittman, Jimmy Cefalo, Chris Marrone, and Todd Blackledge.

Michael Robinson arrived. He'd landed in State College after a red eye from Honolulu and two more planes at 11 AM, slept for an hour, wrote his speech, and here he was. Of all the people, this would be the toughest for him because of the travel, and he hadn't yet had a chance to come to grips with this.

Before the service I went out on the floor to talk to Ohio State coaches Urban Meyer and Luke Fickell. I spoke to ESPN's Kirk Herbstreit. South Carolina coach Steve Spurrier was there. The number of former players was staggering.

Jackson led the event off with some loving words, words that a son would speak to a father, and words for my mother. I listened to all the speakers. It was never just about football with the players. The addition of two students and an academic dean drove home the point of this man's legacy away from football.

Cefalo talked about how Joe recruited his mother and father more than him. Blackledge told about a key moment in the national championship game where Joe trusted him. Michael made a forceful speech about Joe's honesty in recruiting. "Joe never lied to me," he repeated over and over again.

In a beautiful speech asking, "Who will be my hero now?" Phil Knight slew the elephant in the room. He told the story of how, having lost his college track coach and hero, Bill Bowerman, 12 years ago he adopted Joe as his new hero.

> "In the 12 years since, through four losing seasons, big bowl wins, 12-win seasons, through All-Americans and players with criminal charges, through 4-point students and players dismissed from the team for discipline—never once did he let me down. Not one time.
>
> "In the year in question, it turns out he gave full disclosure to his superiors, information then went up the chain to the head of the campus police and the president of the school. The matter was in the hands of a world class university and by a president with an outstanding national reputation. Whatever the details of that investigation are this much is clear to me: if there is a villain in this tragedy, it lies in that investigation and not in Joe Paterno's response to it."

The arena erupted in a standing ovation lasting nearly a minute. Phil had spoken what everyone in our community had felt. But he had more arrows left and he pulled the bow again.

> "And yet for his actions, he was excoriated by the media and fired over the telephone by his university. Yet in all his subsequent appearances in the press, on TV, interacting with students, conversing with hospital personnel, giving an interview with Sally Jenkins, he never complained, he never lashed out. Every word, every bit of body language conveyed a single message: We are Penn State."

Another standing ovation. Phil continued.

> "So I do not follow the conventional wisdom. Joe was my hero, every day for 12 of the last 12 years. But it does lead me to this question. Who is the real trustee at Penn State University?"

He'd taken dead aim, landing a direct hit.

At that point it was time for me to go backstage. Just before I went onstage, I went to the bathroom. When I returned the folder with my speech had gone missing. I frantically searched the area.

Panic.

Then I noticed Phil Knight smiling. He handed over my folder.

Relief.

I walked to Guido and asked if he wanted me onstage while the video was playing before my speech. He told me to hold on. It was set to "Nessun Dorma" sung by Luciano Pavarotti. Images flickered in color, black and white, slow motion, and full speed—a beautiful tribute to Joe's life.

As the video played, Guido said, "Be ready. You're going to get a standing ovation. Don't let it catch you. Everyone is watching, so stay strong."

It was a good thing he warned me because it would have caught me off guard. As I started up the stairs, Guido cracked me across my back. I turned, laughed, and saw him smiling. Between Knight's stealing my speech and Guido hitting me, I was at ease being surrounded by good friends.

Still, as I walked the stairs, I was reminded of John Proctor's last words to his wife Elizabeth in *The Crucible*: "Give them no tear! Tears pleasure them! Show honor now, show a stony heart, and sink them with it!"

I held steady through the entire eulogy. After I finished a lone soloist from Penn State's Blue Band came out and slowly played "Hail to The Lion."

Then I walked offstage, where Guido stood along with Knight. They were so proud. Guido grabbed me and said, "You done good, son."

Out of sight backstage, the emotions I'd held in check flooded me so I sat down and cried before heading out to see anyone.

After the service I sat in my home surrounded by family and loyal friends realizing how lucky I'd been in my life. My mother and sisters were there, and the laughter and smiles helped everyone's spirits. My mother genuinely enjoyed seeing the love and support there for her family.

The funny stories made us smile.

Kerry Small related how his wife, Meg, kept noticing him crying during the speech just before an emotional story came up. He knew when the emotional parts were coming.

Another friend was seated next to Kirk Herbstreit. In the speech I asked everyone to hold hands and recite the Lord's Prayer. "My wife is jealous because I got to hold hands with Herbie. That Dove men's skin care he does commercials for must work. His hands are very soft," he said.

Many told me how proud they were of my speech. But there was only one voice I wanted to hear. We toasted my father with glasses of his favorite bourbon, Old Grand-Dad. How I wanted to call and just ask him how I'd done.

The next day I was contacted by American Rhetoric. They had seen my speech and wanted my permission to list my eulogy among the most important American speeches of the century.

I was so surprised. Then I looked at a picture of my dad and said aloud: "I hear you, Dad."

But he wasn't done speaking.

A few weeks later a female college student stopped me in town. She hadn't gotten a ticket to the memorial but watched it at the student union building with other students. In my eulogy I asked everyone to hold hands and recite the Lord's Prayer. She told me all the students there stood together and held hands. "It meant a lot to us," she said.

"Not as much as it means to me to hear your story," I replied.

The next day I received correspondence from a Jewish man who watched the eulogy on television. In his home he and his son had stood up to recite the Lord's Prayer. He knew the prayer but had never contemplated the non-denominational aspects of the prayer that Joe liked. "My family and I will continue to recite it as a prayer," he wrote.

I put down the letter and looked at my dad's picture again. "I got it, Dad," I said. "You made the sale."

Chapter 31

The Stretch Run

Calling a seven-year span "The Stretch Run" may seem odd, but in the context of a 61-year career, it is apropos. After a disastrous home loss to Iowa late in the 2004 season, many believed Joe Paterno's run needed to end.

At my house after the game, even my good friend Paul Levine asked what I planned to do after the season, assuming this loss would doom Joe Paterno. "Paul," I said, "don't worry. We'll be fine."

Paul looked at me like I had been drinking. "This team's lost the confidence to win," I said. "It's lost the ability to close in the fourth quarter."

We were in every game and we'd lost them by making mistakes. Already I'd evaluated the talent we had coming back in 2005. The last piece was to get one or two speedy playmakers to give us the finishing kick. "If this team wins one game and learns how to win, we might not lose another game until 2006," I stated.

Paul was probably now convinced that I needed a reality check. But I explained the talent coming back and told him we'd get two of the nation's top recruits in Justin King and Derrick Williams.

But just in case, that week I visited Joe at his house as a coach—not as a son. We were 2–5, nearing a second straight losing season with a restless fan base. He was in his den during lunchtime. "What's on your mind?" he asked.

"We're in a tough spot."

"I've been here before," he said.

"Not like this. This is bad."

"We'll be fine," he said.

"I know once we start winning we'll get on a roll, but we both know we have to get to a bowl game this year. We have to win the next four games."

"Well, that's what we'll do."

"I know. But if we don't, they'll be calling for your head."

"I'll be okay."

"I'm not so sure. But I want to say something."

He tried to cut me off, but I raised my hand, indicating he wasn't going to keep me from saying what I had come to say. "This team is close to winning big next year. I want to be sure that you're here to guide that team," I said. "If there is pressure to get rid of someone, I'm willing to go if it will keep the wolves at bay. You'll get this team back where it belongs. I know there are plenty of reasons why we're losing. *But if you have to fire someone, then I am okay going as long as you get to stay.*"

Silence. He knew I meant what I said. I knew there was enough blame to go around for all the losses, but I also knew there was intense public pressure aimed at me—the easy target for fans' ire. If my leaving would give Joe a chance to stay, I wanted him to know I was okay with it.

Across the den from me, I could see the pained expression in hearing my offer. All his life he wanted to protect others, and here I was offering to do that for him. "I appreciate what you're saying," he said. "This isn't your fault. You're doing a good job. You've had guys get hurt and you've kept slugging away. We'll be okay."

A few days later there was a tough loss at Ohio State. That weekend when we returned from Columbus, Ohio, the top recruit in the nation, Williams, came to visit us. It was a tough sell, and his family wanted some glimmer of light.

But at 2–6 we knew there'd be another holiday season spent at home. That week I went to see Joe again. When I arrived at lunchtime, I asked him straight up if he was going to call it a career.

Though he denied it, I saw doubt. As I left the house, I mulled what I should do. If anything, I'd quit before I allowed him to quit. We were on the cusp of something big with this team, and I knew only he could lead that rebirth.

I got back to my office and called a former player in town. Expressing my concerns to him, I suggested that he may want to call Joe and give him a boost. I don't know what was said, but I do know that at practice that after-noon Joe pulled me aside and told me who'd stopped by. I acted surprised, but I suspect he knew.

Joe decided to fight on. He knew he was holding a hand that had three of a kind, and if we could land the recruits we targeted, he'd have a full house.

Days later we lost another close game 14–7 at home against Northwestern. The newspaper headline stated, "Rock Bottom." We were 2–7 and all alone in the Big Ten basement. As we drove from the stadium, an older man seated in a lawn chair by the Bryce Jordan Center yelled at us, "Give it up Joe, you're too old."

Joe didn't hear it, but I did as I rode in the back of the pickup truck. I hurt, not for me, but for him. We were close and just needed a win.

The next week we traveled to play Indiana. We stayed at a hotel outside of town on Lake Monroe. In summer, boaters and vacationers fill the place, but on a dreary late November weekend, the setting felt more like the camp Crystal Lake in the movie *Friday the 13th*.

It was the low point, Penn State playing a meaningless game that no one cared about.

In all the years in the conference, we'd never lost to Indiana, and a sparse crowd felt this would be their year. We fought through three and a half quarters, making a better offensive showing but still trailed.

On a third and 9 in the fourth quarter, we were in field-goal range. That would give us the lead. I called for the Z post play, a post-wheel combina-tion despite some coaches wanting to play for the field goal and not risk an interception. It was the only time in a game I ever cussed at a fellow coach in anger. "I'm sick of the negative shit," I said. "We're gonna run the damn play and get a first down. We need a touchdown."

A season of frustration had bubbled to the surface. I regret my lack of poise. Joe had told us to stay aggressive and show this team we had faith in them to make plays and win. Michael Robinson was covered, so quarterback Zack Mills stuck a pass to freshman receiver Mark Rubin, who made the catch with a defender draped on his back. We went on to score a touchdown, taking a 22–16 lead.

Indiana got the ball. Near midfield they threw a pass that defensive back Anwar Phillips had in his hands. He dropped a game-winning interception. In more than a few minds, I am sure there were thoughts of, *Here we go again*.

Through the headsets I heard Joe encouraging everyone to keep hustling and something good was going to happen. He didn't bemoan the lost opportunity.

Indiana threw at Phillips again, and he missed the play. Indiana's wide receiver had the ball with nothing between him and the end zone. All 11 defenders raced after him, and at the 2-yard line, Phillips made the tackle on a play that was all effort and pride.

Upstairs the offensive coaches talked about what we would do in a two-minute situation to win the game after Indiana scored. But I sensed this had to be our moment. We'd learn how to win. We'd rolled the dice to get the touchdown and now had a chance to stand and win.

After three Indiana plays later, it was fourth down. The touchdown we'd scored following Joe's directive to be aggressive meant Indiana had to go for a touchdown. They tried another run, and the defense stood their ground.

After the win there was elation and excitement. In a cramped postgame locker room, players whooped and cheered. The faces were alive with the joy of a hard-fought win, one requiring everyone to stand and deliver.

By the time we landed back in State College, we were aware that Michigan State had destroyed Wisconsin, the nation's No. 4 team, by a score of 49–14. Our game the next week against the Spartans looked like a big challenge.

But now with our Indiana win, my theory would be tested.

We dismantled Michigan State 37–13 in front of over 100,000 fans, many of whom thought they were seeing the end of Joe Paterno's career. The whispers had been around the state and the country all week. In the tunnel before the game, ESPN's sideline reporter asked if this would be Joe's last game, and I told him no. But I really didn't know.

From the outset we took control, and the crowd got behind it. Joe Paterno had coached this group positively through the losses, and it was paying off now. We pulled away behind Michigan State turnovers and two Zack Mills touchdown runs.

We'd won again, and looking around that locker room, there was a confidence there that had been lacking all year. If we could've played another five or six games that year, we'd have won them all.

The last two wins started our momentum. In December two of the country's most highly sought recruits, King and Williams, announced they'd come to Penn State. They were among the missing ingredients that would enable the team to restore Penn State pride. But there were underdogs who came to the rescue. One was walk-on Deon Butler, and another was unheralded wide receiver Jordan Norwood, the son of our safeties coach Brian Norwood.

Jordan had some injuries in football, but Joe had watched him play basketball. At State College High School, Jordan had helped the team win an unexpected state basketball championship. Joe gave Jordan a scholarship. Butler talked his parents into paying his way to Penn State. Both players were undersized but amazingly intelligent football players.

They were all here in the spring semester of 2005, and Joe Paterno's mind told him he'd assembled something unique.

I can recall a discussion I had with defensive coordinator Tom Bradley in March that year. After looking at the running test results, Joe was struck by the amount of speed we had on our team. As fast as our defense was in 1999, a defense featuring the first two picks of the entire NFL draft, I mentioned to Tom that the 2005 defense would be *faster* than that group.

Everyone we'd put on the field could really run.

Late in 2004 and all through the winter, Joe Paterno would repeat one thing to his team. It was a challenge to win every game in 2005. The believers—Matt Rice, Tamba Hali, Paul Posluszny, Robinson, Tony Hunt, Williams, King, Alan Zemaitis—pursued Joe's goal every day.

In March just before spring break, I called Robinson in to talk to see where he felt we were as a team. I was keenly interested in his leadership. He'd played a lot of football and had made big plays. Also he was one of the most committed students and hardest workers on the field. That gave him great credibility among his teammates.

But I felt he could go further. As he sat across from me in my office, behind him in the windows, I could see across the practice fields and beyond to Mount Nittany and the ridgeline that formed the eastern line of the Nittany Valley. The mountains stood tall and strong, and that was what we needed from the student-athlete seated in front of me. "Michael, this is it for you," I said. "This is your last season. This team can do some great things. We have the talent to shock everyone."

"I know."

"But *your* leadership will be a key. What I want you to think about is this: were you in the best shape you could have been last fall?"

He hesitated, so I continued.

"At the end of the Northwestern game last year, you dropped a touchdown pass that would've tied the game. You told me you were tired. You were carrying about 10 pounds too much."

"You're right."

"My challenge is this: from now until the end of the season is nine months. In college nine months seems like an eternity. In the grand scheme of life, it isn't a long time. I believe you were not in your best shape because of alcohol. Drinking during the season zaps conditioning and adds weight to carry. You can't perform at peak level. Now in 1997 I challenged a player to stop drinking, and he said I shouldn't ask him to if I didn't. I stopped."

"What are you saying?"

"What I'm saying is this: I'm challenging you to stop drinking for nine months. You'll have the best season of your life. You'll carry less weight, you'll never be tired in games, and there's one other thing."

"What's that?"

"You will be a more effective leader. You can challenge others, influence others to do what you're doing, and we'll be better as a team."

"Are you telling me to do this?"

"No. This is all your choice, but I want you to think about something. I mentioned nine months, right?"

"Yes."

"Now, I know your mother smokes, but when she was pregnant with you, she stopped smoking. She sacrificed so your life would be better when she carried you for nine months. For the next nine months, you give up drinking and you'll be able to change her life. You don't have to tell me what you decide to do. It's completely your call. But think about leadership and think about changing your life and your mother's life."

Shortly after spring break we began spring practice. We changed our offense and were more aggressive, using all the speed and skill we had assembled around Michael. It was fun to watch these guys practice.

Joe Paterno was always willing to try new things and new technology. One of the projects we undertook was to put our playbook and our terminology onto the memory cards for the *Madden NFL* game for the PlayStation. We gave all of our players "*Madden* playbooks."

Using the Madden playbooks with our terminology, they learned to converse in our language. With four freshmen playing offensive skill posi-tions, it was vital they pick up and learn our system rapidly. When I ap-proached Joe about the idea, he laughed. "Television games?" he asked.

He always referred to them as television games and not video games. In every team meeting, he'd tell the guys to stop playing so many television games and study more.

"Yes," I responded, "we can use the video games to our advantage. When they play they'll learn our offense."

"If they're gonna play those silly games, they may as well get something out of it." He laughed.

By the time our spring game rolled around, they'd learned the offense. The key now for Joe was to sell our fan base on the new team. In a staff meet-ing three days before the spring game, he told us what he wanted from us.

Normally spring games are pretty dull. Joe needed to get the fan base excited so he told us to open it up during the spring game. He understood the power of marketing to the fan base. He argued that their excitement would rub off on our players during the summer and give them a confidence boost.

The day of the spring game, we did all kinds of stuff we normally wouldn't do. We made a lot of big plays. The plan worked as everyone left excited for the fall. From the depths of the Northwestern game, Joe orchestrated positive momentum, winning the last two games and recruiting wars and using video games and an exciting spring game to help us.

The stretch run of his career was underway. No one suspected it would last another seven seasons.

Chapter 32

2005 and
Michael Robinson

Even now in Joe Paterno's den, *his* pictures remain on dark wood walls. Very few of them involve football. There is a black-and-white photo of his bespectacled, white-haired father, Angelo, in a coat and tie seated at his desk.

There's a black-and-white photo of young Joe Paterno at four or five years old, standing with his parents. There is a print looking across the East River toward the 1930s Manhattan skyline. There are photos of Joe and Sue Paterno, smiling and laughing. There's a photo from the Sugar Bowl win that clinched the 1982 National Championship.

Highest on the wall nearest his desk is a photo of Joe Paterno standing next to the 2006 Orange Bowl Trophy. To Joe's left stands Michael Robinson, smiling but sweaty from a triple-overtime win against Florida State. His right hand is on Joe's shoulder. The joy of the victorious moment is visible. On that photo Michael wrote: "To Joe, Thanks for helping me become a man! Go Penn State. Michael Robinson #12 2006 Orange Bowl Champions."

That is the only autographed picture of a former player that hangs in his office. Why? Michael represented so much and so many. He was a leader of the team that justified Joe's relevance, resilience, and existence after the worst stretch of his career.

Michael's own path to a stellar 2005 Big Ten MVP season was an epic saga of patience, persistence, and seizing destiny by the throat when his chance arose, the kind of story Joe loved.

Michael was a highly recruited football player from Richmond, Virginia. In November 2000 he came to visit Penn State on the weekend of our season-ending win against Michigan State. We finished a tough 5–7 season marked by disappointments and a catastrophic neck injury to freshman cornerback Adam Taliaferro.

Something about Michael clicked with Joe Paterno. He had poise and a sincere commitment to education. More importantly for Penn State, something about Joe Paterno clicked with Michael Robinson.

Joe's approach convinced another player, Tamba Hali, to come to Penn State. Born in Liberia, Tamba and his father fled to New Jersey to escape their nation's civil war. Tamba had great college football programs chasing him, but he remembered something Joe had said to him. "'Tamba, if you don't want to come to Penn State, don't come,'" Tamba recalled Joe saying. "I realized Joe had more to offer me than I had to offer him."

Tamba was intrigued; he bought in.

That was Joe Paterno's approach. We have something special here, and if you can't see that or get that concept, then this isn't the place for you.

That same idea clicked with Michael. On a bitter November afternoon, Michael, his brother Anthony, and cousin Biz rode in the open-air back of a beat-up pickup truck as we left the stadium. Joe rode up front. When we piled into the back, Joe made no apologies for the "deluxe" mode of transportation. "Mike," Joe said, "when you get to be my age you can ride up front."

In the previous summer when Michael was on campus, I was honest with him. Some of our staff doubted he could play quarterback for us. On the outdoor deck of the Lasch Building, I told him that if I didn't believe he could be our quarterback that I would tell him. That fall after watching him play on film and spending time with him on his visit, we were sold. He was the first quarterback I picked to recruit as the quarterbacks coach.

Bill Kenney was recruiting Michael for us, and we were convinced Michael could play the style of quarterback that we wanted to coach. Joe Paterno saw a warrior who could use his mind to lead his team.

Bill and I made many trips to Richmond. We always stopped in a restaurant called Yesterdays, where Bill and I plotted the home visits before finishing our meals with coconut pie.

I can still hear Bill saying to Michael in his house: "Michael, there is a reason God put you and Joe Paterno on this Earth at the same time. Your paths intersected, and there's a reason for it. What exactly that is, I don't know. But I know you can see it."

Bill believed the two were destined to do great things together. This was classic Joe Paterno/Penn State recruiting. The recruiting coach doggedly pursued the young man while challenging him to prove he belonged at Penn State. We never apologized for demanding high expectations on and off the field.

Joe connected with Michael, his mother, and stepfather. Joe's strength was showing the vision he had for *your* future while reminding you he offered the road less traveled: honest striving to reach the goals he had for you. Those goals were often beyond what most young men and even many parents could see for themselves.

In the summer of 2011, when Urban Meyer and I were talking about the student-athletes he'd met at Penn State, he asked how we got such a great group of young men on our team. I explained it was all in how we recruited. Joe was comfortable in who he was. He did not apologize for high standards and he understood no recruit was bigger than our program.

Joe used to get criticized for losing certain big-name players. Joe rarely, if ever, lost a kid. Mostly they just couldn't or wouldn't see what he saw.

Michael and his mother, Rita Ross, came to believe what Bill Kenney had told them. They had a chance to walk a path with Joe Paterno. They took it.

In every joyous life moment, there is a tendency to see that moment only in the glow of the accomplishment while forgetting the often difficult path it takes to ascend life's summits.

That 2006 Orange Bowl victory was one of those moments.

Michael's career started in 2001 as we struggled to an 0–4 start, including a loss to eventual national champion Miami. There was tremendous pressure to play Michael at running back to give us a boost. But through the next seven games, we went 5–2 and managed to hold Michael out, saving his redshirt year. Joe would not shortsightedly sacrifice Michael's long-term future for a short-term fix.

The next year in 2002, we'd have a rebirth, and Michael was one of the catalysts. He remained at quarterback and was the *original* Wildcat. Joe discussed ideas to get Michael in the game plan. He'd line up at tailback and receiver, and we would shift the starting quarterback to wide receiver with Michael lined up at quarterback.

We called it the "Mike Package." A few years later when everyone had Wildcat offenses, Joe would laugh and recall what we'd done years earlier.

We kept it clandestine. At Joe's suggestion starting quarterback Zack Mills, Michael, and I practiced the plays indoors with no one else around until three days before the Nebraska game. I told Michael he couldn't even tell his mother what we were up to. He only told his mom to get to the game on time.

We caught Nebraska unprepared, beating the top 10 Cornhuskers 40–7. After Michael scored two touchdowns against Nebraska and three more the next week, he became a valuable weapon. But he still wanted to play quarterback, and we still worked toward that end.

As the season wound on, his role varied from week to week. Some coaches wanted him less involved and some wanted him more involved. The toughest moment came in the bowl game that year.

Starting quarterback Zack Mills was struggling, so we put Michael in to spark the team. He led us on a scoring drive that gave us a fourth-quarter lead. Auburn rallied to go up 13–9. We got the ball with a chance to win. Because Mills had led us on several fourth-quarter, game-winning drives, we played the odds and put him back in the game but fell short.

In the postgame locker room, I approached Michael. I wanted to introduce him to former Penn State quarterback Todd Blackledge, then a college football analyst with CBS. With Mike interested in a television career, I figured Todd would be a good contact.

Michael was in no mood to meet anyone. He wanted to know why I had taken him out. My explanation didn't sit well with him. "When will I get *my* chance to prove I can win the game if you never put me in?" he asked.

The heated discussion remained respectful. It happens in locker rooms all the time and it was *never* personal. All these years later, we laugh about it.

In 2003 and 2004, we suffered the worst seasons of Joe Paterno's career. There were many calls from Michael's mother, Rita. She knew I had no problem hearing her out. In fact I encouraged her to call. I appreciate it more than the parents who bitch behind your back. That was never a problem with Rita. There was no hesitation when it came to speaking her mind. After a game at Iowa, I returned home, and within a few moments, my home phone was ringing. I knew it was Rita.

The conversation went as expected but ended with a mutual expression of respect for the other's opinion. "Jay, I hear what you're saying," Rita said. "I respect that, but I still think you're wrong. Michael should play more."

"Rita," I said, "I expect you to feel this way. You may be right. We may have won if we'd played him more. But we make decisions in the course of a game based on practice and how that game is going. All we are trying to do is win. Michael has a great future ahead of him. It may be next week. It may not, but it is there."

"Thanks for talking to me. I respect the job you're doing. I respect that you're willing to hear me out. But," she said, laughing, "you know I still think you're wrong."

Through those two seasons, I informed Joe about Rita's calls, just so he knew where she was coming from. He'd laugh and tell me how glad he was that she was calling Bill Kenney or me and not him. "If she gets too tough for you guys," he said, laughing, "I'll talk to her."

But Joe Paterno kept an open dialogue with Rita. One spring they came up, and Michael, Rita, and Mike's stepfather, John, all sat at the round kitchen table and talked. That settled everyone.

Make no mistake, even in those tougher days, Michael was completely committed to our team winning. At Wisconsin in 2004, our starting quarterback Zack Mills was hurt, and shortly thereafter Michael was knocked unconscious, taken off the field in an ambulance, and immobilized on a backboard. Guido D'Elia was at the hospital when a still-immobilized Michael emerged from the MRI. "Did we win?" he asked.

Guido could only shake his head. Immediately he noticed a tear run from Michael's eye. Even then Michael was more concerned about the team. The next two weeks as he recovered, no one I ever coached was more eager to play despite the risk of further injury. But he grudgingly listened to the doctors' advice and followed their orders.

Michael always listened, so Joe kept communicating and talking with him throughout it all. He always knew he'd hear the truth. Michael stopped by more than maybe anyone else who had played for Joe.

Occasionally I'd get a call from Joe. "Jay, Michael wants to stop by," he said. "Is everything okay?"

"Yeah, he's fine, Coach. As strange as it sounds and as hard as it is for me to understand, he likes talking with you," I said, laughing.

Then Joe would sit down with him, and they'd talk. Deep down it meant as much to Joe, maybe more, than it did to Mike. It built trust, a bond where both men knew neither would blink in the face of adversity.

There were difficulties. Michael was human like all of us. But he was a good young man who made some mistakes common to many in college. But it was the trials of the previous couple of years that had forged Michael, his teammates, and all of us for the 2005 season. There was no turning back. We knew no one believed in us, we knew we were all alone.

That team had great leaders. Alan Zemaitis, Matt Rice, Paul Posluszny, and Hali were strong people. But there were others; Calvin Lowry and Chris Harrell led the secondary. They had resolved not to allow this team to lose.

Joe Paterno challenged them before the season in a team meeting. He told them that a lot of people were excited, that perhaps we'd rebound from a 4–7 season to win seven or eight games and get to a bowl game. "You guys didn't come here to win seven or eight games and get to a bowl game," he said. "You came here to compete for a national championship. That's it. We know how to get you there. We're going to push you. This can be something special."

In Joe's notes he wrote he'd retire if he failed and defined failure as an 8–4 season. He told his team we were here to "win them all." Despite everyone outside the program doubting them, they bought in and worked every day to make it happen.

At the Big Ten media gathering in Chicago, Michael and his teammates sensed the complete lack of respect for our team and for Joe Paterno. As Joe spoke Michael heard guys from other teams mumbling that Joe should just shut up. When he returned from Chicago, he came into my office irate at our treatment by the media and other teams. It became motivation.

The season began with three home wins before we headed on the road to Northwestern. In the pregame locker room, Joe had vomited and could barely stand on wobbly legs. His body was chilled, and he was shaky. As his son I was concerned.

He couldn't be seen as old or vulnerable; he knew he had to answer the bell.

But above all he wanted to be there for the team. How he summoned the strength to go out that day I will never know. Both of our team doctors thought there was no way he'd be able to stand, but he stood strong, never betraying how violently ill he'd been before the game.

If he hadn't already been ill, the way we started the game would have made him so. Just before halftime we trailed 23–7 mostly due to four turnovers. Michael had a hand in all of the turnovers, but three of them were beyond his control, including two interceptions that had gone off receivers' hands. Just before the half, Michael led us down the field and threw a touchdown pass to Deon Butler to close the gap.

At halftime I talked to Michael and reminded him that the mistakes of the first half were beyond his control. Joe was roaming all over the locker room, encouraging the defense and reminding our guys that we were in the game.

"Look," he said, "we've made just about every mistake we could make in the first half, and we're still in this game. They can't cover our guys. We have more speed. Keep hustling, and good things are going to happen."

His voice was strong, but I watched him go back into the coaches' locker room and sit down. When I came in, I could see he was still shaking. When I asked if he was okay, he was honest. "Not really, but I'll make it. This is too important to this team," he reminded me.

In the fourth quarter, we were still clawing our way back when Joe came down and called the reverse to Justin King, who ripped off a big gain, setting up a Robinson touchdown run behind a crushing block by tackle Levi Brown.

We had finally climbed ahead 27–26, but Northwestern came alive and went ahead 29–27 with 2:10 to go. We got the ball and three plays later faced fourth and 15 with 1:39 to go. If we didn't make it, we would lose the game. We went to a go-to play for long yardage, Triple Right Gun Red 8, one we'd worked all week.

Northwestern played the coverage we expected, and Mike found tight end Isaac Smolko, who made his first catch of the game, for the first down. He'd told Mike he'd be open and that he'd catch it.

From there we moved down the field and faced third and 6 at the Northwestern 36-yard line. We called another of Joe's favorite plays the 7-lane. On the line Mike saw the blitz coming and changed the protection. He noticed a safety matched up on receiver Derrick Williams and knew he had a favorable matchup there.

When it came to one-on-one matchups with safeties, I'd taught our quarterbacks this truism: "If safeties could cover one on one...they'd be corners." Mike made the throw to Derrick, who caught it, avoided the tackle, and scored the game winning-touchdown.

After the game I checked on Joe, and he seemed much better. It's amazing what a win will do for you. "Jay, I'm happy for us, for you and I'm happy for Mike. Tell him that now he's a quarterback," he said.

I relayed the message to Michael who smiled. It sank in that he had led us to a comeback win after a disastrous first half.

Two weeks later we'd host Ohio State. We had finally risen into the national rankings after routing 18th-ranked and undefeated Minnesota 44–14. At 5–0 we debuted in the top 25 ranked No. 16. Ohio State was ranked sixth.

Before the game we had a couple of goals from Joe Paterno. Both defenses were fast and tough. In the staff meeting and in talking with the team, he reiterated that big games featuring great defenses were more often "lost" by one's team's mistakes rather than "won" by one team making great offensive plays. His goal was to have no turnovers, protect the football, and win the game in the fourth quarter.

We coached Michael to be patient, to take what the defense gave us, and to move onto the next play. If we had to punt rather than force a pass that might get intercepted, so be it. This fight was going the distance.

Our students began camping out Sunday night, a full six days before the actual game. They dubbed the tent village "Paternoville." The weather was warm all week. The ESPN shows *College GameDay* and *Cold Pizza* were both broadcast live from the stadium. Paternoville was college football's original Woodstock complete with drinking and God only knows what else in those tents.

On gameday the clouds hung low, shrouding Mount Nittany, but the rain only magnified the intensity of the crowd by the nighttime kickoff. At various times during the game, the entire stadium was shaking. Ohio State took an early 3–0 lead with a field goal.

There was suddenly doubt in the air…

Then we answered. We lined up receiver Williams at tailback and pitched him the ball to the short side. It was a play Joe had worked on with the offensive staff to get Williams on the edge. As Derrick followed the crack block of receiver Ethan Kilmer, he outran Ohio State linebacker A.J. Hawk down the right sideline for a score that blew the roof off the building.

Suddenly, doubt exploded into belief.

Then the mistake happened. Ohio State quarterback Troy Smith threw an interception to Lowry. Robinson scored, and we were up 14–3.

From then on it was a defensive slugfest, and we held a 17–10 lead late in the game. As Joe had predicted, we had no turnovers. Guys like Hali, Jason Alford, and Posluszny were showing why we had a great defensive unit.

Our lead held late into the fourth quarter. Ohio State got the ball with a chance to tie. As they were driving, Hali, a young man born in Liberia and drawn to Penn State because Joe Paterno sold him on something bigger, made a play that will forever live in the hearts of Penn Staters.

Ohio State quarterback Troy Smith dropped back to pass. Tamba came around the right end and jarred the ball loose. Defensive tackle Scott Paxson scrambled to cradle the ball, sealing the win.

The crowd's eruption shook the stadium to its foundation.

It was a night to remember. As I stood on the field after the game, I heard "Oh What A Night" over the sound system and voices of happy people singing along.

But every hero needs a tragedy to overcome.

The next game at Michigan, Michael led us on an epic late fourth-quarter drive to take the lead. All year Michael never left the field for the last time without a lead. But Michigan had one possession left. They took the ball and scored on the last play.

Joe challenged the team to regroup. In the 1999 season we had lost a heartbreaker when we were undefeated only to lose two more games and a shot at the Big Ten title. Joe wanted this team to be different.

They responded by tearing through the rest of the season with one game left to win the Big Ten. We won that game at Michigan State and as we flew home we kept hearing about the other teams ahead of us—Miami losing to Georgia Tech, and USC trailing Fresno State.

As we made our final approach to the University Park Airport, our 737 hit the runway too hard and bounced back up in the air about 60 feet before the pilot regained control and safely got us down. No one knew how serious it was until the bus driver waiting for us described what he had seen. It resulted in serious damage to the plane and an FAA accident report, but none of us cared.

We'd won the conference championship after being picked to finish eighth. We were now ranked fourth in the country. On the ride to Rec Hall for a Big Ten title celebration, we learned that No. 3-ranked Miami had lost. Rec Hall was packed with thousands of jubilant fans, including the smiling faces of my children.

Joe spoke, and then the captains spoke. There was justifiable pride in their accomplishment. If Fresno State could hold onto their lead, we'd play for the national championship. But Reggie Bush exploded, leading a USC comeback. We were left at No. 3 in the country, tantalizingly close to playing for the national championship.

The Orange Bowl trip was our reward for the Big Ten title. As we readied to take on ACC champion Florida State and legendary coach Bobby Bowden, we knew we were in for another physical game. There were multiple NFL first-round draft picks on their defense all back and healthy for our game.

There was so much speed on the field. It was a brutal game. The hitting was as intense as any game ever played at the college level. In the second quarter, Michael took a hit to his right throwing shoulder that team doctor Wayne Sebastianelli noticed. He asked Mike to look at his shoulder.

Mike refused to get checked out. It was not the first time he'd been hurt that year and played through it. In his last home game, he took a big hit to his sternum against Wisconsin and was wheezing. When I asked if he was okay, he just about ripped my head off. "Jay I am *not* coming out of this game. Their guys keep saying they were gonna knock me out. *I am not coming out of this game.*"

He did come out of the game a few minutes early, but it was with a big lead and only a couple of plays left. Joe pulled him out, setting up a rousing standing ovation unlike any I'd seen at Penn State.

He would not leave the Orange Bowl despite a shoulder separation to his throwing arm. On the next series, he threw a pass to a leaping Kilmer, who made a circus catch for a 14–13 lead just before halftime.

We won the game in the third overtime, well past midnight. As the Penn State band played, I saw Michael get up and direct them. I saw Tamba and thought of his career. I remembered how he'd dominated Wisconsin in his last home game, a game when a child battling cancer named Jake Solomon had attended with his family to see his favorite player—Tamba Hali. After that Wisconsin game, I took Jake in to see Tamba and I'm not sure who that meeting meant more to.

In the afterglow of that Orange Bowl, I saw smiles and faces beaming from knowing they had worked hard and accomplished something that would thunder through the generations in the memories of Penn Staters forever.

Someone snapped that photo of Michael and Joe Paterno. That memory and photo remain even after the coach is gone.

Part of me believes Joe put Michael's picture on that wall because of all he represents, an image capturing the triumph of hope realized, fate delivered, destiny fulfilled.

But beyond that moment, Michael symbolizes so many over many decades. A skinny kid no one wanted became the legendary Shane Conlan. The last guy in one year's recruiting class became Pro Football Hall of Famer Jack Ham.

That uniform symbolizes Courtney Brown, who spent a Saturday in April being the first selection in the entire NFL Draft before returning to campus the next week to finish his degree.

It stands for Mike Reid, a renaissance man who played football not only because he was among the best ever to play, but also because it was a means to an end. He left the NFL at the height of his ability to pursue a wildly successful music career.

That image stands for the adversity and pain John Cappelletti played through while winning the 1973 Heisman Trophy, which he dedicated to his leukemia-stricken brother, Joey.

I could go on and on.

In that player in the picture, Joe saw a young man whom everyone wanted as a football player, but few wanted as the quarterback to lead their team. In that picture Joe saw Michael as the longer road taken, the right path chosen that led to a destiny never to be forgotten. He did not see one player but one who was symbolic of a team that no one believed in, that everyone doubted.

In that moment Joe saw a picture of team joy, love, and a bond formed that no one can ever forget or take away. It was something I'd heard him talk about often but most notably while he sat on the couch at NFL great Walter Payton's home. We were there to recruit his son, Jarrett, but once Joe and Walter started talking, the rest of us all listened in awe.

At that point Walter's health had already begun to falter, the whites of his eyes yellowed from jaundice. The most striking point was their discussion of a championship attained. Both Walter and Joe talked about how no bad day could ever take away the memories of the pursuit of a championship.

Both champions agreed that being handed a trophy was just a moment.

It was the journey that mattered. It was bonds formed in the struggle. It was when in-fighting amongst each other was ultimately defeated by shared pains and joys to form a unit battling as brothers-in-arms.

That is the ultimate symbolism of Michael Robinson and Joe Paterno in that picture and why I believe that he placed it so prominently in his den. It was the fulfillment of perhaps Joe Paterno's and Penn State's most improbable journey.

Michael represented a team willing to trust Joe Paterno when the whole world thought they were fools. Joe Paterno trusted them back when many thought that he placed his hopes in an unworthy team. But that trust would be the catalyst for a wonderful stretch run in Joe Paterno's career, a stretch run that was the envy of any program in the country and a run worthy of capping a grand experiment.

Chapter 33

Vindication

After a big win in 2005, ESPN's Holly Rowe asked Joe if he thought that "Penn State was back." He responded, "Well, I don't know that we ever left."

That was how he truly felt. Joe Paterno hated the word vindication and would never utter it. But there was vindication in his record over the last seven years of his career—unsurpassed achievement at the highest level academically and athletically. From that cold 2004 November day at Indiana through his final game, Joe Paterno led Penn State to the sixth-best record in the country.

During that stretch we were the only football team in the country to win over 77 percent of our games and graduate over 80 percent of our student-athletes. No one else was even close. In his last run, Joe Paterno had restored Penn State to the nation's elite *on his terms*.

In 2012 some tried to advance a narrative that Penn State needed to "Restore the Roar," but when the administration fired Joe Paterno, we were 8–1, well on our way to a fourth top 10 finish in seven seasons and a third Big Ten title in seven seasons. The program was well positioned for the future, and that's why he'd decided before the 2011 season that it was ready for the next coach to be successful.

Some try to diminish what was accomplished in Joe's last years, claiming he'd been a figurehead having little to do with the team's success. Those who were in the meetings and saw his input know better. Was Joe calling every offensive and defensive play like he had done in the 1960s and 1970s? No. But no one else has done that since either. But he had great input on our schemes.

The 2003 defense had struggled against the run, so in 2004 he demanded that it best utilize the talent on hand. He forced the defense to a base stack alignment, allowing defensive ends Tamba Hali and Matt Rice to get up field from leverage positions. From 2004 through 2011, Penn State played from that base alignment, consistently ranking among the national leaders on defense.

In 2005 to utilize the skills of mobile quarterback Michael Robinson, he wanted us to return to the things we'd done in 2002 and add a couple of wrinkles. In 2008 he returned us to that offense to utilize the similar skill set of Daryll Clark. The results were three years of All-Big Ten quarterbacks who won the Big Ten MVP award two times.

In many years the 9–4 seasons in 2006 and 2007 would have been seen as successful rebuilding years. But following the magical 2005 season, they were disappointing to some. But what I learned from Joe Paterno was loyalty. Despite criticism from fans, Joe realized that quarterback Anthony Morelli had come to Penn State at a time when many high-profile recruits turned away from us.

Because he was following Robinson, perhaps the most popular Penn State quarterback ever, Anthony dealt with unfair criticism. During Anthony's two years starting, we finished among the top 25 both years, including wins over Iowa, Tennessee, Texas A&M, Michigan State, and routs of Notre Dame and Wisconsin.

The 2006 season was tough. Our young team had to play at No. 4 Notre Dame and at No. 1 Ohio State in the first four weeks. Of our four losses, three of them were to teams in the top four. The fourth loss occurred at Wisconsin, and during that game, our tight end Andrew Quarless collided with Joe on the sideline.

Joe's tibia was fractured in two or three places, and his ACL would need to be repaired. As it happened I didn't see how serious it was. I saw that Joe had gotten back up and was standing again, so I assumed he was okay.

After a few plays, he knew he was in serious trouble, but who could've even stood up for one play after that injury? That is how tough he was. I knew it was serious when he had to sit and then ultimately leave the game. The next week he was still hospitalized when we beat Temple, but he returned to coach from the box for the season-ending win over Michigan State.

We were the better team, but as the game wore on, we trailed. Joe kept handing us notes and making play suggestions. He wanted counter plays, play-action passes, and misdirection. They worked, and we came back to win 17–13.

By the end of the year, we were 8–4 and were headed to Tampa to the Outback Bowl to play Tennessee, an SEC team considered too fast for us. Joe knew we actually had more team speed. We started the game throwing to receivers who beat Tennessee's corners, forcing them to respect the pass game. Then we hammered tailback Tony Hunt right at them. By the end of the game, we'd beaten heavily favored Tennessee 20–10.

The 2007 Notre Dame game was most notable because it started a new tradition at Penn State. In 2005 we won a wild game at home against Ohio State. All 22,000-plus students wore white—creating a "White Out." The intense game environment became the college football topic of the year. It was a watershed moment in college and professional athletics. People all over the country remembered the crowd as much as our win. At halftime ESPN's Kirk Herbstreit said, "That's the best student section in the country. They're crazy." *Sports Illustrated On Campus* magazine called Penn State home games, "The Greatest Show In College Sports."

In the NBA Finals the following spring, the Miami Heat had White Outs. The next college football season you saw Blue Outs, Black Outs, Maize Outs, Red Outs, and all kinds of schools picking up the theme. We wanted to take it to another level.

In the offseason before the 2007 season, the tradition started as Guido D'Elia and I were talking about how we could trump Michigan's stadium nickname of "The Big House." Our stadium game day atmosphere was light years ahead of theirs and everyone else's. I said to Guido, "They may have the Big House, but the White House is the most important house on the planet." Something in Guido clicked. *Everyone* in the stadium, not just the students, would wear white for the Notre Dame game. The idea caught on, and there was a lot of excitement for the Notre Dame game.

By kickoff 110,078 people (all but the roughly 5,000 Notre Dame fans) were clad in white. The atmosphere was electric. With 1:14 to go in the first quarter, we trailed 7–0 as Notre Dame lined up to punt. On our own

22-yard line, Derrick Williams caught the punt just off the top of the grass in heavy traffic. He made a few guys miss before weaving all the way for a touchdown, creating an eruption of noise. It sparked us on a 31–3 run and a 31–10 victory over the Fighting Irish. That initial success of the first White House made it a Penn State tradition that remains today.

At season's end we headed to San Antonio for the Alamo Bowl against Texas A&M. In practices our team was going through the motions. We needed a spark. Joe found one a few nights before the game at a dinner with both coaching staffs and bowl officials. After the meal both head coaches got up to speak. A&M coach Gary Darnell spoke about his respect for Penn State and Joe Paterno. Then he said, "Coach, I respect you and your program, but we're gonna kick your ass."

Joe laughed along in front of everyone, but on our way to the bus, I saw his competitive fire stoked. The next day Joe held a team meeting and relayed what had been said by Texas A&M's coach.

That got the team's attention.

Then it got more interesting. Two nights before the game, the Alamo Bowl hosted a rally for both teams. The teams boarded flat boats on the Riverwalk and then floated up to the amphitheater for the rally, one of the great settings for any bowl game event.

As our boats were waiting, the A&M team boats floated by, and their players started shouting at our guys and talking smack. Our guys kept their mouths shut but took note. After Penn State went through the pep rally, it was A&M's turn. An A&M cheerleader made a comment about Joe's age and about needing to get him a coffin.

It had all come together, the "kick your ass" comment, the smack talking at the pep rally and team dinner, as well as the comment about Joe's coffin. Our guys had all the motivation they needed. They were focused and ready to go.

We'd also planned a few plays on offense to get backup quarterback Clark into the game. It was the start of our offense for the 2008 season. After falling behind quickly 14–0, the comeback began when Morelli threw a pretty fourth-down pass to the end zone to Deon Butler, who made a clutch catch to score a 30-yard touchdown. In the second quarter, we put Clark in the game with Anthony. Daryll racked up 50 rushing yards and a touchdown. He gave us a spark, and we won 24–17.

After the game I knew we'd get asked about the new plays that Daryll had run. I also knew that Michigan had just hired West Virginia head coach Rich Rodriguez. The media hyped him as the man who would bring the spread offense to the Big Ten conference. We'd already run the spread offense in 2002 and 2005 with a lot of success. Before the bowl as we put in the plays for Daryll, I decided to nickname our offense the "Spread HD." Our more advanced level of the spread offense would co-opt the Michigan/Rodriguez hype—particularly in recruiting.

Joe was on board as I explained pre-empting the coronation of Michigan's new coach as the Big Ten spread offense guru. Joe liked the idea, but he reminded me that we'd better deliver the next fall. He reminded me that the worst thing we could do was over-promise. "The backlash if you over-promise is twice as bad. This better be good," he said.

I promised him we'd deliver.

We talked about the Spread HD with some of our players before the bowl game. I prepped wide receiver Williams to let the term Spread HD *accidentally* slip out in his postgame bowl interviews. Within a few days writers were calling to ask about the Spread HD.

After the bowl game, we also had to make sure that our team knew Daryll's play in the game was not an anointment of him as our starter for the following year. On New Year's Day, I had a long conversation with quarterback Pat Devlin's mother and father to explain just that. His parents, Mark and Connie, are great people, and I understood that they had goals and hopes for their son.

All through the spring and preseason practice, I tracked and charted every pass the quarterbacks threw in practice. The toughest part is making the call between two talented players—particularly when you like both guys and their parents.

When it finally came time, it was decided that Daryll would be the starter. But we did play Pat early in the games at the start of the season. He played in the first half in the early games and did well. We knew we had two guys who would be ready to play.

The Spread HD took off like wildfire. We scored 66 points in the opener and then rolled up 45 points on Oregon State—who would three weeks later beat USC. We rolled up 55 at Syracuse and 45 at home against Temple. The country was watching this offense go up and down the field, and the term

Spread HD had taken hold. The offense would finish the year ranked among the top 10 offenses in conference history.

After five games the Spread HD had its own feature article in *ESPN The Magazine*, telling the story of the diverse offense from the point of view of the football. The concept behind the offense was that all five skill players had to be able to know all five positions. It came from reading Boston Celtics legend Bill Russell talk about his teammates. The Celtics knew what every guy on the floor had to do and could adjust. Our group of guys all could handle the demanding mental aspect of the offense.

The toughest stretch was a three-game set in October. We had a night game at Wisconsin, a home game against Michigan, and another road night game at Ohio State. The tone was set when we blew up the Badgers in Madison 48–7, and then we fell behind 17–7 at home against Michigan before exploding to win 46–17. Finally, at Ohio State we won a defensive battle 13–6. It was a big night for us in Columbus, and though we moved the ball, neither team could break through.

The night before that game, we met as an offensive unit. I brought out the tape of Illinois beating Ohio State in Columbus from the previous season. Late in that game, Illinois took control of the ball and ran it right at the Buckeyes to seal the win.

I mentioned how no one believed we could win, but that tomorrow was to be our day. I even mentioned the biblical concept of faith being the hope and belief in something as yet unseen.

Late in the third quarter, we trailed 6–3, and our starting quarterback, Clark, got knocked out of the game. He fought with the medical staff to go back in, getting so argumentative that they hid his helmet. In the fourth quarter, safety Mark Rubin stripped Ohio State quarterback Terrelle Pryor of the football, and we took over near mid-field.

This was the moment. We ran the ball over and over to take a 10–6 lead. We got the ball back and ran it every play before kicking a field goal to go up 13–6. The game was finally clinched when defensive back Lydell Sargeant intercepted a pass in the end zone. As all the coaches got into the elevators to head down, we heard on the broadcast in the hall that the play was under review. "Tell their guys it's under review," Joe said.

I went to the elevator and told the Ohio State coaches to wait for the review. The play stood, but that act of sportsmanship was noticed by ESPN's

Ivan Maisel who wrote about it. It shouldn't have surprised anyone—it was the way Joe played the game and the way I was raised.

> One thing and one thing only—a single focus for an entire life.
> Turn the boys into men, the team into a title holder.
> The whole town into believers, the whole nation into fans.
> That's what this 81 year old has done, and continues to do...
> With another installment of Nittany Lions that has national championship hopes.
> He's still got it all, the desire, the drive, the DREAM.
> Tonight Joe Paterno will add a few lines to his long and legendary life story...
>
> *—Brent Musburger in the ESPN introduction*
> *for the 2008 Ohio State game*

The heartbreaker came at Iowa City. Late in the game, we had a 23–21 lead. Iowa got the ball back in their own end and marched into field-goal range to kick the game-winner as time expired.

Lesser teams might have thrown it in, but we won our last two games. The finale was a 49–18 rout of 15th-ranked Michigan State in a game we absolutely had to win to win the conference. The day was brutally cold and snowy, but nearly 110,000 fans showed up to be a part of it. Early in the game, Joe said to the coaches, "Let's not be uptight for this game. The players know we're playing for the conference championship, and they will feed off you. Be aggressive, and we'll be okay. Let them play fast and loose, and we'll win."

He was right. Despite windy weather Clark and Devlin combined to throw for over 400 yards. Butler caught only three passes for the game—all of them for second-half touchdowns.

We loved coaching that group of players. They were smart and fast and tough. Between Clark, running back Evan Royster, and receivers Butler, Williams, Jordan Norwood, Brett Brackett, and tight ends Mickey Shuler and Andrew Quarless, those eight players left Penn State with 10 degrees.

The offensive line featured two Academic All-Americans in Gerald Cadogan and Stefan Wisniewski.

It was a true Penn State team with young men excelling in the classroom and on the field.

Before the bowl game, Devlin's parents came to Joe Paterno's house and wanted to talk to him about Pat transferring. It was not easy for my father to release Pat. He was a great young man on and off the field. We envisioned playing him some again in 2009 and then having him take the reins of the team in 2010. It was not to be as he transferred to Delaware.

In the 2009 season, we fell one game short of repeating as Big Ten champions but still finished with an 11–2 record and in the top 10 after defeating LSU in the Capital One Bowl in Orlando, Florida. That comeback on a muddy, sloppy field resulted in a 19–17 win.

Clark had graduated with two degrees. He had come a long way from his high school in Youngstown, Ohio. The story of how he got to us is complicated. In the late winter and spring of 2003, everyone was chasing Chad Henne, a junior quarterback from Wilson High School outside of Reading, Pennsylvania. In early May, Chad called Joe Paterno and committed to Penn State.

A week later I was in his high school, visiting his Wilson coach, who told me that the commitment was so secret that Chad's parents didn't even know. That got my attention, so I kept looking around at other quarterbacks.

I'd kept in touch with Daryll's high school because I had seen him play the year before when I had gone to see Daryll's senior teammate—Louis Irizarry. While I was there, I noticed Daryll, a junior quarterback with a strong but still inaccurate arm. He had tools to build on.

That night sticks out because sometime in the third quarter, after the fifth or sixth fight between the two teams, Jody, the high school's athletics staff assistant, came over to Bill Kenney and me. "I don't want to alarm you, but…" she began, "the police think there may be some gun play after the game. If you back up against the wall, you'll be okay because they usually fire from over there behind you."

It wasn't said with even a hint of alarm—just a matter of fact. Both Bill and I tried to act tough and shrug it off. About 10 minutes later, Bill looked at me and said, "We don't need to stay for the whole game. We know Louis is good enough, don't we?" It didn't take me long to agree. There was no need to stay and see if the police were right. But we had seen enough of Louis and enough to know I should I keep tabs on Daryll.

As May turned into June, I was worried about the "commitment" from Henne. We were hearing about his high school coach taking him on trips to Miami, Tennessee, and Michigan. As July turned to August, his coach repeated to Kenney that Chad was all set for Penn State.

Ultimately, he announced his decision to go to Michigan in August. We weren't totally surprised so we were ready with other quarterbacks. On an off day that fall, I drove to Philly to see one quarterback play an afternoon game and then flew to watch Daryll play that night. By the time the game was over, I knew Daryll was our guy.

Then Anthony Morelli, who had committed to Pitt, contacted us to say he wanted us to reopen his recruiting. Tom Bradley, our western Pennsylvania recruiter, and I spoke with Joe about it. Joe said to us, "If he talks to Walt Harris [Pitt's head coach] and tells him that he's going to reopen the recruiting, then you can talk to him. But I don't want to talk to him until then. He made a commitment to them and if he's got the guts to tell them, then I can respect that. If he doesn't talk to Pitt, then you stay away."

To Anthony's credit he talked to Pitt and was upfront about it. In late January we went to see him at his uncle and aunt's house. As we were getting ready to leave, Anthony gave Joe a picture from his official visit to Penn State's campus. He told us to open it in the car on the way to the airport. Joe opened it, and on the back, Anthony had written a message: "Coach, it would be an honor to play for you."

Several years later Anthony and his wife walked into my father's viewing. Seeing tears in his eyes, I remembered that moment. Anthony always understood how special a man Joe Paterno had been to him and so many others.

A few days prior to that visit to Morelli, we had gone in to see Clark. We had to make a proposal to Daryll. His grades were not where they needed to be. Having spent time with him, I knew Daryll had the ability to do the work. He just hadn't applied himself. As we sat in Ursuline High School athletic director Jim Maughan's office, Joe made his pitch. "Daryll," Joe said, "whether you make the NCAA standard or not, I want you to go to Kiski Prep for a year before you come to Penn State. You need a year to go there so that you are ready for college academically. You're not ready now."

That was not exactly the recruiting pitch Daryll had anticipated when we got there. He and I had talked about it, but now it was real. "Look Daryll," I said, "it's hard being young and thinking about this. But you've got to ask yourself what you'd say to yourself if you were 40 and talking to your 18-year-old self."

Daryll and his father talked with us about what the prep school year would entail. He could have gone to Nebraska, Iowa, or West Virginia without going to prep school. "Look," Joe said, "it's hard at your age to be patient. When you get older, you'll see that one year is a relatively short period of time. But remember it doesn't matter where you are when you start college, it's where you're at when it is time to get out."

Then Joe told him a story about a young man he'd recruited decades earlier. Everyone in his family told him to major in engineering. He visited Penn State and met with an engineering professor. The professor sensed hesitation in the young man. "I'm not sure what I want to study," the young man said. "But I know when I am 60 I don't want my life to have been decided by an 18-year-old kid."

Joe shared that story with Daryll, and it hit home. He challenged Daryll to make the decision as a mature man who would look back to advise him. This decision was bigger than the next year. "Coach," Daryll said, "I'm gonna make the decision a man would make. I will go to prep school."

All in all, Michigan ended up with Henne, who had a great career, and we ended up with two-time All-Conference quarterback and Big Ten MVP Daryll Clark.

But when Daryll left, we had big shoes to fill.

In 2010 we'd settled on Rob Bolden, Kevin Newsome, and Matt McGloin in the last week and a half of preseason practice. The week of the first game, Joe was ready to decide who would be the starter. Joe had a staff meeting and asked the entire staff for their thoughts. I was the last to express my opinion, and by the time it got to me, the vote was unanimous in favor of Bolden. The genius of Joe's method was in making them all weigh in, so they couldn't gripe about the decision later. They'd gone on the record.

The 2010 start would not be easy. After a very good performance in the season opener against Youngstown State, we had to go play at top-ranked and defending national champion Alabama. It was going to be a rapid ascent up the learning curve.

The trip to Alabama was one we'd looked forward to for years, and the atmosphere did not disappoint. But the greatest moment came at the end of pregame warm-ups. As Joe walked off the field toward the Alabama student section, they rose and gave him a standing ovation that was joined by everyone in the stadium. It stills gives me chills when I think about it.

For our seventh game, we headed to Minnesota. We came out on fire with Bolden hitting his first nine passes and going 11-of-13 before suffering an injury. McGloin came in. "Don't get conservative," Joe said, "keep throwing it. They'll expect a run play with a new quarterback."

We called a play-action pass. I told the coaches on the sideline to get the extra-point team ready because I knew Matt would throw for the end zone. He did, and Derrick Moye pulled in the touchdown. It confirmed Matt's tremendous self-confidence, which carried him through the rest of his career.

The next week Matt started as we beat Michigan in a wild shootout. No matter how far ahead we got, it seemed the Wolverines were three plays (or less) from scoring. Ultimately, they couldn't stop us, and we won 41–31. After the game I was at my parents' house. I saw my mom and stopped her for a moment. "Mom," I asked, "are Diana and her family coming up for the game next week?"

"Why would they?" My mom asked.

"Mom, tonight was Dad's 399th win. Next week should be number 400."

"So?"

"Mom, it's huge. No one at this level has ever done it. If we win, they may not want to miss it."

It never dawned on her to think about those things, but I saw Diana in the house and gave her more information than I gave my mom. Diana asked if we were going to win the next week, and I guaranteed it. "Don't say that. It's bad luck," she said.

Coaches' Quotes on ESPN Pregame before the 400th Win

"It's amazing to me that when he went to Penn State, I was 10, and he's still there. And he's been able to adjust and adapt." —then-Texas coach Mack Brown

"He's set a great example of how a coach should conduct himself in doing things the right way." —Oklahoma coach Bob Stoops

"I had the opportunity to work for Coach Paterno for six years and probably not a day that goes by that I don't call upon something he taught me." —then-Rutgers coach Greg Schiano

"His longevity, his loyalty, his character, I am a great admirer of Joe Paterno." —then-Florida coach Urban Meyer

"I don't think there'll ever be one like Joe Paterno." —then-Ohio State coach Jim Tressel

In pregame warm-ups, Joe told McGloin to be ready. Bolden hadn't played in three weeks, and he wasn't sure if Rob was completely ready. Rob moved the team, but we didn't finish drives. After a couple of series, we put Matt in the game, but we still couldn't get on the board. With 56 seconds to go in the first half, Northwestern pulled ahead 21–0. The stadium just died. My superstitious sister, Diana, was mad that I had guaranteed a win.

After Northwestern's kickoff we started on our own 9-yard line with under a minute left in the half. I suggested to Joe that we run a draw to start the next possession. If we made good yardage, then we'd go into the no huddle and try to get a score before the half. His response was classic Joe. "Why hold back now? The stuff we were doing before wasn't exactly killing them," he said.

On third and 3 from our own 32-yard line, we called the draw, and Stephon Green broke it for 21 yards. With 18 seconds left, Matt hit a pass for 20 more yards. The next play he hit fullback Joey Suhey to the 7-yard line. We had eight seconds left when Matt hit Brett Brackett in the back of the end zone.

At halftime our team ran into the locker room. The place was alive with energy, and everyone could sense something special was happening. We'd just gone 91 yards in 53 seconds to get back in the game.

In the locker room, you could see belief in everyone's eyes. Joe's fiery manner was infectious. He told the defense to stop them a few times, and we'd be right back in this. In the offensive meeting room, he had a lot of suggestions, and we made adjustments. Right before we headed back out, he encouraged everyone and reminded them that momentum was on our side and that if we played hard and eliminated the mistakes of the first half, we'd win.

Joe's prediction snowballed, and the field seemed to tilt in our favor. We scored on our next four possessions, building a 35–21 lead that held.

The stadium energy grew with each score and stop until the last seconds ticked away. Joe was hoisted on the players' shoulders and carried to a stage brought out for the occasion.

That night I felt a magic that I'll never forget. My wife and children had come down on the field. My siblings were there with their families. There were good friends on the field, too.

Then I saw Diana, pointed at her, and said, "I told you so." She smiled.

As Joe spoke on that podium, I felt the weight of decades of history and a long line of young men who had worn those uniforms. "I know you all wanna get home," Joe said. "I want to thank President Spanier and Tim Curley for making this such a special night. But most of all I want to thank the guys who have played for us and I mean us, I mean Penn State. People ask why I stayed here so long and you know what? Look around, look around. I love you all."

Tom Rinaldi's ESPN broadcast opening for the 2010 Northwestern game

It's not a number; it's a narrative.

It's not a total; it's a tale.

Written across autumns, forged by generations, made by dozens of teams, guided by one man.

The ancient glasses, the classic look, the lasting touch, and the steady way.

Formations come and go; schemes thrive and fade.

Commitment endures.

It's not just longevity...

It's consistency, integrity, history.

And soon, it's the same ending for 400 game days...It's called victory.

Chapter 34

Tales from the Gridiron

Joe Paterno loved good stories—both telling them and hearing. Over the years I heard many: Joe watching Jim Brown play high school basketball or saying Lenny Moore was the greatest football player he had ever been around. He told us about Al Davis trying to get Penn State standout Dave Robinson to sign a contract on the hood of a car in Rec Hall parking lot before Dave signed with Green Bay. Another time Joe had his lunch at The Corner Room downtown interrupted to take a call from Vince Lombardi who wanted his input on a player they were considering for the NFL draft. He'd led an interesting life, and I was blessed to witness or be told about much of it.

Twice when I was a young kid, I answered the phone to hear a thick recognizable Southern accent on the other end. To my amazement I realized it was Coach Bryant from Alabama. Another evening in late 1975, Coach Bryant phoned again; this time my mother answered the call. At the time Penn State had an invitation to the Gator Bowl, and Joe was trying to get into the Cotton Bowl. This was long before BCS and conference contracts tied up all the bowl slots.

Coach Bryant was calling to invite Penn State to the Sugar Bowl. Joe was unsure how serious this offer was. "Coach," Joe said, "now you and I have never done business together. I have a bid to the Gator Bowl and I may have one for the Cotton Bowl, but I can't turn them down and be left with nothing."

"Joe," Bryant said, "I'm telling you; you got the bid."

Joe asked if the director of the Sugar Bowl was with him, and Bryant put him on the phone. Joe asked if Coach Bryant was serious in extending Sugar Bowl invitations. The director assured Joe that while Bryant had had a few drinks, he was good for the invite. "Okay," Joe said, "put him on."

When Bryant got back on the phone, he reassured Joe that the bid was his. Then Joe asked why he wanted to play Penn State. "Because your team is not as good as your record, and I need a bowl win," Bryant said.

Both statements were true. Penn State was not a great team, and Bryant had not won a bowl game since the 1966 Sugar Bowl, a streak that had seen him go an uncharacteristic 0–7–1 in bowls. In the end Bryant got a tight 13–6 win over Penn State on New Year's Eve in the first Sugar Bowl played inside the Louisiana Superdome.

Bryant came out to coach without his houndstooth hat. During pregame, Joe asked Bryant where his hat was. "My momma taught me to take my hat off indoors, and there's a roof here," Bryant said.

That stayed with my dad because he required his players and his own children to remove their hats indoors. In fact Penn State's locker room door had a sign, reminding people to remove their hats when they entered.

In 1978 the two teams met again in the Sugar Bowl, this time for the national championship. A few days before the game, I was in a New Orleans Hilton suite with my father and his brother, my uncle George, watching Ohio State play Clemson in the Gator Bowl.

Late in the Gator Bowl, Ohio State threw an interception that ended the game. Legendary Ohio State coach Woody Hayes lost his cool and grabbed the Clemson linebacker. I remember the look on my dad's face. He really liked Coach Hayes and hoped this wouldn't end his career.

Early the next morning, Joe's phone rang, and it was Bryant. As Joe sat at a desk in the suite, he could see the barges coming up and down the Mississippi River in the early grey of a foggy New Orleans morning.

Joe and Coach Bryant had a scheduled joint press conference later that morning, and the subject of Woody Hayes was bound to come up. Bryant wanted to discuss how they'd handle the questions. After talking, Bryant told Joe that if they were asked he'd take the question. At the press conference, Bryant essentially said Woody Hayes was a little old man and the kid from Clemson was a big strong linebacker wearing a helmet and full pads and that he was pretty sure no one had gotten hurt. There were no more questions about it.

Despite two bowl setbacks to Bryant, Joe Paterno was arguably the best bowl coach in college football history, having won more bowls than anyone and with one of the best winning percentages in postseason history. But the setbacks drove him to success.

On January 1, 1993, after a bad bowl loss to Stanford, we were watching the Alabama-Miami national championship with my father. Earlier that year Penn State had played Miami and should have won the game. In the Sugar Bowl, Joe saw Alabama employing the same defensive schemes Penn State had used. But Alabama played with a faster nickel back rather than keeping all of their linebackers in the game as Penn State had done.

When Alabama made the defensive play to break open the game, Joe threw down the yellow sheets of paper he was making notes on and pointed at the television defiantly. "Aw nuts!" he shouted "You see that? I wanted to use a nickel back and I gave in. *We* should be in that game. But mark this down: we're going to get right back in it. I'm not getting talked out of anything again!"

After a 9–2 regular season in 1993, the first year of Penn State's Big Ten play, the team was invited to play in the Citrus Bowl in Orlando, Florida, against heavily favored and sixth-ranked Tennessee.

Joe re-evaluated his bowl preparation, going back to his 1960s bowl training plans. He took the team to Melbourne, Florida on December 19th for a tough five-day camp, including two-a-day practices. By the time they got to Orlando, he wanted them familiar with the game plan, so bowl activity distractions wouldn't interfere with their readiness. But he also used the bowl practices as a training camp to evaluate the talent he had on hand for the following year.

After falling behind 10–0 in the Citrus Bowl, Penn State took control and won 31–13. For the rest of his career, Joe used that blueprint for bowl preparation. Bowl mini-camps became a tradition, and from 1993 on, Penn State compiled a stellar bowl record of 10 wins against four losses.

The bigger picture from 1993 bowl preparation was the momentum for the 1994 season. Penn State assembled what may still be the greatest offense in college football history.

Despite holding starters out of over 12 quarters of lopsided wins, the team still averaged more than 500 yards per game and nearly 50 points. The offense boasted five first-team All-Americans and five first-found NFL draft picks. The top 14 players on the depth chart logged a combined 112 years in the NFL (an average of eight years)—and 92.8 percent of them graduated.

Penn State finished the year 12–0 with a win over Oregon in the Rose Bowl. Just two years after he'd predicted he'd be back, he was hoisting the Rose Bowl trophy after an undefeated season.

The next season, 1995, I joined the coaching staff. At season's end in the Outback Bowl, we beat Auburn 43–14 behind a dominant final performance by receiver Bobby Engram despite a torrential downpour of biblical proportions. Bobby finished as one of the great Penn State players of all time.

After the game he dropped in to the postgame party to see Joe and thank him. Joe invited him to stay since Bobby was done as a Penn State player. His receivers coach Kenny Jackson was in the suite as were several other notable Penn State players. NFL first-round picks Kyle Brady, Ki-Jana Carter, and O.J. McDuffie were there.

An argument began about the best receiver in Penn State history—with every receiver in the room voting for himself. The argument lingered late into the evening, getting louder and funnier. Joe had gone to bed, but he re-emerged with a box of cigars the Outback Bowl had given him. "Here, if you're gonna argue, take these cigars and smoke them. It should at least quiet you down, so I can pack and then get some sleep," he laughed.

After that run of bowl success, Joe got calls from Ohio State's John Cooper and Michigan's Lloyd Carr, asking for his bowl preparation schedule, so he sent them all of his bowl schedules. I was one of the coaches who asked why he helped those guys out. He replied that if Ohio State and Michigan won their bowl games it made the conference stronger and we'd all benefit.

Michigan and Joe Paterno had some history. After Penn State's undefeated 1968 season, Michigan athletic director Don Canham, a man Joe greatly respected, contacted him about their head coaching vacancy. They met in Pittsburgh and after some consideration, Joe politely declined the offer, indicating that he felt Penn State had a great future.

A few days later Canham called back and asked about a former Woody Hayes assistant named Bo Schembechler. Joe did not know Bo, but something Canham said jumped out at him. "Joe," Don said, "Woody Hayes said he was the best assistant he ever had."

"If Woody said that, you'd better hire him," Joe said laughing.

A few decades later Michigan was forced to fire their head coach after an off-field incident in the spring of 1995. Joe Paterno got a call from a Michigan administrator to ask his advice. They wanted to make Carr the interim head coach and go look for a national candidate. Joe's advice was to hire Lloyd and forget the interim tag. "Look, if you make him the interim coach, it will hurt your recruiting," Joe said.

With a chance to help his own recruiting, Joe was giving honest advice to a rival school. Ultimately, they kept the interim tag until the fall when they hired Carr permanently. In 1997 Carr delivered Michigan's first national title in 50 years.

The Michigan and Ohio State games were always special for Penn State. In 1995 we were hosting Michigan in November. On Tuesday that week, we received an early winter gift of 18 inches of snow. The university bought snow shovels and offered anyone $5 an hour to help clear the stadium. Fraternities sent their pledge classes to earn beer money for the weekend. Inmates from nearby Rockview State Prison came in to shovel. On Wednesday night I shoveled but also presented the stadium crew with a case of beer.

The day before the contest, Joe talked to his team about the dramatic setting of a snow game. "When you were kids, if it was snowing, you'd be out playing football in it," he said. "Tomorrow will be no different. It is a game. Have fun. You will remember this game the rest of your lives. Make them great memories."

Michigan's field-goal rush had been consistent all year and presented an opportunity to run a fake I'd brought from James Madison University the year before. On the previous two field goals and two extra points, they were still in the same alignment. Upstairs we kept telling Fran Ganter that we had the fake.

With under three minutes to go, we led 20–17. Facing fourth and goal, Fran told Joe he wanted the fake, and Joe nodded. A touchdown would put us up 10 points and ice the game. The holder, Joe Nastasi, took the snap, the blocks came off perfectly, and he walked in for a 27–17 win. It was indeed a game we will remember the rest of our lives.

The next year before the 1996 game at Michigan, Joe Paterno delivered one of the most memorable Friday night speeches I'd heard him give. Joe inspired his team using a recent sports story to help him. The week before

Evander Holyfield defeated Mike Tyson in a stunning 11-round upset. Joe stood up that Friday night and started to talk about the fight. "When Tyson fought Holyfield, Tyson landed some early punches," he said. "But Holyfield was not afraid. Tyson has intimidated and bullied and scared the men he's fought. They've been beaten mentally before they even got into the battle. Tyson saw he could not bully or scare Holyfield. He was forced to trade punches and battle through 11 rounds. Holyfield took some punches, stood his ground, and fought back."

All the guys in the room were eerily silent; Joe had their rapt attention. He used an event they had all watched and was drawing them to his ultimate lesson. "Now tomorrow you're going into Michigan," he said. "This is their stadium. They have a great tradition and they are used to intimidating people. Our tradition takes a backseat to no one. *Be proud.* They'll land some punches; they will make some plays. But stand unafraid, and when the time is right, we'll deliver our counterpunches to ultimately knock them out. It is something that you will learn tomorrow that will carry you through your life. You will take punches, and as long as you are not scared, as long as you stand your ground, you will get your opening to win the fight. Tomorrow will be a fight. But stand firm, find your opening, and you will win."

The team did not say a word as they filed out of the room. When I went to check my guys in, they were ready to play.

The next day we took some punches, delivered some punches, and late in the game on a key third down, our tailback Curtis Enis broke free for the knockout touchdown that put them away in a 29–17 win.

Penn State games with Michigan and Ohio State were also the catalyst for one of the biggest changes in college football, which occurred in the fall of 2004. That season the Big Ten conference began a trial run in instant replay. What many have forgotten was the driving force behind instant replay.

In 2002 at Michigan, our game was tied late in the fourth quarter. On a third down and 4 from the Michigan 48-yard line with 49 seconds left, Zack Mills made a great throw to Tony Johnson, who got both feet clearly in bounds. He was incorrectly ruled out of bounds. The correct call would've put us in field-goal range to win the game. The game went to overtime, and we lost.

After the game Joe Paterno talked to Tim Curley and president Graham Spanier about instant replay. In the offseason after 2002, only two schools were against it—Ohio State and Michigan. "What do they know that we don't?" Joe quipped in a staff meeting.

The next season we hosted Ohio State. On a late drive, Ohio State faced a critical third down. Their tight end dropped a pass he then landed on. It was called a completion, giving them a first down. On Monday a photo surfaced, showing the tight end a good two feet off the ground, the ball on the ground, and the official looking right at the ball.

Joe Paterno made it his mission to get instant replay instituted. He became impossible to ignore, and the Big Ten adopted instant replay. That year it was a rousing success and by 2005 it was in use nationwide.

There are a lot of happy memories from the years coaching with my father. So many fall Saturdays watching pregame warm-ups and seeing how much joy he had being in the stadium. Every week before I went up to coach from the box upstairs, I would shake his hand last.

There was always the smile from seeing his black shoes and white socks laid out at his locker. At home there was always a sandwich—ham and Swiss on rye; on the road there were two hot dogs.

There were great games—some wins and some losses—but for him it was the competition that he relished. It was working to prepare against someone else who was working to win and then seeing how you stacked up.

He loved big games. In the late 1970s, he added games for the 1980s against Notre Dame, Nebraska, Miami, and Alabama. When we joined the Big Ten, we won non-conference games against USC, Nebraska, Notre Dame, Miami, Louisville, Pitt, and Oregon State and bowl games against Tennessee, Oregon, Auburn, Texas, Kentucky, Texas A&M, Florida State, and LSU.

Before the 1999 season, we were approached by the Pigskin Classic about opening the season against Arizona. The Wildcats had a great 1998 season and were the preseason favorite for the Pac-10 title. Everyone wanted to play the game.

Joe went to work feverishly, designing schemes for that game. Every week or so in June and July, the staff would find notes and plays in Joe's writing under our office doors.

On June 15 a 17-page packet appeared followed by more packets. July 5 had 14 pages, July 7 had five pages, July 8 had six pages, July 8 (2 PM) had five more pages, July 12 had 24 pages, July 15 had six pages of run game and nine pages of pass game, and July 26 had three run pages and nine more pass pages. All told that summer, we received 108 pages of hand-written notes, suggestions, ideas, and plays for the opening game and for the season. By kickoff between our third-ranked team and fourth-ranked Arizona, we were prepared.

The defense featured two All-American linebackers in LaVar Arrington and Brandon Short as well as All-American defensive end Courtney Brown. But what surprised everyone was the explosive offense that destroyed Arizona's vaunted Desert Swarm defense. By the time the game had ended, we'd made a powerful opening statement with a 41–7 win.

A few weeks later we went to play at eighth-ranked Miami and found ourselves in a dogfight. Miami took the lead and faced a fourth and 1. If they made it, the game was over. Backup linebacker Maurice Daniels was in the game and made the key stop.

A play later Kevin Thompson made a sideline throw to Chafie Fields that he caught before outrunning the entire Miami defense for the game-winning score. The play was supposed to be a quick hitch play, but when Miami's cornerback pressed, Chafie converted to a fade, and Kevin made a great throw.

Joe's notes had paid off. Using two quarterbacks, Thompson and Rashard Casey, the offense averaged 36 points a game against a schedule that included seven games against nationally ranked teams.

Even later in his career, he was always plugged in. He could see more from field level than any coach. That ability was unique to him.

In 1996 we'd worked on a risky double reverse to fleet-footed wide receiver Fields. In the third quarter of the Fiesta Bowl, we led by seven and had the ball at our own 11-yard line. Joe ran over to Ganter and said, "I want the reverse—7 transfer."

Fran pointed out that we were on our own 11-yard line and that it might be too risky. "They're flying to the ball, we need some misdirection," Joe said.

Every offensive coach wanted to wait, but Joe overruled us. As we broke the huddle, we all held our breath, but Joe was coolly pacing the sidelines. Fields got the reverse, broke into the clear, and went all the way down to the Texas 2-yard line, setting up the touchdown that broke open the game and led to a 38–15 win over the Big 12 champion Texas Longhorns.

The funniest one was in 2005 against Wisconsin in our last home game of the season, a battle for first place in the Big Ten. Our tailback Tony Hunt was the type defenders got tired of trying to tackle. As we were driving for another score, Joe came down and told graduate assistant coach Kermit Buggs what he wanted. "Kermit," he said, "tell them I want the draw."

We were inside Wisconsin's 15-yard line, and their safeties were up around the ball, so we didn't want to run the draw. Joe came running back and asked for the draw again, to which Galen Hall relayed to Kermit that we didn't think it would work because Wisconsin's safeties were around the ball. "Kermit," Joe said, "tell them to call it or I will."

Joe sent in the draw play. Before we even broke the huddle, Joe said to Kermit, "I don't care if the safeties are on the line. They're tired of tackling Hunt. He'll score."

In the box I looked at Galen and said with a laugh, "You know this will score." Sure enough, neither safety tried to hit him as Tony crossed the goal line.

There were a number of those plays.

At Alabama in 1986, he called a reverse to wingback Blair Thomas inside the 5-yard line that scored. In fact he loved reverses inside the 10-yard line, an area of the field where most people aren't thinking about reverses. Michael Robinson lined up at receiver and scored on a reverse against Nebraska in 2002; Derrick Williams scored on a reverse against Minnesota in 2005 and on another one against Illinois in 2008. Later that year he wanted a reverse call against Indiana. Finally, on a third and 7 (not usually a reverse situation), he called it. Sure enough, Williams had carried the reverse in for a touchdown 36 yards later.

He loved throwbacks, and the week we played defending Big Ten champs Illinois in 2008 he was bugging me to design a throwback pass. "Think of something and keep an open mind," he said. "You never know when inspiration will strike you."

The next morning in the shower, I drew up the throwback pass on the foggy glass shower door. I came in, drew it up, and he gave us the okay. Just before the end of the first quarter, we threw it to a wide-open Williams for the game-tying touchdown. We went on to win 38–24.

There were moments of trial, too.

After the 1997 season, we finished 9–2 and were invited to play Florida on New Year's Day in the Citrus Bowl in Orlando. Early in December our starting running back went to a Harrisburg mall with an agent who bought him a suit. It was against NCAA rules for him to accept any gifts from an agent. By the time we arrived in Orlando on December 19, someone had broken the story.

The running back initially denied the story, but Joe kept him from practicing. Joe had already left our best receiver home because he had not performed as well in school as Joe felt he was capable of doing. He was eligible to play, and some members of our staff knew we'd need him to win the game. "If I play him, what message am I sending to him and to the team?" Joe asked. "That football is more important."

Playing the sixth-ranked Gators in Orlando was not going to be easy, especially if we lost both of those players. Even as the agent story began unfolding, our NCAA compliance coordinator received word from the NCAA that we would be okay if we played our running back.

Joe gave him one more chance and he admitted he had broken the rule. No one else had to know, but Joe knew, and that was all it took. He sent him home. As he told me, "I'd rather lose a game the right way than win a game the wrong way."

This was one game and certainly not worthy of risking a lifetime of integrity to win. It all went back to a quote Joe had spoken many times: "Losing a game is heartbreaking. Losing your sense of excellence or worth is a tragedy."

There were milestone moments.

In 2001 we began the season, and Joe was one game behind Coach Bryant in the all-time major college football career victory list. We opened with Miami—who would go on to win the national championship. We were outclassed. Then we lost to Wisconsin, Iowa, and Michigan.

We had an off week before the Northwestern game, and Joe decided to change the offense. He put in an old-school, three-back attack to utilize a stable of talented running backs that included future pros Larry Johnson, Eric McCoo, Eddie Drummond, and Omar Easy.

Our previously feeble running game exploded and with renewed offensive balance we went up and down the field. Late in the game our starting quarterback was knocked unconscious, and freshman Mills came in and led us down the field. Inside the Northwestern 10-yard line, Joe ran over and said, "Tell Jay I want the Z-Post." We called it, McCoo caught it coming out of the backfield, and we won the game.

The next week we faced Ohio State, and Joe had a chance to break the record. We moved the ball well but trailed Ohio State 13–9 before the half.

To open the second half, they got a big score to go up 20–9. On the very next series, Mills threw a short pass to a wide-open receiver who tipped it straight up in the air and into the arms of an Ohio State defender, who ran it in for a 27–9 lead.

All hope looked lost.

Joe came down and told us not to panic. We were moving the ball and just killing ourselves with mistakes. "There is a lot of time left. Just take it one play at a time," he said. "Something good will happen."

We got the ball back and ran a running play that went just about nowhere. Ganter asked me what I thought we should run. "Fran, they are blitzing a lot," I said. "Let's run the option into the boundary, see if we can at least get a first down."

"Call it," he said.

"Lucky Gun 2 Speed," I said.

We lined up, and Ohio State blitzed. Mills turned upfield, hurdled one guy, bounced off a tackle by Ohio State safety Mike Doss, and then ran 69 yards for a touchdown that became the signature play of that historic win.

Every Penn Stater can still see Zack in the air frozen in that moment for all time.

The crowd exploded and came alive. The defense cranked it up, and before we knew it, Zack hit another touchdown pass, and it was now 27–22. In the fourth quarter, we had the ball and were driving again to take the lead. Joe came down and told Fran, "Tell Jay not to forget the Z Post again."

The Z Post he wanted gave us pass protection to the field. If Ohio State kept their field blitzes coming, McCoo, an excellent receiver, would be covered by a weaker defender. After a big play and penalty put us on the 17-yard line of Ohio State, the time was ripe. "Fran, tell Joe he's getting his Z Post," I said.

Sure enough, McCoo was matched up with a linebacker, and Joe's play put us in the lead, completing an improbable comeback and a 29–27 victory for his record-breaking 324th win.

After the game I brought some old friends over to my father's house. JB Morris and Mark Kavanaugh were among them. They'd known my father since we were all kids. At the house family friend George Middlemas was there with a bottle of French Armagnac.

As if drawn from across town by the presence of an after-dinner drink, Kevin McHugh stopped by. His son, Sean, was on the team, and at that time,

Kevin's wife, Jeanne, had been diagnosed with cancer. My father encouraged Kevin to stop by and talk any time he was in town.

I was no longer drinking, but after that win, it was a special occasion. There were family and friends all over the house, and the smells of my mother's pasta sauce filled the kitchen. It had been a chilly day, but inside the hearts were fired by great camaraderie and by the warm Armagnac we sipped.

Kevin's son, Sean, had been a highly recruited player from Chagrin Falls, Ohio, and we were battling Michigan, Ohio State, and Notre Dame for him. In March of 1999, Sean and his family came up for an unofficial visit.

When we went to lunch, I explained that on an unofficial visit NCAA rules dictated that they had to pay for their own meals. As the waiter came by, we all ordered, and then Kevin ordered his lunch and a cocktail to go with it. I knew immediately I liked this guy when he said to me, "Jay, you're working, but I'm on vacation, so I'm going to have a cocktail with lunch."

They had a remarkable family, a strong Irish Catholic family with two beautiful daughters who doted on Sean, the baby of the family.

On April 9 Kevin wrote a letter to my father, thanking him for the visit. It was funny and heartfelt.

> I thought it was a terrific opportunity to witness one of college football's greatest teams, not to mention greatest head coaches. Oh I know you must get tired of being revered, but whatta' ya gonna do? Anyway Joe, it was an honor, it was fun, and we took it as a high sign of Penn State's interest in Sean that you would meet with us for breakfast. Your feedback to Sean about UCLA was priceless.
>
> One last thing. I want to take this opportunity to applaud and compliment Jay's recruiting methods and style. He has been a professional, a gentleman, and a regular guy all at the same time. He's established an excellent rapport with Sean. We've enjoyed working with him. I am sure it is not always easy following in the footsteps of "Joe Pa" but Jay appears to have it all in perspective and just does the job he sets out to do.

He sent a copy of the letter for me in the same envelope so
that Joe would see it with a handwritten note on the bottom:

Hello Jay—Thanks for a fine visit with Sean. We enjoyed
our visit. That last paragraph stops just short of asking
for a raise—but I'm setting it up.

After that Ohio State game in 2001 when Kevin walked in the door, we welcomed him with open arms and he helped salute Joe. Joe always had a special place in his heart for Kevin. It was the least we could do for a man watching his wife and the love of his life battling cancer. I still can hear his eulogy of Jeanne a few years later when he spoke about their partnership using a phrase, "The part of me that is you."

I'll also neither forget seeing a busload of our players get out at the church all dressed in coats and ties for Jeanne's funeral, nor can I ever erase the memory of the lonely bagpipe player on the snowy cemetery hill as we walked away after the graveside service.

Sean went on to marry a Penn Stater, have kids, and started the game when the Pittsburgh Steelers opened in a two-tight end set in a Super Bowl XLIII defeat of the Arizona Cardinals.

The celebration of the 324th win lingered into the following week. Someone had dropped off a large sheet cake with white and mostly blue icing. My mother sent the whole cake into the locker room, where the guys ate it up. Monday afternoon Mills had to excuse himself from our meeting.

When he came back he had a concerned look on his face. "Are you okay?" I asked him.

"I'm not sure, I just went to the bathroom and..."

I laughed because I knew what he was going to say. The blue icing had added a bluish hue to the bowel movements of everyone on the team. "Blue turds?" I asked, laughing.

"Yeah," he said, "how'd you know?"

"Me, too. It's from the blue icing on the cake."

The rest of the guys in the room chimed in, too. We had an epidemic, but it passed when the cake was all gone. It made for some good laughs, though.

But there were serious illnesses and injuries in Joe's career.

In 2006 a trophy fell off his bookshelves the morning of a home game and hit him on the head. Had Diana not been there, he may have bled to death on the floor. Dr. Wayne Sebastianelli stitched him up, and he coached in a cold rain. Both Wayne and I were in awe that a man nearing his 80th birthday could still get there and stand in the rain coaching his team for hours after significant blood loss. He was a man who truly had a mind-over-body will that almost never failed him.

His was an indomitable will to better Penn State in anything and everything. That came through in December of 1989 when Penn State announced it would join the Big Ten. That rejuvenated Joe, and he pushed to be ready to join the conference in football for the 1993 season. In notes made in April of 1993, he sketched out ideas for promoting Penn State and the Big Ten.

PROMOTION:

Penn State
Big Ten

You	You are in Big Ten Country
Athletics	Show stadiums and arenas around the conference
	Focus in on Beaver Stadium
	Construction of our new arena
	Flash attendance facts
Academics	Research
	Top Schools
	Zero in on Penn State
Exposure	To Over 300,000 alums
	How Many TV Sets
	How Many people In Big Ten Country

MEDIA MARKETING:

I. Image Themes

Credibility-Authenticity-Performance

298

Video Productions: Penn State Big Ten
and You—Athletes, Students, Fans,
Alumni, Media

Stadium

Experience

Academics

Alumni

Job Opportunities

Tradition

First Big Ten Game—Minnesota

Big Ten week—Seminars, lectures, etc.

½ Time show—All our sports
Represented, Research, Alumni

We have to Develop Conference Mentality

Job Opportunities # of CEOs who are Big Ten graduates, etc.

Social Life

Image

Theme

Create   a. Authenticity
              b. Credibility
              c. Performance

After opening the conference in 1993 with a 10–2 record and a top 10 ranking, he was back at it promoting Penn State and the new Big Ten affiliation. In March of 1994, he came to a promotions meeting at the Nittany Lion Inn armed with more notes of what he wanted to get done for Penn State both on the field and academically.

He was always thinking about the whole picture, about how he could build a better university in all areas. Years before it happened, he was already thinking about a $1 billion fund-raising campaign for academics.

Coincidentally, the "Big Ten Country" idea became the mantra for the first Big Ten Network commercials 14 years later.

MARKETING + PROMOTION MEETING

I. Why we are here

    A. We have a great opportunity to Put Penn State not only at the Very Top of the Big Ten ($1 Billion Campaign) But the Country

        We have the resources and (with another boost) the facilities to move ahead of anybody—

        Plus we have a 50 million population base in 250 mile radius

(Page 2 of Notes)

1. Make Tickets Cheap
2. Don't require Contributions to Buy good tickets
3. Tailgate Parties & Use Press Box in the Stadium as VIP Lounge

What we do make it 1st Class

Travel 1st Class

Travel Better than other people

Chapter 35

The Recruiting Trail

JOE PATERNO NOTES ON RECRUITING:

The staff should try to come to a consensus as to who is #1. #2 etc. in the pecking order for each position and whether it is time for some people to say Yes or No. If we aren't sure we have the best people to ask and at some positions we want to "wait-see" until after our camps that is OK.

But be careful we don't lose our momentum.

One other factor= the better Student + Person should be our choice

In big-time college football, recruiting 17- and 18-year-old kids is the most challenging part of the job. It's never easy to get inside the head of a young man being bombarded by information, misinformation, and advice from everyone. Society builds up their decisions as ones that will make or break the history of the world.

Joe always tried to downplay the pressure. He had a simple philosophy that he would share with our staff and with the young men he recruited. "It's hard enough for any student to decide where they want to go to college," he said. "These guys have everyone in their school or town telling them where *they* want them to go. They have to pick the best place for themselves. I don't want to be a used car salesman. We're dealing with people's lives. Remember this is a little like getting married. You can't tell a bunch of lies because sooner or later you have to live together."

Then he'd tell a recruit something that surprised them. "Look, I can't tell you that this is the best place for you," he said. "I don't know you well enough to say what is best for you. Anyone recruiting you who tries to tell you they know what's best for you is being dishonest. Only you and your family know what's best for you. But I will tell you we have great people here who will see that you reach your full potential in the classroom and on the field."

The honest approach wasn't always the most effective tactic. One big-name running back met with Joe, who told him that he wasn't going to make a hard sell and that our school and tradition spoke for itself. "No, Joe," the running back said, "go ahead and sell me."

His attitude made Joe question if this young man would fit at Penn State. Joe would find out. "You want me to sell you? You *will* go to class, you *will* have freshman study hall four nights a week," he said. "You *will* be expected to follow team rules and be on time and cut your hair and shave. You *will* be on some great football teams and you *will* graduate, but this will *not* be a picnic. It is a challenge not everyone can make. If you want that challenge, come to Penn State."

After the meeting he asked what I thought about what he had said, and I laughed.

"If he's our kind of kid, he'll come here. If he's not, he didn't belong here. It's better to find that out now," Joe said.

It was vintage Joe Paterno. His pitch: what we have for you is more valuable than what you have for me. There are plenty of great players who want what Penn State is all about, plenty of guys we can win with. There is only one Penn State.

Sometimes there were too many guys who wanted what Penn State had to offer. In the recruiting class of 1990, there were several quarterback prospects in Penn State's recruiting area. John Sacca from Delran, New Jersey, was the younger brother of Tony Sacca, who started several years for Penn State. Kerry Collins from Wilson High School near Reading, Pennsylvania, was out there as was Frank Costa from Philadelphia.

Penn State was going to take two quarterbacks, and Kenney was involved in the recruitment of them. Bill had done a great job, and all three wanted to come to Penn State. Down the stretch Penn State had John Sacca committed, and it was down to Costa and Collins. Joe had a feeling that Kerry Collins was the guy he wanted to lead his team, but Kerry wasn't quite ready to make that decision. But Joe knew he was close.

Bill Kenney was on his way to Philadelphia when Joe got ahold of him. "Bill, whatever you do, do *not* go see Costa, and do *not* let him commit."

"Joe, I think he's going to tell us he's coming."

"Exactly. I want to give Collins another day," Joe said.

So Bill had to cancel the home visit with Frank Costa. Then Collins committed to Penn State. Frank Costa went to Miami, and Collins emerged as Penn State's starter in 1993 and 1994.

There were awkward moments. Joe and an assistant coach went into the home of a star running back to visit with him and his mother. Out of nowhere the father appeared. He had not been in his son's life until he saw an opportunity to cash in.

After Joe made his recruiting pitch, he asked if they had any questions. The father spoke up. "Coach, if my son were to go to Penn State," he asked, "what would come to the family financially?"

He was asking for a payout. Joe was surprised by the blatant request for money, but he answered. "Well, there is the value of his tuition and room and board and books," he said. "Plus there are Pell grants he may qualify for and the value of his Penn State education. But that's all we can do legally."

It wasn't the answer that father was looking for.

Taking Joe Paterno into schools wasn't easy. The day we visited Gary Berry, a running back at St. Francis DeSales in Columbus, Ohio, the Bishop was saying Mass, and the kids were running out to see Joe.

We hid Joe in coach Bob Jacoby's office, where Joe had a cup of coffee. Bob kept that mug, and it is still with him in his office. He never washed it. When Mass ended we spent time with Gary and his mother who, unfortunately for us, worked at Ohio State. He was a great kid, but the hometown pull was a bit too strong.

I took him out to see Mac Morrison in Port Orchard, Washington. Mac had come to camp, and we were sold on him. He committed to us, but Washington and Nebraska kept pounding away at him. I flew out one Friday morning to see him play in the pouring rain in the Tacoma Bowl and then turned around to catch the red eye back on the same day.

He signed with us, completing a recruiting process jump-started by a letter Joe got from Mac's father in the spring of his junior year. Mac had gotten a recruiting letter from us. Being a linebacker, Mac was intrigued by our great tradition.

Mac's father wrote to Joe, "Are you really interested in Mac or is this one of hundreds of bullshit letters you send out to everyone?"

Joe read the letter in our staff meeting and laughed. He passed the letter down to me. "There's something about this that I like," he said. "Check him out and see how good he is."

Morrison turned out to be a three-year starter for us, and only a neck injury after college kept him from being a pro football player. It was his attendance at camp that really got our attention. We had a great camp advantage because Joe Paterno was the first guy to start college football camps. Ours was the biggest and best run in the country.

As the tight ends coach, I was able to pick several NFL tight ends from that camp. Sean McHugh, John Bronson, John Gilmore, and Tony Stewart were all guys who made great camp impressions. There were other guys who jumped up in camp. Anthony Adams, Bryant Johnson, and Michael Haynes were all relative unknowns in recruiting until we saw them in camp. They were all drafted in the first two rounds of the NFL draft.

There were tough stories, too. One year we recruited and got a commitment from a young man who was later named the big school Ohio Defensive Player of the Year. At the end of his senior year, he just missed the SAT score he needed to be eligible so he agreed to enroll in Kiski Prep for a year.

Before he went, the headmaster at Kiski wanted to be sure that the young man would not bolt after one semester. Joe made the young man promise that he would go for a full year even if he made the score he needed in time to enroll at Penn State in January. "This is not about getting a score," Joe told him, "you need the full year of college prep to be ready to compete in the classroom here."

The young man promised he would stay. The trouble started after he got there and did not like the non-coed atmosphere. He busted his tail and got the score he needed by December. Then he called me to tell me he was leaving Kiski in January.

Finally, Joe told him that he would not take him at Penn State if he left Kiski early. Despite having given the school his word, the young man left Kiski in January and called Joe's bluff. Joe was adamant, telling me, "We gave our word to Kiski, and he gave his word to Kiski that he would stay. He needs to learn that his word should mean something."

There was no question that when it came to recruiting, Joe Paterno was a man who believed and acted in a way that left no doubt he meant what he said. For decade after decade, he did his very best to uphold his word because as he always reminded us: "In recruiting always remember that we are dealing with people's lives."

Chapter 36

Frozen In Time

Through the years I have found that between equal teams the winning formula is a thin margin above which to remain requires fidelity to fundamental principles and a team faith that abhors mediocrity and moral victories.

The pride of accomplishment which only comes from sacrifice and superior performance.

Father Cox taught Lombardi at Fordham said:

"Character is an integration of habits of conduct superimposed on temperament, the will exercised on disposition, thought, emotion and action."

Remember we are going to have a great team—not a good one

A <u>Great</u> one

I don't think we are a great one Right now but the guys who do what we have talked about will be the guys who will be playing as we work to become a great team.

It will be fun but only if we pay the price.

—Joe Paterno's notes for the first
team meeting of the 2011 season

307

Not many people believed the 2011 Penn State team was a great team before the season began. There were question marks at quarterback, and as such both Joe and I suspected we'd start the year playing two and see how it progressed. As with many of Joe's teams, he planned to build a great 2011 team with defense, the kicking game, and an offense that took care of the football and was successful in key situations.

This team was still full of younger talent, enough that the team would have enough guys to compete for the Big Ten title in 2011, 2012, and 2013.

Joe knew that if we could stay close in the fourth quarter that we'd know how to win. These guys had played enough football. Even the quarterbacks Rob Bolden and Matt McGloin had started games against teams like Alabama, Michigan, Florida, and Ohio State.

That summer Joe was driven. Ridiculous health rumors hounded him the previous season. One rumor had him near death in Hershey Medical Center on the same day he was in Clearwater, Florida, at the Phillies Spring Training complex running our practice for our bowl in Tampa and meeting with the press.

In the summer of 2011, he was 84 years old, had stopped drinking, and was walking seven miles a day. His weight was down, and he was in fighting shape. He'd already decided that it would be his last season and he wanted to do something special to leave the program ready for the next guy.

That summer Urban Meyer came to State College for ESPN to interview one of our players and also to have his son go to Penn State's football camp for a day. He had become friends with my father on the Nike trips and when he was contemplating getting out of coaching my father spoke to him about staying in the game.

Urban's presence on campus sparked a lot of rumors about his potential future coaching at Penn State. Todd Blackledge was also in town, and the three of us went to dinner. Urban had great curiosity about our program and the type of kids we recruited.

All the while Joe kept walking, plotting, drawing up plays, and looking at moving players to insure we got our best athletes on the field. He put together a Wildcat offensive scheme to use, but the players he planned to run it were hurt. He told me to file it away for when they got healthy.

Joe kept going. A friend bumped into me and asked what Joe was doing out on the far edge of the golf course on a path that was a couple of miles from Joe's house on a 90-degree day. "He's walking," I said

"From his house?"

"Yep. He's doing about seven miles."

"Jay, it is 90 degrees."

"You try to stop him," I said, laughing.

At the late summer Big Ten media days in Chicago, the new Joe Paterno was the subject of a lot of discussion. He was tanned, in fighting shape, and amazed everyone there.

About a week into preseason practice, luck would turn on him. He was run into by a player on the practice field and broke his hip. It was a complete fluke that would've caught anyone half his age. I saw him hit the deck, and my heart instantly dropped.

It was a bad break, forcing him to coach from the press box for the first few weeks of the season. But he was on the mark as we got going.

We faced a schedule where we'd play Alabama at home in Week Two. That would be a good gauge as to the kind of team we had. At quarterback we decided to start Bolden but also play McGloin.

Against Alabama we opened with a 3–0 lead. Late in the second quarter, we trailed 10–3 and faced a third and 10 near midfield. Rob hit the tight end on a crossing route who ran for the first down. But just before he hit the ground, he fumbled. Alabama recovered, and a few plays later they led 17–3.

We ultimately lost to the eventual national champions, the last loss of Joe Paterno's career.

Despite McGloin's rough day against Alabama, we wanted him to keep playing. We decided to keep using them both. We kept playing Matt because we knew we could win with him.

For the rest of Joe's season, we made the right call. The next week we trailed 10–7 at Temple, a team that finished the season with a bowl win and 9–4 record. We got the ball near midfield late in the game, and Joe asked who I wanted in at quarterback. I told him Bolden would handle it. "Are you sure?" he asked.

"Yes," I responded.

Two plays later we faced a third and 7, and Rob found a receiver for the first down. On a fourth down, Rob zipped a pass to Derek Moye for a first down. Finally we reached a fourth and 1 on Temple's 3-yard line, and the decision was to kick the field goal and play for overtime.

I pled my case to take a timeout and go for it. Joe relented. "Okay, you got your timeout now make your case," he said.

"If we don't make it, they're stuck inside their own 5, and we'll get the ball back. If we kick the field goal, we kick off, they have better field position, and they may get a field goal. The best we get is overtime. If we make it and score they have to get a touchdown to beat us. Right now there are less variables. We know what we need."

"Okay, you made the sale."

We made the first down, and on the next play we scored a touchdown to win the game 14–10.

A week and a half later, I was approached by the captains, who wanted to talk about the quarterback situation. We walked out onto the loading dock, and they asked me to play McGloin and not play Bolden anymore. "Have you guys talked to Joe about this?" I asked.

"No."

"Let me tell you where we're at with this."

I understood they wanted to win and they have opinions. I wasn't angry. "Look," I explained, "neither quarterback is playing really well. Would you agree with that?"

"Yes."

"Okay, if one guy was clearly better, we would play him. We haven't reached that point yet. We may get there and we may not. I hope we do. Until then we have to see what we have. If you feel strongly, you guys ought to talk to Joe."

I thanked them and appreciated that they spoke to me rather than gossip around the locker room.

There were other close games. Against Iowa we led 6–3 in the fourth quarter, and I put McGloin in for the game-clinching drive. He had the confidence that day. He led us down the field to a touchdown and a 13–3 win. All that mattered after that were the victories. It seemed as long as we won our team knew we were progressing toward a Big Ten championship.

We won a tight game against Purdue. Against Northwestern, McGloin started and played well in a wide-open shootout, which we won 34–24. We returned home to play 6–2 Illinois, a good defensive football team. Joe Paterno was well enough to coach from the sideline for the game.

It was late October, and we were the only team that was undefeated in Big Ten conference play. The lessons of that preseason team meeting were coming through. We were staying above that thin margin through hard work and fundamentals.

On a cold and blustery Saturday morning, we woke to several inches of snow falling. Jack Frost brought winter to Happy Valley several weeks early. The snow postponed Joe's return to the sideline.

By Illinois, McGloin had become our starter at quarterback. We'd planned to play Rob for two or three series in the second quarter and then put Matt back in the game. At the end of the first quarter, we hadn't scored, and Rob went into the game. During his second series, some of the defensive players voiced their opinions that they wanted Rob out of the game. I passed that information to Joe. "Play Rob another series," Joe said. "Stick with what we have planned."

Just before halftime Joe grabbed me and gave me instructions for the locker room: "Jay, tell those guys to keep up the good work on defense, but we'll decide who plays. That's not their job."

"Got it."

I went down and relayed the message. What happened next was something that is best left among the men who were in the room, the men who were actually playing in the game, and not discussed outside the locker room.

I will say this: one writer's characterization of the language I used was completely inaccurate—not that he ever bothered to call me. After the game the player, who actually shouted at me, and I talked, understanding completely that we were involved in an emotional game. We both laughed it off and looked forward to the next game.

In the second half, there was continuing drama. We trailed 7–0 before we got a fourth-quarter field goal. Then we got the ball back and went with Matt to win the game. The brutal weather had taken its toll on both teams' quarterbacks, making it tough to throw the ball. The wind and snow had been tough, but when it mattered most, Matt got a hot hand.

He hit a big pass to Moye, who jumped in the game during the fourth quarter despite still healing from a painful foot injury. A few more passes got us inside the 5-yard line, where tailback Silas Redd crashed across the line to put us up 10–7.

But Illinois moved the ball down the field. On the final play of regulation, the Fighting Illini lined up to kick the game-tying field goal. Their kicker had not missed a kick the whole season.

Joe Paterno had coached 408 wins and was tied for the most wins in NCAA Division I football history. He was even with legendary Grambling coach Eddie Robinson, one of the true giants of our profession.

In the box I was getting our playlist ready for overtime, but during the timeout, I witnessed something wonderful. In the cold, dark late afternoon, some students had left the game early. The ones who remained moved en masse to pack in the end zone and distract the kicker.

At that moment we saw how special our students were. They were willing us a win.

As the Illinois kick left the kicker's foot, it looked like it was going through. Something happened. It faded a little and bounced off the upright, falling futilely onto the wet grass and leaving us with a hard-fought, record-breaking win on a frozen afternoon.

At game's end we had the best record in the Big Ten at 5–0. We were becoming the great team Joe had envisioned before the season with so much left to play for.

In the media room, athletic director Tim Curley and Penn State president Graham Spanier presented Joe with a plaque commemorating his 409th win, which made him the winningest coach in Division I history.

When Joe got up to speak, he praised Eddie Robinson and the job he had done for so many black players when many of them had nowhere else to play in the South before desegregation. He also praised coach Jake Gaither, who had coached at Florida A&M, another black school.

When he stepped down he was tired, and his leg was sore. Already he was looking forward to coaching from the sidelines again against Nebraska. Most of all he was looking forward to a three-game run to the championship.

In the locker room, there was a buzz, a sense that we'd earned seven wins in a row and stood on the cusp of something really big.

But we didn't know the future. The late touchdown, missed field goal, the 409th win in the wind and snow, and the images of Graham Spanier, Tim Curley, and Joe Paterno remain frozen in time waiting for the light of truth to melt the ice and unlock that moment for all time.

Chapter 37

Where Is Rock Bottom?

From Bleacher Report

Penn State Football: It Doesn't Feel Right to
See Jay Paterno on the Sidelines
By Dr. SEC(Analyst) on November 12, 2011

One of the lessons that I learned at a young age is that family might mess with each other, but nobody messes with family. As I watched Jay Paterno take the field today for the Nittany Lions, that lesson came to mind.

I understand that Joe Paterno was in the wrong by not pushing the issue harder when the AD did not respond to allegations outlined in this grand jury summation. Public opinions differ on the issue of his firing. Perhaps he should have been allowed to finish the season. On the other hand, his immediate firing might have been the right choice.

Either way, he is now gone and the Paterno era at Penn State is over. When Joe Pa was fired, Jay should have resigned with him.

Jay should consider the emotional aspect of the players. Sometimes it is better to just rip the Band-Aid off in one pull.

Jay did nothing wrong as far as I know. However, he is a constant reminder of his father. Joe Paterno might have been the face of the Nittany Lions for the last 46 seasons, but this game should have been about the seniors.

Although Paterno had delegated much of the work of the head coach to his assistants, these players still loved Joe Pa. The events that have transpired over the last week have devastated them.

As hard as it was to go on the field, once the first hit transpired, it could have become a safe haven—instead, Jay was there as a reminder.

Secondly, Jay should have considered the emotional aspect of his father. Yes, Joe Paterno allegedly messed up. Yes, he should have gone to the police. However, at the end of the day, he is still Jay's father. His dad needed him by his side more than the Nittany Lions did.

Joe Paterno is known as a coach who was not overly emotional. He just believed that every player and coach went to work and did his job. He might have even told Jay that he should coach in the game. However, this was probably the hardest moment of his father's life.

He needed his son to be there and hug his neck. Much of the world has turned on Joe Pa, and it is understandable. As a result, he needs those closest to him. The reality is, this is likely the death of his career and public image.

Perhaps Jay did nothing wrong by coaching in today's game—however, he did nothing right, either.

SENT: Monday, November 14, 2011 8:12 PM
TO: Jay Paterno

Jay, "The ultimate test of a man is not where he stands in moments of comfort and moments of convenience, but

where he stands in moments of challenge and moments
of controversy."

Martin Luther King, Jr.
27 January 1965

You did a great job exemplifying this quote this past
weekend,- for your family, players, and nittany nation.
Like most Penn Staters, my thoughts and support go
out to you and the team as you face this moment of
challenge and controversy. I know it will be done in
a manner befitting the legacy of JVP- with dignity,
humility and honor.

All the Best,
Kyle '04

After the Nebraska game, we turned to the next game at Ohio State. But Monday night brought more bad news. My mother told me my father had "treatable" lung cancer.

No one hears the word "treatable" when they're first told someone they love has cancer.

I went to see my father Monday night to see how he was doing. He shrugged his shoulders, said he'd be okay, and changed the subject. "Jay," he said, "I want you to know how proud I am of the way you handled everything on Saturday."

"Thanks, Dad," I replied, "I only did what I learned from you."

"Well, I have to tell you that what you did was noticed by a lot of people. I heard from Presidents Bush today. They both called. The father called first and then the younger President Bush called. In fact he told me how proud I should be of my son and how you coached."

Hearing what former President George W. Bush had said meant a great deal to me. For the generation that produced my father and President George H. W. Bush, loyalty was everything. When my father needed it most, I saw where they stood.

SENT: Wednesday, November 16, 2011
TO: Jay Paterno
SUBJECT: Sorrow

Jay..I neither know what to say or how to say it. My
devastation pales in comparison to what you and your
mother and father and siblings must be enduring.
My admiration for you under unbelievably trying
circumstances is more profound than ever.

The impersonal aspect of an Email is embarrassing...
but...it would be an emotional experience I couldn't
handle to confront any of you.

My life, as well as Charlotte and my sons lives have
been enriched, thanks to years of association with
the Paternos.

Please give your mother and father a hug for me and
tell them I love them.

                              Fran Fisher

SENT: Wednesday, November 16, 2011 9:47 AM
TO: Jay Paterno
SUBJECT: Ohio State Gameplan

You are a useless douchebag. And your brother is a
stupid fuck. The only reason you have a job is your
last name. I think it was former President Clinton who
said that it isn't the screw up that brings you down,
it's the cover up. How does it feel to work for Pedophile
State University? I hope you die in prison of pancreatic
cancer if you were in on the cover up. ....

He is not a man. He is just a senile guinea. You are just
a greasy cocksucker. You should do everyone a favor

and kill yourself. You are a gutless maggot. I hope your
entire family dies of pancreatic cancer. Fuck you and
fuck everyone at Pedophile State University.

Jef

Media stories circulated, insinuating we knew about Jerry and either looked the other way or covered for him. Media people, who should've picked up the phone to get the truth, went on national television with false narratives destroying our reputations.

The university was no help. In a meeting days after the Nebraska game, the firm the school hired stated it wasn't in the school's best interest for us to respond. I responded that soon most of us would no longer work for the school. We needed to defend *our* best interests. We coached with integrity. The firm Penn State had hired had no answers and would have to consult with the board.

On Wednesday the administration decided we'd do an interview with ESPN's Tom Rinaldi on Friday, a full two weeks after the story broke. In this media age, two weeks is like a thousand years.

As for my father's cancer, my family wanted to keep it private, but he'd been seen coming and going from the hospital. We had no choice but to issue a statement that would come on Friday.

Shortly after the team plane took off on Friday, I told the assistant coaches and interim head coach Tom Bradley about Joe's cancer. I waited until takeoff, so that all media members would hear it from my family first. I wish it could've been handled differently. By the time we got to the hotel, most of our student-athletes had already seen it on their phones.

SENT: Friday, November 18, 2011 11:08 PM
TO: Jay Paterno
SUBJECT: New

Your father is a worthless piece of worm shit. Who gives
a fuck if he dies? The shit hole you and your perverted,
maggot eating family live in is irrelevant to the rest

of the United States. You are a shit head. Your father
should get raped with a broom.

Have a great holiday
Bill

Saturday morning we had a meeting with the offense. I wanted to
address the pressure our university put on the student-athletes when we
took the field against Nebraska the week before: a pregame prayer service,
the media, and the constant repetition of how this game would help heal
the community.

After we watched the films in our morning meeting, I stood up to say
a few words. I hesitated, unsure that I should say what I was about to say,
but my silence grabbed their attention. "Guys, this afternoon we *play* a
game," I said, "just one game between Penn State and Ohio State. You're
better than they are. If we play like it, we will win. But there's something
else I want to say. This afternoon's game is just that, a game. I regret that
last week the university administration made you the ones to heal the
community. That's crap. None of you did anything wrong. In fact no one
in this program caused these problems. But you guys were asked to atone
for sins you did not commit."

I could see many were nodding their heads along with what I was saying
to them. "Last week we coached and played the first half with a weight on
our shoulders," I said. "It cost us the win. This afternoon be selfish, focus
on yourselves. Despite what you've been forced to hear, today's game is just
that—a game of football. You will not heal any victims today, you will not
heal Penn State's problems, you will not save the world, and you will not
cure Joe Paterno's cancer."

With that last line, my voice started to catch, but I stayed poised. "He
will be watching. You will make him proud," I said. "But today it is about
you. It is about your chance to win the Big Ten and go to the Rose Bowl. It
is just Penn State versus Ohio State. So go out and play. Ignore all the crap
that people have tried to put on your shoulders. Play to win one football
game for you and your teammates."

As they left the meeting, many of the players thanked me for what I'd
said. Maybe it helped, maybe not, but my convictions wouldn't allow me to
leave those words unsaid.

Playing in Ohio Stadium is special. Their 100,000 fans bring an intensity that is tough to beat. As I boarded the bus to the stadium that Saturday, I was nervous about how they would treat our team.

My fears were unfounded; the Ohio State fans were so supportive. They stopped me getting off the bus, yelled to me from the stands, shook my hand, and patted me on the back. Before the game and even after we had won the game, they were the same. "Your dad is a great man, what they did to him was wrong," they said

"Tell Joe to get well soon."

"We love Joe."

"We miss your dad."

After the win outside the locker room, the white-haired man who'd guarded the door every year we'd come to Ohio State took my hand in both of his hands. Under the stadium lights cutting through the dark night, tears glistened in his eyes. He spoke in a pained voice. "Jay, tell your dad I miss him. It will never be the same without him, never. I hope he gets well...I just miss him."

From the Ohio State fans came recognition of my humanity and my father's humanity. They showed so much class. I'll never ever forget that day in Columbus—not because we won but because of their fans. I'll always have a special place for them in my heart; they put aside team allegiance for a moment to help me.

When I saw my father on Sunday, I relayed all the well wishes from Ohio State fans. It meant a lot to him. I could tell in his half-smile, a smile brought on by memories of games past.

"I missed them too," he whispered.

> **SENT:** Saturday, November 19, 2011 6:41 PM
> **TO:** Jay Paterno
> **SUBJECT:** I'm Your Fan
>
> Dear Mr. Paterno,
>
> I'm not sure if you read e-mail. I know it is a difficult time and that a lot of people are probably saying a lot of foolish things via e-mail. I just wanted to tell you that my husband and I are now pretty big JayPa fans. We

are both alums from 2005. I've been watching you on TV over the past few awful weeks and my respect for you has grown and grown. I didn't know much about you before but I think you have demonstrated yourself as a class act. We as a family-my in-laws, my side of the family, my little kids, my husband, our fellow alum-support you, your father, and all of your family and we're pulling for you and praying for all of you.

Today, you guys all made me proud to remain Penn State Proud.

Sincerely,
Bethany

Joe-

It has been alleged that Jerry Sandusky sodomized young boys on the campus of Penn State University.

If you knew, or suspected, this to be true and did not report it to police then I urge you to take your own life immediately.

—Anonymous letter sent to me in November 2011 to give to my father.

November 20, 2011

Dear Mr. Paterno,

My 3 year old son noticed how upset my wife and I have been over the past few weeks, and wanted to know why. I told him we were sad, because part of our family was sad. Then I showed him "our family" on the television, and did my best to explain to him how important you are to us.

At the end of the Nebraska game, when we saw you being interviewed, we were holding back tears as you were "wishing Joe was there". It was then that he asked us if he could draw you a picture to make you feel better.

In this crazy world where the media take heroes and rips them apart; please know that there are others out there wishing nothing but the best for you. We will continue to call you our family, even though it takes a while to explain to a 3 year old why you aren't coming over for Thanksgiving dinner.

So if you ever have any doubts about your support, please know that on 3rd down there is a 3 year old yelling "Defense!" at the television, right along with his mom and dad.

We are...

John '98 HHD

Note: enclosed were two pictures drawn
by their three-year-old son.

My last months at Penn State, my immersion into my job's details helped block out the distractions. But there were calls from people my dad had known over the years that lifted me, as they checked up on him. Michigan State basketball coach Tom Izzo, Bobby Bowden, and former Florida football coach Urban Meyer were among many who called to ask about my dad. Through it all I made time to walk with my father. It was critical to this mental and physical well-being that he got outside and walked.

Joe enjoyed visits from former players. They came every day. They cried, vowed to fight for him, prayed with him but all thanked him. When I saw him, he would light up as he told me who'd stopped by or who'd called. When so much of the world was fleeing, the players ran to him. I mentioned something relevant. "Dad, I think Twain said he wanted to be at his own funeral to hear the nice things people would say about him that they never said while he was alive. You're hearing that now while you're here."

321

He laughed, allowing that maybe I was right. He appreciated moments with the guys who'd been on the fields on so many Saturdays with him—the memories of their games and the roar of the crowd still thundering in their heads.

On the field we fell short of getting to the Big Ten Championship Game. The week after our last regular season game, I had my interview with the Freeh Commission. We were told we could not bring counsel, but in good faith, I sat down with former Federal Judge Eugene Sullivan and a former Delaware state trooper.

At the start I asked if I could tape the interview. They said no. I asked if they were taping it. They said no. It was obvious that they had an agenda. Very few of the questions were about Jerry Sandusky. There were a lot of questions about Joe Paterno and the power relationships as they related to president Graham Spanier and athletic director Tim Curley.

At the end of the interview, the most interesting part of the conversation occurred. I asked for copies of their notes of the interview. They denied my request insisting that all of the interviews were privileged information and were the property of their client. "Who is your client?" I asked—expecting the answer to be Penn State.

"The board of trustees" was the answer.

It was a curious answer.

Later we would learn that the privileged information had been shared with the state attorney general's office and the NCAA.

The next week my father asked if I had gone in front of the Freeh Commission yet. "Yes," I responded.

"I'm supposed to talk to those guys to help them. What do you think?" he asked.

"Well, I am not supposed to get into specifics."

"I don't want the specifics. Are they doing the right thing?"

"No. Not even close."

"Don't be cynical," he scolded. "Why do you say that?"

"Dad," I began, "they are going to issue a report, alleging lack of institutional control of football as the reason for this. Then Penn State will ask the NCAA to sanction the school."

There was a look of shock.

"Why would they do that?" he asked.

"To burn this to the ground and take credit for everything that happens next. They want to destroy all the good things done here and blame you for it. Then they can claim *they* made Penn State football."

"Whatever happens, we must defend this university and the program. This is not a football scandal. We must fight. We owe it to the student-athletes, coaches, administrators, faculty, and alumni who have done things the right way in all sports for decades. We can't let them take that away."

Unfortunately I would be proven right.

• • •

A week later the walls really started to cave in. Sunday morning, the day of our Senior Football Banquet, I got a call from my mother to bring my minivan to the house to help get my father to the hospital. He'd fallen in the middle of the night because he didn't want to turn on the lights and wake up my mother. Despite breaking his hip, he crawled back to bed and stayed there until morning so they wouldn't disturb me in the middle of the night.

The next Saturday, the saga got stranger. Starting quarterback Matt McGloin fought with another player, fell onto the floor, and hit his head. By the time I got to him from the equipment room, our doctors were there, but Matt was turning blue and convulsing. It was scary.

As I rode with him in the back of the ambulance to the hospital, I reassured him that he'd be okay. Out the window as we headed up University Drive, I saw the Penn State logo on the new lacrosse field. The realization came over me that it was over. Soon that logo would symbolize a chapter closed.

> **SENT:** Friday, December 16, 2011 5:49 PM
> **TO:** Jay Paterno
> **SUBJECT:** hope your dad rots in hell!!!
>
> U and your father are sick motherfuckers!! He is just as
> guilty as the pedophile piece of shit that he covered up for.
> How could you dad allow and enable someone to rape little
> boys just for the sake of not disturbing the penn state officials
> weekends?!!!!!!!!!!!!!!!!!! ur and ur family are disgusting!

A few days later, my father came home again. More people came to visit him. My friend Mike, the guy who'd probably spent more time with my dad than any of my friends, came by with me to see him.

We talked about the current events. Joe looked Mike dead in the eyes and reiterated how he hadn't known, but if he had known that he certainly would've been more aggressive. But the truth was that he didn't know.

Four days before Christmas, Joe celebrated his 85th birthday with his wife, his five children, their spouses, and all 17 grandchildren. The medical news was positive, and my father was in great spirits. Instead of complaints he reminded us how lucky he was and to treasure the good in his life. That's how he looked at things. Be thankful for what you *do* have; don't complain about what you don't have.

Underlying it was the bowl trip, and as I left the house Christmas night, my family wished us luck. My heart sank, knowing that I would go without him on the bowl trip. My mother and father and my siblings would not be along. I also sensed this would be the last game I would coach for at least a year—maybe ever.

We were headed to a bowl game with a team that was at best lukewarm to the idea of playing in the Ticket City Bowl.

The night the bowl bids were announced in early December, I was at the Penn State basketball game. Our team expected a trip to the Gator Bowl in Jacksonville, Florida, or to the Insight.com bowl in sunny Tempe, Arizona. Despite being division co-champions, we slid all the way to the eighth pick of Big Ten bowl teams.

At Penn State we'd recruited a smart group of student-athletes—bright enough to know the Big Ten didn't go to bat for us. A year earlier Big Ten commissioner Jim Delany lobbied the NCAA to allow key Ohio State players to play in a bowl game after they had violated NCAA rules. Where was he to defend the Penn State players?

That Sunday night I received a text informing me that the players were meeting to decline the bowl trip and announce their decision on social media. Interim head coach Tom Bradley was out of town. There wasn't time to talk to anyone, so I reacted.

I left the basketball game, arriving at the football building, where the team was gathering. I asked senior Quinn Barham if it would be okay if I talked to the team.

After discussing it with other seniors, he felt it would be okay. I stood in front of the team in a quiet meeting room. There was genuine anger, palpable to all in that room. I understood their anger. All I wanted them to do was to sleep on it.

I headed back to the basketball game to find acting athletic director Dave Joyner and fill him in. He had already left, so I called him. "Dave," I said, "I just want you to know that the team is meeting. They were going to vote not to go to the bowl game."

Dave was silent. I assured him they'd told me they would sleep on it, but that we were not out of the woods. They would meet tomorrow. Ultimately, the next day they decided to go to the bowl game.

While the administration could hide in the shadows, these young men soldiered on in public. They had to face reporters, hear the questions, and drive through the wreckage every day. The players had to carry the burden, and I could sense their hearts weren't there.

Who could blame them for wanting to get it all behind them? I know I didn't.

Once we got to Dallas for the bowl game, all week long everything we did was awkward. When we went to a team dinner, it was as though people were waiting for Joe to show up. At media events Joe was an unseen presence. We simply wanted to coach and play a game, but the events of the past nine weeks sucked the oxygen from everything we did.

For my part I was determined to enjoy the week. The people from the bowl game were fantastic, going out of their way to make us feel welcome.

The bowl functions were strange. Acting AD Joyner was one of the trustees who had voted to fire my father. University legal counsel Cynthia Baldwin, who had botched this case every step of the way, was at every free event or meal. On New Year's Eve, she approached me and asked how my father was doing. "We're praying for him," she said.

"We're praying for you, too," I responded.

There was a puzzled look on her face. She wasn't sure how to take it, but I meant it in the most sarcastic way I possibly could.

Finally, it was gameday on January 2. I dressed in a coat and tie and hugged my family. We took a couple of photos. Looking at the pictures now, it is evident how bittersweet the moment was. Even in the smile of my son Joey, I can see sadness. He was hoping this wasn't an ending. Kelley was sad because she knew better.

We pulled into the Texas state fair grounds and to the historic Cotton Bowl Stadium. In pregame it was chilly but dazzlingly sunny. There was a buzz in our opponent Houston's warm-ups and on their sideline while our team seemed flat. When you sense that dynamic, all you can do is hope that you get a lucky bounce or two and that it gives your team a spark.

It didn't happen.

We played uninspired football. I can't blame our team for that. From the start of the whole mess on November 4, everything became a chore; the fun was gone. Once we'd had the joy, the bounce on the practice field the morning of November 4. All seemed possible until that night. It was all taken away.

As I walked off the field in Dallas, that is what broke me. The journey should have ended so much differently.

That evening I spent with friends who stopped up to our hotel suite. I finally fell asleep, dreaming about the game and what I could have done differently. I woke up a half-dozen times with a different play call or a different take on our game plan.

Early the next morning, I walked down to Dealey Plaza, where JFK had been shot. Most of Dallas was getting back to work after the long holiday weekend, and the cars were starting to move. But it was still quiet for me. The dream of Camelot had died there.

I knew that a part of my own life was ending. There would probably never again be a moment when I put on a headset and called plays or an afternoon spent on the practice field.

It was early morning, and I was alone with most of the pieces of my life already in wreckage. In less than three weeks, the damage would become total. Here as I stood at Camelot's end, the magical run of my own father's career and my career with him were now gone forever.

Alone I walked from that plaza back toward the hotel and into an uncertain future. I reflected on the moments that we could only dream of that were never fated to have been.

• • •

Within a week of getting back from Dallas, a new coach had been hired, and I knew I would not be coaching at Penn State anymore. It was difficult to pack up an office after 17 years, but all good things in life come to a conclusion.

I had another round of questioning. Our attorney, Wick Sollers, accompanied me to the interviews because we now knew that the university's relationship with Joe Paterno had turned adversarial.

My father had become a tenured faculty member in 1957, and as such the university was unable to fire him without a hearing. They backpedaled and said they hadn't fired him yet so they had an executive committee meeting via speakphone to fire him.

It was too bizarre to be believed.

Wick and I went in to meet with a university attorney that Thursday. After meeting the university's attorney, we met with a state police officer a few miles from campus.

Once inside the office, we sat at a conference table, and the officer started to ask me questions. He showed me pictures of people and asked if I recognized any of them. I racked my brain but found that I didn't. Then he asserted that several victims had stated they were at practices, on team planes, and on bowl trips after Jerry had retired. "How many times do you recall seeing the victims with Jerry at practice or on trips?" he asked.

"After he'd retired?" I asked.

"Yes."

"None," I stated.

"You never saw them?"

"Never, because they weren't there."

He asked how I could be so sure. Our practices were closed, and there were rarely if ever any kids, including my own, at practice. Jerry didn't even come to practice himself. They weren't at practice, they weren't on team planes, and they weren't on bowl trips with us.

The next question was even more puzzling. "We understand that Jerry was able to arrange for his victims to dress for football games," he said.

"You mean in uniform?" I asked.

"Yes."

I allowed that I didn't personally check every uniform, but I doubted that story. We would notice a 10- or 12-year-old in uniform among oversized college players. "We have a picture of one," he said.

He showed me the picture, and I laughed. "This young man is one of the victims," he said, pointing to a player in uniform without his helmet on and standing right next to Joe on the sidelines of a game.

"No, it's not." I said. "That is Shane McGregor."

He wanted to know how I was so sure. I explained that Shane was still on the team, that I had coached him for four years, and that the picture he was holding was from the Outback Bowl on January 1, 2011.

If they were so off on this, I wondered what else they might have gotten wrong.

After I was finished, we headed home to meet Sally Jenkins from *The Washington Post* and have a family dinner. This was going to be the first interview Joe had done since being fired.

My father was still wheelchair-bound from breaking his hip in December, but he was in good spirits. Sally Jenkins got to see a family dinner close-up. There were arguments, laughs, and great food from my mother. It was a typical dinner. We talked about politics, current events, old stories, and everyone weighed in. The conversation, as it typically does at our dinners, wandered all over the place. "You know, Sally," Joe said, "I always had tremendous respect for your father."

"Well, Joe, he always spoke highly of you," she replied.

I always had great respect for Sally Jenkins as a writer, so that moment stuck out for me. That dinner would turn out to be the last family dinner Joe would have in the house he called home since August of 1969. The last one.

That round table had been the scene of so many things. How many recruits had been at that table? How many millionaires and even billionaires had sat in those seats? But most importantly how many meals had my mother served and my parents presided over across the decades as one by one their five children grew up day by day, week by week until we left the house one by one?

Memories of the dinners still remain. Good Friday meant shrimp scampi. New Year's Day meant pork and sauerkraut for good luck. Saint Patrick's Day meant corned beef, potatoes, and cabbage. Mixed in with all that was a steady run of pastas, lasagna, spaghetti, and all smothered in the homemade sauce my mother cooked up and jarred every August when central Pennsylvania tomatoes would be fresh off the vines.

That dinner would be the very last one, but no one even suspected that.

The next morning my father was too weak from the treatments, so we moved him from the wheelchair to his bed. He insisted that he would finish the interview from his bed. When I asked if he should do it at all, he scolded me. "Sally came all this way, and I want to make sure she can get everything she needs. I owe that to her," he said in a voice that was a whisper of what it once was.

From his bed he struggled to finish the interview. Shortly afterward he left the house to go back to the hospital. He would never return.

Annie Marshall @KarlMarx35 1/22/12

@JayPaterno @THON Be careful not to rape any children like Joe Pa did. Thank god he's dead

From Twitter

LeBron James @KingJames 1/22/12

R.I.P Joe Pa! Met him before while I was out at Nike campus with @BrandonWeems10 @mavcarter @RichPaul4 @ErnieRamos32. He was great man!!

From Twitter

After Joe died the Freeh Commission continued their investigation. Our attorneys offered to help and were told the report would be completed in late August or maybe earlier that month. We were also told we'd have a chance to reply to any allegations about Joe.

In late May I saw an athletic department member's email, stating Joe's role in this whole thing would be seen in a darker light based on what he was being told. In June a trustee mentioned there was evidence of a cover-up. I sensed trouble.

In June Sandusky's trial took place. On late Friday evening June 22nd, the jury had reached a verdict.

As the verdict was announced, the people outside the courthouse cheered. The cheering seemed out of place; there are no winners in stories like these.

tom foster (@tmatfost) 6/23/12 9:03 AM

@JayPaterno wish you're dad could of spent his life in jail with jerry too bad he took the easy cancer and death way out

From Twitter

A week later the final Freeh warning came. CNN went on air with leaked emails, reportedly showing a cover-up and insinuating that Joe Paterno knew about a 1998 incident. I was seated in a restaurant with friends. I excused myself to talk with my brother Scott and Dan McGinn. "Dan," I said, "I bet this report is coming out over the All-Star break. ESPN has *nothing* to talk about then. It is the deadest day in sports. They'll release it to do the most damage. This is an opening salvo."

We were all in complete agreement.

A little over a week later, I successfully pulled off a surprise 20th anniversary party for my wife. I stood on my patio to say a few words to gathered friends and family. Despite the happy commemoration, I knew there was trouble on the horizon. "I want to thank all of you for being here and for sticking by us through the events of the last several months," I said. "I appreciate all of your loyalty. Understand it may get worse before it gets better, but we'll see it through together."

Four days later, the night before the report was to be released, I was on a conference call with my family. We talked about what to expect the next day. There was great uncertainty about what was in the report.

I remember clearly what I said on that call. "Look, I know what will not be proven in that report. There is no academic fraud. There are no NCAA rules violations. I know Dad didn't commit a crime, witness a crime, or cover up a crime. They have the ball, they will make their case. But then we get the ball, we're on offense from here on out. This is a long game."

The next morning as planned, the NBC News satellite truck for the *TODAY Show* arrived at my house at 5 AM. The plan was to do one interview with them and then see what happened. I did the interview with Matt Lauer before the report came out. It was tough to talk about a report that had yet to be issued. Given that we were both in the dark on the report's contents, both Lauer and I did the best we could.

But I reiterated that we did not fear the truth.

As soon as the report came out, we started to print it. As it came off the printer, we were highlighting sections and passages. My phone rang, and it was Dan. "Jay," he said, "you're going to have to go back on and do more interviews."

I took a deep breath: "Okay."

"Jay, I wouldn't ask you to do it if I didn't have to. It's up to you. But I'll tell you this, there was a time when Eisenhower had to send Patton into the fight. Our best course of action is to have you go in and fight. You've got to be Patton."

"If I'm Patton, we're screwed," I said, laughing.

We read frantically until Freeh's press conference at 10. My initial reaction reading the report was positive because he had *zero* evidence. But in his press conference, he stated things that I knew to be lies unsupported by evidence. He took some questions from the media; none had actually read or analyzed the report to see the flaws.

It was well planned, a setup all the way. The 24/7 media spent the rest of the day drumming the accusations into everyone's brain. Massive repetition gives even outrageous lies the aura of truth.

We decided to go back on air in the afternoon. We thought out possible questions. Dan called in, Scott called in. These would not be easy interviews. I had to counter a false narrative that my father had helped cover up for a convicted pedophile.

There are three distinct interviewing situations; it's like a game. The first—things are good, and you can easily answer to score points. The second—events are open to interpretation, so you must play some defense but can still score some points. The third—events are bad, and all you can do is limit the damage, hold ground, and retain the ability to credibly respond more forcefully later.

That day was the third situation. Play defense, limit damage, and give the people in our corner some ground they could stand on when it came time to rally back. It was the first part of a long, long road back.

The toughest moment of the day came when Nike announced that they would be taking Joe Paterno's name off their daycare facility—The Joe Paterno Child Development Center.

I would get that question right away in the next round of interviews, particularly since Phil Knight had spoken so forcefully in defense of my father at his memorial service in January. I knew the answer I had to give.

I looked at Guido D'Elia and Mike Clements and said, "Here is what my dad would say. Phil is the CEO of a publicly traded company with a responsibility to his board and his shareholders. I don't fault him for making that decision. We still consider him a friend, and my family and I still love him."

When I got the question, I answered it along those lines. Months later Phil said he watched my interview. He thanked me for how I'd answered it. I assured him it was exactly what my father would have said.

The rest of that day included over a dozen interviews with national and state outlets. The toughest setup was a taped interview with CBS News. They asked me 10 questions to use and would only use two. I knew I could get eight of 10 just right, and they'll use the two you missed. Eight of 10 is really zero for two; nine of 10 is one for two.

The longest interview was via satellite live on *SportsCenter* with Tom Rinaldi. He is a great interviewer—tough but fair.

All afternoon long the satellite trucks came and parked on the street, and the television crews filed in and out. The furniture in the living room was moved all over the place. Friends took our kids to play with their kids, and so many people helped out on a horrible day. It was humbling to feel their loyalty and their love.

I took a break and walked with Guido through Spring Creek Park, out to Millbrook Marsh, and back home. On the way back, I saw a neighbor and apologized for the trucks and the mayhem I'd created in the neighborhood. "Don't sweat it," he said. "You're doing the right thing; for *all* of us."

Just before 8 PM we had a last interview with CNN's Erin Burnett. I am a fan of her show so I knew her pace of questioning. It varies, so you can never get too comfortable in the batter's box. I relished the challenge. I felt my strongest answer came when I said that, "Joe Paterno, Penn State, and above all the victims deserve more than reasonable conclusions. They deserve the truth."

It was in response to Freeh's repeated use of the words "reasonable conclusions."

It was a tough day, but we'd stood up and held ground to defend and may have even scored points. But the report damaged the reputations of Penn State, Joe Paterno, and the other accused men. What saddened me most was Penn State's board of trustees willingly accepting the report's false narratives about our university.

The story Freeh sold was not true. Despite all we'd done to defend Penn State, their narrative would stain the school for the foreseeable future.

> Joe Paterno was a liar, there's no doubt about that now. He was also a cover-up artist. If the Freeh report is correct in its summary of the Penn State child molestation scandal, the public Paterno of the last few years was a work of fiction. In his place is a hubristic, indictable hypocrite.
>
> —*Sally Jenkins in* The Washington Post, *July 13, 2012*

"When the fall is all there is, it matters."—Richard III in *The Lion In Winter*

It was a quote my brother Scott had shared with me. As we kept falling, I just hoped we'd reached rock bottom, so we could push off and try to swim back to the surface.

Chapter 38

Gimme Shelter

In February 2013 the doorbell rang a day after I'd been on ESPN, CNN, and national radio shows to present our reports. It had been months since the damage of the Freeh Report, but we'd started to rebut those lies.

When I got to the door, there was a police officer there. I invited him in to sit down in the living room. He explained they were looking into multiple death threats made against me on social media. The police were alerted to the threats by Penn Staters who'd seen them. I hadn't seen them, so I'm thankful to the people looking out for me.

The officer assured me they'd keep me posted, and I thanked him.

Kelley came into my den. Quietly I assured her that everything was under control, but it wasn't easy. Since the story broke, we'd had a tree cut down, and our house was egged. We also had stopped putting our garbage out the night before trash day because we feared media members going through it.

She was concerned. When someone posts they will come to town and *kill* you and your family, that gets your attention. But with a new understanding of sexual abuse issues, I suspected the threats came from people harboring anger from unresolved issues with it in their own lives. "Look," I said to Kelley, "I have a feeling that some of these people were victims of abuse and maybe never got help. I'm a target for that anger because I'm defending Penn State and Joe Paterno. They don't have the information and don't realize that Joe reported it. I don't blame them for being angry."

That moment was when months of hateful emails and letters crystallized in my mind. There are people who live with or know people hurt by sexual abuse. There is a lot of pain and with that maybe a desire to lash out at someone. For those who don't have all the facts, we're the easiest target.

Later that day the police called back and had found one of the people who'd made a threat. My prediction was correct. There were some issues there. "We've talked to him and to the police in his area. What action do you want us to take?" the police officer asked.

"I don't want an emotional tweet to ruin someone's life. If they promise to get help, I won't do anything."

We offered to provide references to people who could help and even pay for the help if needed. "Okay," the officer said, "I will pass that along."

Later the officer called back and reported that the person had agreed to get help and apologized. I hung up the phone, knowing I had done what my father would've wanted me to do. I hope that person got help and found peace.

I thought back to July just after the Freeh Report put my father in the crosshairs. The 11 days after the Freeh Report were among the toughest of my life. As the Central Pennsylvania Festival of The Arts began in State College, thousands of alumni flooded back into town. As I walked around the festival, people stopped me to thank our family for standing up for Penn State.

Going on behind the scenes was a coordinated effort to tear down Joe Paterno once and for all. After the initial two-day surge of the Freeh Report, the university leaked details of Joe's last contract to a reporter from *The New York Times*. The attempt was to imply Joe added a retirement bonus to his contract because he knew this was coming.

It was clearly written by someone working hand in hand with board members to make Joe Paterno look greedy and, after his death, to make our family look bad for simply asking that the terms of his contract be honored. But it also gave insight into the paranoia that some board members felt about what one board member had termed in an email to a friend as "a narrow band of Paterno worshippers."

The article reported: "During a conference call, one board member worried aloud that failure to make good on what was owed to the Paterno estate could lead to another 'reign of terror' by Mr. Paterno's supporters, according to a person who was on the call."

Monday the mess continued. I got a call from someone close to the Paternoville group, a student organization that camps out before each home game for the best seats. They planned to meet that night to remove the name Paterno. During my daughter's birthday, I left to take a call from the Paternoville students. They told me they were voting to take the name off. They were upset. But I knew what was happening. I told them, "Look, I know what's going on and I know you're being pressured. You don't have to tell me. I know."

"We feel so bad because your family has been so supportive," the student said.

"Don't worry about it. Call it Nittanyville or whatever you have to. Joe would want you to do whatever you have to do to keep camping out to support the team."

They thanked me, and I thanked them for calling me so I could explain it to my mother. After I told my mom, she excused herself to head home. "I want to get a picture of the Paternoville sign on the way home before it gets dark," she said.

About 15 minutes later, I got a call from my mother, and she was upset. "What's the matter, Mom?" I asked.

"The sign is already gone," she said.

She had gotten there within a half an hour of the time I had been told the name would change, and already the university had removed the metal sign that was anchored in the ground. The sign's rapid disappearance confirmed the name change was a premeditated push from the administration.

The next day it got weirder with a plane appearing over State College, pulling a banner behind it that read, "Take The Statue Down or We Will." The statue of Joe Paterno had stood outside the stadium since November of 2001. Students started to guard the statue, even camping overnight. By Wednesday and Thursday, a news event had been created with speculation running rampant about the future of the statue. Satellite trucks returned to State College and parked across the street from the statue.

Thursday night in Colorado, a national tragedy occurred as a lone gunman went into a movie theater and shot dozens of people on the opening night of a Batman movie. For the first time in months, Penn State was seemingly out of the news and fading a bit from the national picture. But media continued to talk about the statue. As late as Friday, Penn State president Rodney Erickson was telling some trustees that he would not make a decision for 72 hours.

Sunday morning I got a call. Six months to the day that Joe died and less than 48 hours after he'd said a decision wouldn't be made, Rod Erickson had the university take down the statue of my father. I refused to watch it. My mother found out from the children of my sister Mary as they were watching it live on television.

The administration had gotten what they wanted, the visual of a public lynching of Joe Paterno—even it was only a bronze statue of him.

The statement issued by Penn State was even more insulting: "With the release of Judge Freeh's Report of the Special Investigative Counsel, we as a community have had to confront a failure of leadership at many levels. The statue of Joe Paterno outside Beaver Stadium has become a lightning rod of controversy and national debate, including the role of big time sports in university life. The Freeh Report has given us a great deal to reflect upon and to consider, including Coach Paterno's legacy. I now believe that, contrary to its original intention, Coach Paterno's statue has become a source of division and an obstacle to healing in our university and beyond. For that reason, I have decided that it is in the best interest of our university and public safety to remove the statue and store it in a secure location. I believe that, were it to remain, the statue will be a recurring wound to the multitude of individuals across the nation and beyond who have been the victims of child abuse."

I couldn't believe what they had written about my father. Shortly thereafter, the leaks about the NCAA sanctions started. The NCAA would hold a Monday press conference, announcing "unprecedented sanctions" against Penn State.

The press conference was grandstanding for NCAA president Mark Emmert. He used the false accusations of the Freeh Report as the basis for the sanctions. It was an appalling moment for all Penn Staters and anyone who believes in due process.

The team received a reduction in scholarships, a four-year bowl ban, and a $60 million fine. Penn State's wins were taken away all the way back to 1998 when, according to Emmert, Penn State had failed to act appropriately in response to an accusation against Jerry Sandusky. That showed how little grasp he had of the situation. Penn State had issued a 1998 report and given it to the commonwealth of Pennsylvania to investigate.

By Monday night the damage was nearly total. In 11 days the Freeh Report, a story about Joe Paterno's greed, the removal of the Paternoville name, a plane flying over town, the takedown of the statue, and finally NCAA sanctions completed an assault from within on Penn State and on Joe Paterno.

So much had been lost that I knew that there was nothing else to lose, nothing else to give. There was no shelter.

Late that night I knew we could finally begin to crack back.

> Donald J. Trump (@realDonaldTrump)
>
> 7/25/12 4:51 PM
>
> I knew Joe Paterno. When he heard what he heard, it just wasn't in his world--a different planet!
>
> Donald J. Trump (@realDonaldTrump)
>
> 7/25/12 4:55 PM
>
> Amazing how fast all of Joe Paterno's friends abandoned him. They ran for the hills.
>
> *From Twitter*

Chapter 39

The Fight Back

"Kites rise higher against the wind than
with it."

—*Winston Churchill quote from
Joe Paterno's handwritten notes*

O n a June Saturday, I took my dog out for our morning walk. I'd finished
morning prayers and tuned in my iPhone to NPR to catch up on the
news. A show came on that caught my attention.

It was a BBC program called *Dream Builders*, focusing on architects and
their craft. Daniel Libeskind, the designer of the Jewish Museum in Berlin,
was talking about his process. In the course of the interview, the host asked
him about his design of the Holocaust Tower, a stark bleak structure lighted
inside by a single slit coming through the walls.

Libeskind told the story of a female Holocaust survivor he'd heard. She
was pushed into a dark cattle train car where all she could see was a solitary
crack of light. She did not know where she was going or what fate awaited
her at the end of her journey, but that sliver of light was her hope. The story
inspired Libeskind and, in his sharing, I was inspired.

From the morning of July 12 when it seemed the world turned on my
deceased father and our university, we found ourselves under siege. But I
drew strength in knowing that if someone facing a situation as desperate as

the horrible unknown of a train ride into the Holocaust could find hope, I could certainly withstand the much smaller challenges of my life.

I knew the truth. The Bible tells us when we find God's light of truth, we do not hide it under a basket. We hold it up to chase the darkness.

That was the fuel of the fight. I went back to that conversation I'd had with my father in December of 2011 when he reminded me that we would have to fight to defend the student-athletes, coaches, administrators, faculty, medical staff, and alumni who had done things ethically in every sport from those creating and promoting lies about our university.

Defending what we did on the playing fields and in the classrooms was in no way taking away from the fight Jerry's victims faced. It was an issue of two wrongs not making a right. Collateral damage to a university and to men and women who were not responsible for the actions of one man should never be a price we carelessly pay to hastily close the chapter of one story so we can move on for the sake of moving on.

After the Freeh Report was issued, we knew that if there was to be a factual review of what really happened it was going to have to come from us. We set out through our attorneys to conduct a thorough and factual review and issue a report that could do some good in educating society and preventing this in the future.

Approached by our attorneys, two of the men, former United States attorney general Dick Thornburgh and former FBI profiler Jim Clemente, had worked with Louis Freeh and were reluctant to get involved. However, once they'd read Freeh's report and seen how terribly wrong he'd gotten it, they agreed.

On the night of October 11, 2012, I had the first dream about my father since he'd died nearly nine months earlier. In the dream I was called to the football office to coach again. When I got to my locker, someone else's name was on it, so I went to see equipment manager Brad Caldwell. As I walked through the locker room, the whole scene was in sepia, a brownish hue that you see in old-time pictures. I heard a familiar voice in the locker room and I turned to see people crowded around someone wearing a blue blazer. They were recruits and their parents, and the man in the blue blazer, the blue being the only color in the dream, looked like my dad.

Initially I was furious that they'd hired a Joe Paterno impersonator to pose for pictures with recruits until I got closer and heard the voice and saw the lines on his face and the unmistakable mannerisms.

It was my father.

He turned and saw me and painfully hobbled toward me. "Jay, you've got to help me," he said.

"Help?"

"You've got to get me home, just get me home. Then everything will be better."

As I walked him slowly from the locker room, the doors opened into a brilliant light, and I shot straight up in bed—wide awake.

I was crying because I knew he wanted us to fight to make things right.

Our patience was tested, waiting to see what would become of the reports, and the dream was probably a symptom of that. Finally, in early February, the reports were ready. I traveled to Washington, D.C., to start reading the reports. About a week or two later, I was home studying the reports and getting ready for a day at ESPN doing all the interviews.

I spent a lot of time on the phone with my brother Scott, discussing the reports after they'd been issued to us and before I went to do the interviews. What many people do not know was that prior to reading the reports we were not even aware of who was writing them. In fact for a long period of time, the men writing the individual reports were not aware if there were others also writing reports or who the others were. These men looked at the evidence individually and came to very similar conclusions.

The week before the reports came out, we went to New York to tape *Katie*, Katie Couric's show. It was my mother's first interview on television. It was an effort to get people to take a second look at the facts of the case. My mom did a great job on the show.

We were in a room backstage where we could see all the cameras, and as my mother talked about losing my father and about what had happened, we could see the shots of the women in the studio wiping tears away. The majority of the women there were unattached to the story. It was good to see they had open minds and had their hearts open to my mother. My mother stated that, given the failure of the experts to recognize Jerry's problems, how were we all to know?

The reports were issued a few days after the *Katie* taping. On Sunday morning February 10, the men who wrote the reports went on ESPN's *Outside the Lines* to talk about their findings. On Monday the full-court press would begin. *Katie* would air that afternoon. As part of the push, I flew up to Connecticut to do the ESPN "car wash," meaning the grand tour of all the television and radio shows.

The day began with *Mike & Mike*, followed by *SportsCenter, First Take*, Colin Cowherd, *SportsCenter* again, *The Stephen A. Smith Show*, and Scott Van Pelt's show. *Mike & Mike* got heated, but I appreciated their willingness to challenge our case with tough questions yet allow me to answer in full. They did not cut me off.

First Take featured Skip Bayless and Stephen A. Smith, and before we went on the air, Skip shared some information with me. "Jay, I see your side of this," he said. "Now Stephen has been tougher on you guys."

But when the show began, I give Stephen a lot of credit for allowing me to correct some false information. Stephen had made a point about Jerry and kids being at our practices and on team trips with us after the incident in 2001. I stopped him to point out he had his facts wrong and I stated very clearly that neither Jerry nor any of his victims were at practices or on team trips after he retired in 1999. Stephen asked me again, and I stated again the truth of the matter in no uncertain terms.

As soon as the interview was over, my cell phone rang. It was my brother Scott. "Jay," he said, "great job so far, but you should stay away from saying that Jerry and the victims weren't at practice. We don't want to contradict anyone."

"I appreciate what you're saying, but what I'm saying is the truth," I said.

To Stephen's credit when I went on his radio show later, he brought up that question for me again, so that his radio listeners who hadn't seen the earlier interview would hear what I'd said. That is what good journalists should do: have open minds willing to hear facts and share them with the public.

After ESPN we flew to Newark and on the way into Manhattan, I called in to Mike North's FOX Sports radio show and to LaVar Arrington's radio show in D.C. before heading to CNN for Erin Burnett's show. While I waited to go on the show, I looked out the window to see a snow-covered Columbus Circle.

Finally, I walked on to the set where Erin and I were seated across a very narrow table from each other—so narrow we could've shared a milkshake with two straws. Former attorney general Dick Thornburgh joined the show via satellite.

As the day wore on, the reaction from Penn Staters and people who wanted to hear the truth was gaining momentum. Our push on ESPN, CNN, and combined with my mother's appearance on *Katie* made for a good first start to letting the world see the truth.

Truth Rule @PCTypesCanSukit 2/11/13

@JayPaterno You're making a Fool of yourself dumbass. Your father Joe Pa did nothing to help stop a Pedophile he absolutely knew all about.

From Twitter

racy Atacheson @tjatcheson 2/11/13

@Jay Paterno @mikeandmike U did a gr8 job! To think ur Dad would cover this up for the sake of PSU is crazy! Goes against everything he stood 4!

From Twitter

Bands4RAINN 2bands4RAINN 2/11/13

@JayPaterno @mikeandmike glad the focus was clearly on the victims too. Please help join my fight http://RAINNmakers.rainn.org/bands4rainn

From Twitter

Note: RAINN is a child sexual abuse prevention group.

Sure, there were people who wanted us to just shut up and go away. My response was simple: if *their* father or their school had been unfairly stained with accusations of covering up for a pedophile, they'd fight, too. Defending Penn State's honor is not an offense to the victims. We should never fear the truth. Moses ben Maimon, a leading rabbinic authority of the medieval period, wrote: "Hear the truth, whoever speaks it."

The truth for Penn State and for Joe Paterno has been discounted because those who should defend the university found it in their personal interests to sell an alternate story. They neglected to defend the university they'd been entrusted to protect.

The rest of the week I did interviews with nearly two dozen more people in cities like Atlanta, Philadelphia, Miami, and Los Angeles. I went and talked with all the local media outlets as well. It was important that the people in our home community hear what Clemente's report had to say about how we miss the nice guy offenders in communities all over the country.

Many people in State College who'd worked for or volunteered with Sandusky's charity, The Second Mile, were carrying collective guilt. I wanted them to know nice guy offenders operate without enablers; they neither need nor want them. I also wanted people to realize there were many young people whose lives had been saved by the work of The Second Mile volunteers.

As we went on the offensive, Louis Freeh hid behind his written statement. He'd been asked to appear and declined. The damage his false narrative had wrought was but a blip in his rearview mirror as he counted his Penn State money.

Subsequently, Louis Freeh and Mark Emmert have declined every chance to appear on camera with anyone from our side.

One of our objectives as we issued the reports was to create awareness of the issues of child sexual abuse in this country. Clemente was given a segment on *Katie*. My mother and I were asked to speak to the Pennsylvania Family Support Alliance at their awareness breakfast in Harrisburg on April 10, 2013.

While I made it quite plain in my speech that I was not there to talk about my father, we were criticized by members of the media, who were not even in the room, for trying to use Abuse Awareness Month to try and "defend Joe Paterno." The media that was actually in the room had a very different take on our message.

Shortly after my speech, I heard from Jolie Logan, who is the CEO of Darkness to Light, a group based in Charleston, South Carolina, that trains people to recognize the signs of child sexual abuse. They asked if I could help Penn State student Lance Chappelle with his prevention walk. I was more than happy to do so in September of 2013 but also noticed the university administration's absence at the event.

As the spring of 2013 moved toward summer, there were more and more positive developments. NBC's Bob Costas took another look at the Sandusky scandal and hosted a show on the NBC Sports Network as we announced a sweeping lawsuit against the NCAA. In the run-up to the show, Costas showed why he is among the most respected journalists on the planet. He openly admitted that he had not read the entire Freeh Report before commenting in July of 2012. With more study and time, he asserted that Joe Paterno wasn't involved in a cover-up.

I was grateful for Bob's willingness to stand as a bigger person than others in the media who refused to further study what had happened here. Journalism should be a constant re-evaluation and analysis of facts as we learn more and more. Bob Costas gets it, and that's why he is among the elite.

Others weren't as ethical.

Christine Brennan from *USA TODAY* stated that she knew everything she needed to know before even reading our report. I laughed as I heard her say that. Good thing Galileo and the explorers of the 1400s and 1500s didn't just accept that the world was flat.

In the fall of 2013, the prosecutors of the Sandusky case told CBS that there was no evidence of Joe Paterno being involved in a cover-up. I am still awaiting Sally Jenkins' retraction from what she wrote in July of 2012 about Joe Paterno being a cover-up artist. I'm disappointed because I respect Sally so much.

The sweeping lawsuit against the NCAA united a broad-based group of people. Faculty members signed on, unafraid of the potential retaliation from the university administration. Five trustees—Anthony Lubrano, Ryan McCombie, Adam Taliaferro, Al Clemens, and Peter Khoury—signed onto the suit. Peter was later forced to choose between being on the lawsuit or be removed from the committee choosing Penn State's next president. He stepped off the lawsuit but made sure the media knew why he'd done so.

Nine former players stood up: Michael Robinson, Anwar Phillips, Justin Kurpeikis, Pat Mauti, Richard Gardner, Gerald Cadogan, Shamar Finney, Anthony Adams, and Josh Gaines. All of them had played between 1998 and 2011 and had wins stripped. Bill Kenney and I put our names in to represent the former coaches. The group stood shoulder to shoulder armed with a slingshot to take on the NCAA Goliath. It might have only been a slingshot, but it was loaded with the truth.

In the summer there was more ammunition for our cause.

On the Thursday of the Arts Festival, former Penn State football player Brian Masella and his wife had joined forces with former basketball player

Brian Allen. They released a list of over 500 former Penn State athletes who'd signed on in support of the lawsuit against the NCAA.

It really moved me to see the names of people I knew standing with us.

The statement was issued the same weekend that three newly alumni-elected trustees had joined Penn State's board of trustees. Not one incumbent had been re-elected in the two alumni elections, and familiar names like Anne Riley and Paul Suhey had been knocked off.

Slowly but surely, the change was coming.

By July 16, 2013, Keith Masser, Penn State's chairman of the board of trustees, admitted in an interview with *USA TODAY* that the Freeh Report's conclusions of a cover-up were "speculation." That followed an interesting legal argument a few months earlier. Penn State's attorneys argued in civil court that, "There was no factual basis to support a cover-up" in a lawsuit filed by a victim against the university.

The truth was slowly emerging, but the pressure needed to remain on so we continue to press the fight. The saddest part? It all could've been avoided because the board failed to learn from history of people they knew well.

In October of 1987, the Dow Jones plunged 22.6 percent in one day while markets around the world followed suit. In the immediate aftermath of doubt and panic, Penn State alum and Merrill Lynch C.E.O. Bill Schreyer recorded a commercial stating Merrill Lynch was still "Bullish on America." His calm message, advocating the long view over short-term panic is widely credited for settling the markets.

Although Bill had died, he had served on the board of trustees with many of the current members. If only they'd have followed his example.

Worse yet, the board chose not to solicit the advice of Larry Foster, a Penn State alum living in State College at the time the story broke. Larry headed up Johnson & Johnson's public relations, leading them through the Tylenol cyanide scare in the 1980s. His direction of that crisis saved the Tylenol brand. Here he was, a veteran of this type of crisis, and his expertise was never called upon.

Even the state police commissioner who, all the way back in November 2011, judged Joe Paterno with his public comment on "moral duty" should have known better. After naming Joe in the presentment and then judging his morality, months later Noonan had this to say about another case: "It's

348

not fair for us to talk about people who aren't charged in the presentment, so I'm not going to."

Maybe someone should remind him that Joe Paterno was not charged in the presentment.

The Penn State board and the state of Pennsylvania made mistakes in their handling of Penn State and Joe Paterno. That is human. But they compounded them over time by doubling down on their initial positions. Maybe it is pride that prevents them from righting the wrongs. Maybe they just can't see what they've actually done.

At this point the cause of the problems isn't what matters. Getting the truth is the lone focus. That is why we got to where we were and why we are still in the fight of our lives to defend Penn State's honor.

The most telling statement in all of this came from a meeting between the trustees and athletic director Dave Joyner in the summer of 2013. One of the trustees asked Dave what had happened to Penn State's athletic department motto, "Success with Honor." Dave responded by insinuating that the university didn't feel right using the word "honor" with Penn State right now.

If the administration won't defend our honor, who will? The fight back is up to the students and alumni. After all, it is indeed our university—not theirs.

Epilogue: Avalon

In August of 2013 as I was finishing much of this book, I returned with my family and some friends to our family home at the shore of Avalon, New Jersey.

Avalon.

In English lore the isle of Avalon held great meaning in the life of the legendary King Arthur. It is said to have been the place where his sword Excalibur was forged, where Arthur was taken to recover from his wounds in battle, and ultimately where he died.

In my father's life, Avalon was his retreat, a quiet private place when we were young. As the years passed, more and more people knew where his home was, but it was his second home. To the end of his life, he resisted the urge to sell the house and go somewhere else. It was just the way he was.

On the sands of Avalon, he would walk early in the morning as the sun rose and then he'd walk again in the evening as the sun began to slip over the marsh that separated the sea island from the mainland.

The deck of that home is one of those places where you can sense his presence. Between the morning and evening walks on the beach, he'd sit here and look at the ocean as he read or studied summer scouting reports or plotted practice schedules for the approaching season. The sounds of the waves became the soundtrack of his summer study.

Here he came to re-invent or re-invigorate or ready himself for the long fall football season ahead. In Pennsylvania the football season starts amid the fiery summer heat of August and lasts through the chilling north winds of November. The weeks and months between promise nights of scarce rest marked by the constant preparation for the next foe awaiting you.

That was what he lived to do, but as he got older, the summer escapes to Avalon became more and more important. It was where he came to heal the wounds, whether physical or mental, from the previous year while girding for the coming campaign. In the summer of 2005, he found the strength to begin a seven-year run to conclude his career at the level with which he started it. In August 2013 I stepped into the Avalon Supermarket, and the owner approached me. "Hey, Jay," he said, "I really miss seeing your dad in here."

"Me too," I said.

As the calendar turned into 2014, we're in the third year without my father. The pain doesn't dull; the void remains. Although I carry him with me, I just want one more moment to sit and talk with him, to walk the park with him, to see him smile, just to be a child again on a Wednesday night, seeing him through the plate glass kitchen windows walk in his bow-legged gait from darkness into the glow of the kitchen table lamp casting its light on him as he walked to the back door.

Bruce Springsteen once wrote a lyric about a neighbor, his wife's friend who had died. He recalled seeing how the light would strike her face as she walked past a window to the back door of their house.

> "Now there's a loss that can never be replaced,
> A destination that can never be reached,
> A light you'll never find in another's face,
> A sea whose distance cannot be breached"

I think of that light in my father's face walking around the back of that house or in the early morning in his den or amid the deafening roar of the crowd as the stadium lights made his eyes twinkle with anticipation of a primetime football game.

There is a time, and the time as I write this is still upon us, when we must fight for that which we hold dear in our lives. As long as I live and breathe on this Earth, I will hold dear the light of my father's life. I will fight for it.

The Native Americans had their core of dog soldiers. The dog soldiers would drive a stake into the ground and attach themselves to it. It told everyone in their tribe and those who attacked that they would not and could not retreat. They were prepared to die defending the ground they held, the village of their families and friends.

As people waged their assaults on Penn State, on my father, on Penn State, and our football program, I thought about the dog soldiers. As I went on television and radio and stood up to blistering, hateful criticism, I knew that there was a stake driven into the ground I held.

My father has gone to his Avalon, to the afterlife that his faith promised him, so we are left to stand the ground his life gave our university. Many stand alongside us.

Faculty members stand with us. Trustees like Ryan McCombie, Anthony Lubrano, Al Clemens, and Adam Taliaferro stand with us. Former student-athletes from across the sports at Penn State stand with us. Alumni, fans, and supporters, most of whom we've never met, stand with us.

As I look down I see *their* stakes driven into the ground alongside mine and I take comfort in knowing the impact he made on so many lives.

All those years ago, his father had told him to "make an impact."

The numbers of people with us and the ferocity of their courageous spirit speak to the impact Joe Paterno made on so many people.

I go to sit at his desk in his den. The notes on his desk blotter remain there in his handwriting. Among them this quote from Lincoln stands as a testament to how my father lived his life: "I do the very best I know how—the very best I can; and I mean to do so until the end. If the end brings me out all right, what is said against me won't amount to anything. If the end brings out winged Angels swearing I was right it would make no difference."

The quote strikes true with me. I read it every time I sit in his desk and I know that he could have uttered those words as his time on Earth began to close. While his mortal time on Earth is past, all of his children and his players walk this Earth without him, but we know he is here.

In April of 2012, I spoke at an alumni association event on campus, a senior send-off for the graduating class. I was introduced to a family and their newborn baby, Jayden Joseph. It didn't strike me until his mother informed me that they had been so impacted by my father's life and by my example in the months since his death that they named their child after my father and me.

A year later as I spoke to the 2013 graduating class of Paterno Fellows in Penn State's College of Liberal Arts, I stood in front of a group of students who'd voted to keep the Paterno name on their elite program. While others had run from him, they stood and re-pledged their loyalty and commitment to the ideals they knew my father held true all his life.

These students had studied or worked in 29 countries on five continents and spoke 25 languages. They represented the best of what my father had hoped to inspire in this university, a school with a reach and a breadth of education that would give Penn State a global impact. These students had carried the Paterno name to the farthest ends of the Earth. Generations after them will do the same.

I thanked them for their commitment and then I shared with them something that I hoped they would find in their own lives.

> I hope you find a moment each day to hold. I was along the banks of Spring Creek and saw an osprey swoop down and snag a trout from the water. Not a good moment for the trout but special to witness. I see the smile and wave from my daughter as she got on her school bus years ago or a walk across a park with my father or the twinkle in his eye before a game.
>
> I hope you fall in love with something bigger than yourself. That term "something bigger that yourself" has almost become a cliché. But it really entails this: make yourself vulnerable, pour your heart into someone or something despite knowing if things go wrong it will hurt so deeply as to gut your soul. It could be family, a cause, a university you love, or to believe in something so real like "Success with Honor."
>
> May you find a cause or a love so precious you will defend its honor to the last, fighting even if it means shouting truth to power over the howling tempest winds as most of the world pushes back against you. If there is one lesson I have learned in my life, it is the pride, the honor that comes when you stand up for right.

As all of us walk into the future without him, I hope that we retain the pride and honor that comes when we stand up for right. I hope that we remain committed to defending that which he left us.

In 2012 and 2013 on Penn State gamedays, I drove to his grave and I knelt down like we did in the locker room before and after every game. Touching the stone with my hand, I said the "Our Father" aloud. Then I walked away from the grave—alone back to the word of the living.

Lawrence Loewy (@LarryL05)

11/24/13, 8:27 AM

@JayPaterno An honor to meet you yesterday at the grave of your dad. My son never played a down for Joe but he affected his life forever.

From Twitter

On September 12, 2013, while doing research for this book, I found a bunch of notes stapled together in a folder. On a small 7.5" x 5" lined piece of paper, he had written notes from Walt Whitman's "Leaves of Grass":

Nothing can happen more beautiful than death.
Behold I do not give lectures or a little charity, when I give, I give myself.
Oh Captain, my captain our fearful trip is done.
The ship has weathered every rack, the prize we sought is won.
The port is near, the bells I hear, the people all exulting.

Yes, Dad, indeed your trip is done. You weathered every rack and won the prize. You gave of yourself until you breathed your last. How noble a journey you concluded, a journey for which bells have rung and people have exulted. The lessons of the way you lived your life and the way you left this world continue to resonate with me.

But the light of his life, the impact he made will guide me until my port is near and my trip is done, until I, too, walk the sands of the next Avalon.

Acknowledgments

No project like this ever occurs without a lot of help, so I owe a lot of thanks to a lot of people.

First, my wife and five children had to put up with long hours of typing and editing. I hope they will see it has all been worth it—to tell this story—one I hope they will share with their children someday.

For their support and understanding, I thank my brothers and sisters and especially my mother. My mother deserves the most thanks for her guidance in my life—she is a living example of so many great values that I hope I can carry to my own family.

Thanks to Paul Levine, who vouched for me to agent Al Zuckerman, who is as good as it gets. I thank Al and Mickey Novak at Writer's House in New York for their efforts, critiques, and honesty. There is no doubt that I tested their patience, but here we are.

Thanks to Tom Bast and Jeff Fedotin at Triumph. They had faith in this project. I've enjoyed working with them to get this book finished and edited. They patiently gave me time to tell the authentic story of my life learning the lessons of an extraordinary man.

Thanks also to those friends who read and reviewed sections of the book—Michael and Megan Flanagan, Ben Bouma, Guido D'Elia, Jill Bailey, Sharon Herlocher, Charles Kranich, Michael Hammond, among others who patiently gave me their perspectives for free. I've always valued the opinions of honest critics and I thank them for that.

To Phil Knight, special thanks for writing the foreword. It is rare to see accomplished men speak so honestly about a difficult decision they've made. My father was proud to call you a friend, and you have remained a friend to him even now that he has gone. Thanks also to Al Clemens, who had the fortitude to publicly acknowledge the errors made in November of 2011. It takes a lot to stand up and own something—for that I have great respect for you.

I want to thank the men I coached with and the people I worked with every day—particularly the student-athletes I coached. I miss the camaraderie of meetings, the practice field, and the team bonds—from quiet pregame moments to a rowdy victorious postgame locker room. There were lots of laughs and tears, and I've taken something with me from so many players.

I now know why my father never gave it up.

Thanks to my friends. Some friends have emerged stronger than before, and some drifted away, and I thank them all. I know the true feelings of those around me. When hard times emerged, I saw the best and worst of people I know and for that I am thankful.

Last I want to thank all those who have been here to support the cause of finding truth: Dan McGinn, Wick Sollers, Mara Vandlik, Paul Kelly, and others who have battled for Penn State's name and my father's name. Thanks to the trustees, faculty, former players, and coach Bill Kenney who joined the lawsuit to right the wrongs wrought by the NCAA and the Freeh Report. I'm grateful to so many alumni, Penn Staters, and students who have supported our fight. Thanks to Penn State coaches like Russ Rose and former players like Franco Harris and Brian Masella, who led countless others. They refused to allow others to tear down what we know to be true.

Over time the truth has emerged, but in the earliest days, it wasn't easy, nor was it politically correct to defend Joe Paterno. The ones who stood to support Joe are the ones I will always remember in my heart until the day I die.

Thanks.